DATE			

Tales of an Old Horsetrader

Tales of an Old Horsetrader

THE FIRST HUNDRED YEARS

By Leroy Judson Daniels

As told to Helen S. Herrick

UNIVERSITY OF IOWA PRESS   IOWA CITY

University of Iowa Press, Iowa City 52242
Printed in the United States of America
First edition, 1987

Book and jacket design by Sandra Strother Hudson
Typesetting by G&S Typesetters, Austin, Texas
Printing and binding by Thomson-Shore, Dexter, Michigan

Library of Congress Cataloging-in-Publication Data

Daniels, Leroy Judson, 1882–
Tales of an old horsetrader.

(A Bur oak original)
1. Daniels, Leroy Judson, 1882–
2. Businessmen—United States—Biography.   3. Horse
industry—United States—History.   I. Herrick, Helen S.
II. Title.
HD9434.U6D36   1987   338.1'761'00924 [B]   87-10932
ISBN 0-87745-173-7
ISBN 0-87745-187-7 (pbk.)

Photographs on title page, from top to bottom: driving team Nan and Nero shown by
a hired hand, trotting horse Governor Burk and hired hand Billy, and Percheron stallion Maxwell with a hired hand. Photographs courtesy of Lee Daniels.

A Bur Oak Original

CONTENTS

Who is more important, the horsetrader or the horse? It's just like the question, Which came first: the chicken or the egg? Neither one would get very far without the other. But I think the horse would get along better without the man than the man would without the horse.

Leroy Judson Daniels

Tales of an Old Horsetrader

ONE

Montana

When I was sixteen my father and I had a disagreement. We had a lot of hired men, and I was supposed to look after everything. That's a pretty big job for a kid that age. Seemed like everything one of the men did wrong got blamed on me. My father said I wasn't doing much, but I thought I was a pretty good man, and I decided I'd just pull out for myself. I went up into Minnesota and got a job hauling water for the engine crew of a threshing outfit. We threshed there all fall. I had to make ten trips a day to haul enough water for the engine. It was several miles to the lake, and the mosquitoes were just wild. After a while I quit hauling water and started hauling and scooping grain. They had big outfits those days—150 horses and 200 men —and worked all summer, June through September, one farm after another.

I stayed with the threshing crew until they left for home. Then I went to work for a man plowing. They treated me real good and wanted me to stay longer, but I got homesick and came home. Believe me, my folks didn't know where I was all that time. I stayed home, but things never were the same with my father. He promised if I would stay home he would give me a team of drivers and a new buggy. He got the buggy, but he wouldn't let me use it.

I finally left home again and went to work for a man at twenty dollars a month. That was top wages at the time. He had a lot of cattle, horses to break, other stock. He knew I could do that job. I stayed there one month and did two men's work. My boss had a son the same age as me, but he wasn't much for work. My boss would go to town every day, and as soon as the old man was gone, the boy would take off to see his

1

girl, leave me with the work to do. I drew a month's wages and bought a ticket to Omaha.

I stayed all night in a hotel and next morning I realized I didn't have much money left. It looked like I'd better bum a ride on a train. So I caught a freight, climbed into an old boxcar. That train happened to be going straight through. Several days later when it finally stopped I was in Deadwood, South Dakota. A nickel was all the money I had left. I was tired, dirty, and hungry. It was dark, sleeting, and cold, but Deadwood looked pretty good after that boxcar. I decided I had to do something desperate but not dishonest, and I had that nickel to do it with. I went into this bar and asked the bartender for a drink. Never did a thing like that before in my life.

At that time you could buy a glass of beer for a nickel and that gave you the privilege of having a free lunch in any saloon. I went into the Log Cabin Saloon and walked up to the bar. I laid my nickel down and asked for a glass of beer. The bartender looked at me and said, "Oh, kid, you're too young to have a glass of beer. What's the matter, you hungry?"

I said, "Yes. I haven't had anything to eat for two or three days. I'm just starved. Now, here's your nickel anyway. It won't do me any good."

He said, "You just go over there and help yourself. Be careful not to eat too much. If you haven't eaten for a couple of days, you might eat too much to start off."

I sure didn't need a second invitation. I went over there and, boy, I was shoving down food with both hands. That bartender was watching, though. He came over and took me by the shoulder. "You just wait a bit now. You'll make yourself sick. After a bit, when you get over your hunger spell, you can go have some more."

I've often heard what good people bartenders are, and I guess they're human. But this one, in my book, is somebody special. He was a real man, a real friend to a young boy who was alone, hungry, and more than a little bit frightened. I didn't have anyplace to go, so the bartender, whose named seemed to be Joe, said if I'd help him there a little I could have a bed in the back room. He fixed me some blankets. I cleaned spittoons, brushed the floor, and polished glass. I did anything anyone had to do in a saloon. Joe said that on Saturday the ranchmen would come in there and they'd often hire men.

Saturday night I was looking, hoping for a job to come my way. That first Saturday night I didn't get a job. There wasn't anybody in the saloon much that wanted to hire a hand. I waited around about two weeks, and I wondered if I'd ever get a job. But my friend Joe didn't seem to wonder. He knew. So I knew too, because he didn't leave any room for doubt. We both knew I wasn't going back home.

The second Saturday a fellow came in who had a horse ranch. He was looking for somebody to help him run it. Well, that was just up my alley. I wanted that job, and I hired out to that man for forty dollars a month. I wanted to break horses for him. This man was pie-eyed drunk when he hired me, and I figured he'd forget it when he sobered up. I don't know how long he stayed drunk, but he came in late one night and wanted to get started.

We hitched up his horses and rode most of the night, catching a couple of hours of sleep and getting on the road again before dawn. Kept going and going. Finally I found out his ranch was way up in Montana where he had his stock, and it took us two, three days to get there. We drove up to his ranch late one night. He didn't have anything but a little old shack of a building to live in—no stable, no corrals, or anything that I could see when we arrived in the night like that. Had an old buckboard that he drove down to Deadwood. No animals except the team he drove up with. They didn't need breaking, but they sure could stand a rest.

He went right to the house as soon as the team stopped. Tossed the reins to me and said, "Take care of the horses now." I didn't know what to do with the darn horses. I couldn't find anyplace to hang the harness except over the wheels of the buggy, so I just turned the horses loose.

Next morning, oh, ten or eleven o'clock, he came to himself and said, "Well, we'll round up some horses this morning and you start work." We saddled the same old, tired horses we'd driven from Deadwood and went out into the wild-horse country. Every time we'd round up a few horses I'd think that was about enough to handle at one time, but he kept us at it two, three days. I guess we had sixty-five or seventy horses, quite a job for two men. When we'd run the horses into a box canyon back at the ranch, I took one good look at them, and if it hadn't been so far I'd have beat it back to Deadwood, but I was stuck. I was out there looking over those horses when I heard the buggy wheels grind on the gravel. He waves at me and says, "Well, kid, there's your job. See you in a month." Away he goes, back to Deadwood, and here I am alone with a herd of wild horses to break.

There've been lots of teenagers far from home with big problems, but not all of them had seventy wild horses to gentle. I looked at these old jugheads and I wished I'd never seen a horse. I felt like turning them all out and heading off down the road. But I decided to stay and give it a try, and I broke every one of those nags.

No, I wouldn't say I ever broke any horse in my life. I hope I didn't. I gentled them. Even then, when I was just a kid, I knew what to do. I'd seen it done all my life. My folks, Dad and Uncle Lee, for whom I was named, they never broke a horse, always gentled them. A broke horse won't ever be much use to anybody, but a gentled horse, ah, that's a horse of a different education, a different training. Makes all the difference. In the old days you'd hear a lot about breaking horses. You'd hear about breaking children, too, which meant teaching them how to take care of themselves, to get to the bathroom on time. We called it a little different.

Gentling a horse means domesticating it. If you gentle a wild horse, you render him fit to live and work with humans with no harm done to the horse or the human. Wild horses had usually never seen a man up close. They reared up and became violent because they were terrified, not because they were mean. Out in their native lands they have to fight for their lives from the time they are colts. Coyotes, wolves, catamounts, many kinds of wild animals prey on wild horses. They are off by themselves, and their minds, their way of life, develop differently than those of horses raised by men. They know every trick in the trade—how to use their front feet, their hind feet, and their teeth. I found out that kindness and sternness are the only two ways to conquer a wild horse. You've got to let them do part of it themselves.

First, the man must know more than the horse.

The first thing in gentling a wild horse the way I do is to put a braided-rope halter on him. Then tie a rope to the halter, oh, five, maybe seven, feet long, so it will drag on the ground. Turn the horse loose right in among the other horses. Well, he'll step on that rope and it jerks him. He'll get scared at first, but he'll come to feel he is doing it himself. But if you tie him up and try to hold him that way, he'll kill himself, or ruin himself for life, often. He'll get his head and neck sore, lame, and it can do permanent damage. He'll throw himself. People will take horses—people who know nothing about how to handle them, nothing at all about horses—and a lot of horses will break their necks. A horse has a very sensitive neck. Some get to be outlaws because they're handled wrong from the beginning. They get a bad name right away. But take one of those horses of marketable age and gentle it slowly and carefully. You will have a friend for life—the horse's life.

That's what I was thinking about as I set a post in the ground and two more posts in the ground on the other side of the corral I had had to build.

My boss didn't have much of anything out there. I found a saddle horse, a good saddle, ropes and one thing and another, a bit of harness. I worked for a couple of days and got a corral made so I could handle these wild horses.

Next I tied a horse to the one post. Between the two posts I put a couple of horses so they could get the feel of being a team. Then I started in on those jugheaded broncs. To gentle a horse, first you've got to *be* gentle. In the corral I tied ropes around their necks, then I left them to learn their own lesson. I went out with another bunch and I roped a horse and snubbed him up to a post. I got an old raincoat I had found in the house. I'd shake that raincoat until the horse gave up being afraid of the noise. You can tame a horse like that, just with an old raincoat. It doesn't hurt him at all. You can just quiet him. In thirty minutes you'll have that horse just lathered up all over. When he's ready to stand, you get on the horse and he won't buck with you. I'd pull his head down tight against his breast so he couldn't buck and I'd get on. I broke that seventy head of horses to ride, and quite a few to drive.

I had two little black horses there, and I thought they were ready to break to drive as a team. There was an old wagon out behind some brush, and I had found a long pole. I put that pole in the wagon for a tongue. That put the horses several feet ahead of the wagon. They couldn't kick me or the wagon as I sat in the seat and drove with two ropes for lines. I tied the heads of the two horses together so they had to go the same way. I thought I'd drive those blacks out the gate and practice them for a while as I had done a team I'd broken earlier. I always let a team run down this lane and out onto the open prairie. I thought I'd opened the pole gate earlier, but I hadn't, and I guess I forgot. When that long tongue hit the poles of the gate, the whole wagon gave an awful jolt. I went into the air and came down on my back. Away went the team.

That happened about ten o'clock in the morning. I must have lain there until close to nine o'clock that night. It was dark when my boss came in, and I was still lying there. I guess he thought I was dead because he stopped his rig and got out and came over and gave me a kick in the ribs. That brought me to. He was drunk and mean—violent. I would have to get away or he would kill me. I ran as fast as I could, started toward Billings afoot. I'd go a little way and I'd have to sit down, my side hurt me so from that fall. After that kick I didn't know but what my ribs were broken. I slept most of the night alongside the road, crawled under a bush.

I had walked about ten miles next morning when a man came along with a buggy. He said, "Where you going, kid?"

"I'm trying to get to Billings."

"Where've you been staying?"

I told him, and he said, "Did he pay you?"

"No, he didn't. The only pay I got was a kick in the ribs."

"You just get in the buggy and I'll go back with you. We'll get your money. Then you can come stay with me, because you'll never make it to Billings. It's forty miles, and you're in no condition, you just can't make it. Just come home with me."

So I went with him. His name was Fred Whittum.

Fred and I went back to my boss, and Fred went into the shack. What he said to my boss I don't know, but he came out with my forty dollars, my month's pay. Several times I asked Fred how he'd gotten it, and finally he said, "Well, I had to use a little force." I just imagine he gave that fellow a darn good choking, which didn't do him any harm.

Fred had a lot of colts that had just been weaned from their mares. He said, "Now, you work at these colts, break them to lead, gentle them. That's your job for the winter." I guess there wasn't any happier boy in this whole world. I just loved those little things. They were practically registered horses, smart as you'd find anywhere. I played with them, roped them, taught them to lead, wear a saddle, teamed them up. I had a ball with those colts, and they'd do anything I wanted.

Fred had a wife, nice couple, just young folks. She might have been twenty-five and he twenty-seven or thirty. They were raising carriage horses, standardbred horses. Everything was right up to snuff—good house, good barns, well-made corrals—it was more like home.

I worked for Fred and Mrs. Whittum until the end of March, maybe April. I gentled a nice black mare for Mrs. Whittum to ride. She was expecting a baby at the time, and Fred wanted this horse broke for her. Well I just gentled that little black mare till she was like a kitten. You could do anything with her. But Mrs. Whittum wouldn't get onto the horse. She was afraid she'd get hurt.

Then I got so homesick to see my mother that I couldn't stand it any longer, even though I liked my job so much. One day I said to Fred, "I've just got to get home."

As if he already knew, Fred said, "Well, I'll take you up to Billings and let you take the train from there home." That was good to hear, and I agreed right away.

Fred said, "We'll have breakfast, but I can't go for a little while yet. Get your things ready." I didn't have much to get ready, just a pair of overalls and a felt hat, that's all the clothes I had.

After breakfast, he got up from the table and went out. When I finished eating, Mrs. Whittum said, "Fred wants you to come out to the barn. He wants to show you something."

I went out to the barnyard where Fred was. He had this little black mare all togged out—new saddle, new bridle, new girth, all the fixings. New felt hat for me, pair of chaps, everything all rigged up. Well I had already told him I wouldn't take any pay for the work I'd done there that winter, and he said, "This is yours. If you take it easy, she'll get you to Deadwood in two, three days."

Boy, that was a real surprise for me! I never thought of owning that beautiful little horse. I got all rigged up and started for Deadwood. I was riding on top of the world that morning, but soon luck turned and I was in a bad spot. I got caught in a blizzard, and the horse and I both nearly froze to death. I got caught in a blizzard, and the horse and I both nearly froze to death. We finally made it to Deadwood about a week later, me and the horse both half dead. My little black mare got pneumonia from that experience.

I stayed in Deadwood and worked for my friend Joe at the Log Cabin Saloon for my board. What money I had I spent trying to get my mare well. She just got poor, she wasn't able to travel, and I was so homesick I couldn't stand it any longer. Joe thought I might get someone to take her to pasture, so I found a place for her. She surely wasn't going to Adair until she could build herself up again.

I took my saddle and rig and caught the train for Omaha and got on home. I helped Dad with the farm work, and my winter in Montana seemed more and more like a dream, something that had never happened.

About the first of July, when the work slacked up, I went back to Deadwood to get my little black mare. Took my saddle and all my paraphernalia and went back for her. Got up there and went out to the pasture and caught her, but she was ruined. Because of the pneumonia, she was so windy I knew I never could make it home with her. She couldn't get her breath easy enough, like a horse normally does, to be able to travel like she'd have to, to go home with me. I went to the man who had rented the pasture to me and asked, "Would you take the mare for the pasture bill?"

"Why, yes, I'd be glad to, why?"

"She's so windy I can't get her home, can't do anything with her."

I got on her and rode a little way. She almost fell down with me. I said, "It's a long way home. If you'll take her for the feed bill, you can have her." He took her.

I came home and went to work on the farm, stayed there that

summer, and the next fall my father gave me my time (paid me what I had earned), and I went to farming for myself.

I thought that was the end of my Montana story, but about forty years later I learned the rest of it. I was in Omaha one day, and I was walking on the boardwalk across the stockyards. Someone hollered, "Lee!" I didn't pay much attention because there was a Lee Commission Company there and I thought somebody was hollering for them. But the voice called, "Lee, come down here!"

I stopped and went looking around, finally went down the steps into the alley where the voice seemed to come from. Here was this man. In a moment I recognized Fred Whittum. Oh, we had quite a visit. He stayed with me all day and all night. We visited—my, how we visited.

He told me a terrible tale, unbelievable, from what I knew of him. Fred said that when his wife had her baby, she died. So did the baby. Fred went all to pieces. He started drinking. He was so broken up about losing her and the baby that finally he sold his ranch and drank up what he got for it. Just let everything go. Lost his ranch, his friends, everything else, I guess. When it was all gone and he was broke, he came to his senses and made up his mind he'd get that ranch back. He must have had one friend left, because he got a little lift from somebody, and pretty soon he had his ranch again. He went into the cattle business. Oh, losing his wife had hit him hard. Fred Whittum was one of the finest fellows I ever ran across.

Years and years after that trip into the Black Hills, I took my wife and children up there. I had chewed tobacco ever since I was five years old, and when we arrived in Deadwood I was clear out of cut plug. The prospect was shocking. I said to my family, "I believe I'll go over by the old Log Cabin Saloon just for the fun of it. Probably if it's still there I can get my brand of tobacco."

I walked over and here was Joe, the same bartender I'd known when I was a starving kid looking for work. There was no way of getting away from him, either. I went out and told my wife and kids, "Go get a cabin somewhere, we're staying over. I'm going to visit with this old friend of mine."

Joe was a great man. No one who came there in trouble, hungry, out of money, out of luck, needing a friend ever left helpless. He'd always help them. I can't tell you his last name, don't know as I ever heard it, but I guess most people never heard it.

Most stories end happy or sad. This one man, so good to everybody else, always carried his money with him. One night he was killed for his money. I heard of that, but after my visit with him there, with my family, I never saw him again.

TWO

The Daniels Family

Well, I guess that Montana story sort of started things off in the middle and I should go back to the beginning and go on from there. I can't go too far back, though. I don't know anything about the Daniels family before my grandfather, where they came from or when they arrived on this continent, but they're here. All that family history never interested me. The name has always been pronounced "Dan'ls," not any other way. A lot of people call me Daniels, the way it's spelled, but I don't care. My grandfather, Henry Daniels, had a place in Putnam County, Illinois, on the banks of the Illinois River, and my father was born there. Henry and his parents had built a house, sheds, barns, and like everybody else in those days, they farmed. My grandmother died, and the father and son lived alone for a few years.

My grandfather Henry was then a young man, and he had some land in Kentucky. About the middle of the 1830s, long before the Civil War, Henry went down to look after his property. It was a big timber tract, all hardwood timber, and I never knew just where it was, guess none of the family knew, even my dad, Lewis. Henry went down to take care of it, sold some timber, I guess. Maybe he had to stay to oversee the buyers taking timber off his land.

He was on his way home, traveling alone through pretty unsettled country, when he heard noises that sounded strange to him, something he couldn't account for, like moaning, people in misery. He started looking in the swamp nearby, where the sounds seemed to come from. Hidden in the tules and rushes of that swamp he found a flatboat, kind of a raft. A woman was on the raft, and eight children, four boys and four girls, aged four to about eighteen. They were a sad-looking lot—thin, narrow faces, huge eyes, all sizes—near starving, Henry said. Had no money and were afraid to go look for help. Didn't know how to find their way north and wouldn't go back south.

That woman looked at Henry so appealing and asked him if he wouldn't go find some food for her children. She wasn't a big woman, and I guess there wasn't much else he could do. They promised not to move if Grandfather Henry looked for food, and if they hadn't trusted him, I guess they'd all have died. Henry Daniels found some food somehow, found someone living nearby, I guess. I don't know what he did, but he fed those people and he took them with him. Wasn't much trouble; they were scared of everything and everybody but him. He took them along with him up north, the woman and her eight children, some of those boys big enough to be a real help to Henry, too, moving that many people back to Illinois. Must have taken a couple of weeks or more getting back to Putnam County, but they did, and a little while later they were all fed up and in good shape. Brought the whole family up out of the South and they lived there on his farm, and they worked—working fools, I guess.

When Henry got around to it, he asked the name of the woman. She said she was called Esther. He asked her last name, and she didn't answer right off. Then she mumbled something. He tried to repeat it, "Service?" She said, "Not quite right, Mister Dan'ls. I spell it Ser-Vis." Nobody alive today knows why she spelled it like that.

When Henry asked about her husband, she said, "Dead." She never explained why she took her eight children and started north through a strange land, or why·she refused to return south, nor did any of the children explain, ever. Later it was discovered that her forebears were Acadians expelled from Grand Pré, Nova Scotia. As Henry Longfellow tells us in his poem *Evangeline,* they settled in Louisiana and became known as Cajuns. But there's never been any proof of that and it doesn't seem like she gave her right name. This is just another one of those mysteries of those slavery days that will never be explained.

My grandfather married Esther Ser-Vis, and all those kids were his. They were a close family and always cared for each other but didn't take anything from anybody. In about a year, Henry and Esther had a little boy whom Henry named Marion, and on June 28, 1845, they had another little boy and named him Lewis. Lewis was my father. Altogether, Henry and Esther had ten kids! But in those days that wasn't a big family. Every kid earned his own way and a bit more, so the more kids the better. The Daniels were a prosperous family for those times, and the kids, some of them, were already adults.

Several years later, just before the states started warring between themselves, Henry Daniels had to go again to look after his property in the South. I guess he went down to Kentucky to sell more timber off his land. After some time the timber was cut and he sent word he was coming home. He never arrived. He must've had quite a lot of money from that timber. Nobody ever knew what happened to him. Must've been killed by someone for his money, we thought. Well, those two little boys of Henry's still had a home, because Esther had promised Henry she would run the farm while he was gone, and when she realized he wasn't coming back, she just kept right on running that farm. Made it pay, too! When the two Daniels boys got a little bigger, they and their mother bought another farm, near the old one. I think that was about 1860.

That awful war started and it went on so long. Young Marion Daniels volunteered, joined the Union Army. He rose to the rank of corporal, and just about that time young Lewis thought he had to get into the fighting too. Lewis never was heavy (though he *was* tall, later), but he joined, became a drummer boy. He was only in ten days when the war was over, never was in any battles. Home the Daniels boys marched, to help with the farm work. You know, my father, Lewis, had an army pension for the rest of his life for serving those ten days. Uncle Marion married, had a little daughter, but soon died of consumption due to exposure during the war. Later his wife and daughter both died, so my father was the only survivor of the Henry Daniels line. The Ser-Vis children all married and were on their own. Lewis and his mother ran the farm for years.

A young widow, Josephine Paine Williams, lived nearby, and she had a little daughter named Hattie. Josephine's father was Judge Judson Paine. My dad must have been as much in love with Hattie as he was with her mother. He always said he married them both in 1876. Hattie was seven or eight years old by then. Lewis was running both farms and taking care of Grandmother Esther, who lived with them until she died. I always thought Lewis had made a pretty good choice when he married Josephine. Not only was she my mother, but for several years she had supported herself and Hattie by dressmaking. If you think that wasn't much, just look at the clothes women were wearing in the 1870s, and almost all made by hand. Not many sewing machines in those days.

Josephine (they called her Phine) was born in New York State. Her parents had moved to Illinois and settled there. She married this Mr. Williams, and six weeks later he got sick and died. It must have been pretty tough on a young woman, a mere girl, left alone like that. But her brother, my uncle Leroy J. Paine, that I'm named after, was a big help to her. She was a great seamstress, they said, and had all the work she could do, and she raised her baby girl alone. It was good that a man she could care for, like my dad, came along.

While I was growing up, my folks often told me about the farm they moved to near Tonica, Illinois, shortly after they were married. They had a new baby girl named Amy then, and while they were building a house they lived in the big log barn. That wasn't unusual in those days, or even now, if there's a good reason. There was a stairway leading up to the loft, and the family lived up there during the summer. They got into the house before the first really cold weather set in.

The saddest thing that ever happened to our family—worse than so many deaths, war, or depression—was the tragedy of my sister Amy. After winter was over in the new house at Tonica, the kids got to play outside again. Well, you know how little girls like to play house. Amy was about two years old and Hattie nine or ten, so of course they played that Amy was the baby and Hattie the mother. My third sister, Abbie, had just been born, and my mother was busy in the house. She usually didn't think much about the kids playing in the barn when the men were working there. But just at the wrong moment that day the men were busy and didn't look up. Mamma Hattie picked up baby Amy, and, wearing a pair of old shoes which had belonged to some woman with big feet, she started down the stairs which led from the loft to the floor of the barn. She held the baby tightly, talking softly all the while, her long skirts trailing behind her on the stairs. But for all her care, she tripped. The big shoe caught in the long gown and it neither fell off nor stayed on. She struggled for her balance and lost it. With Hattie hanging desperately onto the trusting baby with her arms, both girls went rolling down all those stairs.

I never did see that barn, but they say there was a long flight of steps. The two children rolled to the bottom. They could've been killed. They were bruised all over and crying, naturally. Hattie was just stricken with concern and feeling guilty, for she knew now that she hadn't remembered all she'd been told not to do. But Hattie's bruises would heal, except the one she would carry on her heart clear to her grave. Baby Amy didn't seem to be hurt too much either—just bruised, same as Hattie. But Amy had hit her back on a lower step of that stairway, as I heard tell many times. Amy wasn't able to speak for a long time after that. She wasn't paralyzed, she could move around slowly, but her mind was affected. There was a spinal injury.

From the time I can remember (I wasn't born yet when she was hurt), Amy had a terrible temper. She never could talk plain, but when she got bigger she'd get mad over lots of things. She'd throw the first thing she got her hands on. Amy lived to be eighty-four years old, but she never could be anything but a child. My parents, Amy's parents, must have been heartbroken. Even so, they little realized all the problems they would have to face as the years passed.

Soon after this accident, my father made a trip to Iowa. He liked what he saw in Adair County, and he bought 80 acres from Dave Eschelman, 80 acres from Chris Eschelman, and 160 acres from a Mr. Grant, and paid twenty-five cents an acre for the whole deal—half a section of Iowa land for eighty dollars. My uncle Lee Paine bought land here too, and the two families moved together. My dad ordered a couple of boxcars for his goods, and I guess Uncle Lee did the same. Uncle Lee and his wife lived near us, and everyone used to help out with farm problems, stock, hay harvest, and all. They moved into their new farm in March 1882, and I was already waiting to be born. Other settlers soon came too—in clumps, my dad always said. Families didn't venture out across that prairie alone then. Soon there were five families living around us, and after a few years most of the Ser-Vis children were out there too, somewhere within a few miles of us.

I remember that old house well. It had been built by some earlier pioneer, and we lived in it until we built a new one several years later. It stood on blocks of wood, it had a strange construction, there was a little cubbyhole in one place where they used to keep the dogs. The hogs? They kept them under the house so coyotes wouldn't get them. Besides, it saved building a pen until they could spare the time. The yard was always rooted up by hogs, looked like a plowed field. No trees, nothing, just right out on the bare prairie. I remember the old hay shed where the horses, cows, and other stock were kept. That shed was made of slew hay, a coarse grass that grows in low places in a pasture or field. I've always called that farm the old home place, sitting out there in the middle of the prairie. I was born there on October 28, 1882, the first one of the family born in Iowa, the first boy in the family, and I lived there much of my childhood.

I've always been glad they named me for Uncle Leroy Paine. As I grew up, they found I was Uncle Lee's Benjy, just like him in every way—looks, thoughts, actions—without even trying. If I ever saw him do anything, I copied him purposely. I was just like him in every way a boy could figure out to be like someone else, but I was like him in ways I didn't think about, too. I don't think my father liked that very much. Why should he? I was his only son for a while. But you can't change such things.

Did I say that prairie was bare? Depends on the time of year. What a sight in the spring! Grass as far as the eye could see, wild flowers of all kinds, wild strawberries, most every kind of wild fruit, millions of prairie chickens and quail, wolves and squirrels, foxes, other furbearing animals. It sure was a paradise for hunters and trappers. Of course, now we can see what we did to that wonderful world, because it is no longer there for anyone to enjoy. They took it away, destroyed what God and nature gave man to support his life. Then there wasn't a fence anywhere, and we had to herd our cattle. Of course, that was a job for a boy. Didn't take many years till I was a cattle herder. We herders would all get together, and what good times we did have—swimming, games, fishing, all the things a boy likes to do when he naturally can.

There were very few chicken eggs; few families had chickens. In the spring all the kids would gather prairie-chicken eggs, and we would "put them down" to keep them from spoiling, preserve them in our cyclone cellar until we needed them. I remember a strange thing that happened. One Sunday our family visited my Uncle Lee. All of us kids were out gathering eggs, and among us was a girl who worked for Uncle Lee's wife. She didn't know that her apron full of prairie-chicken eggs also had a snake's egg among them. Hadn't noticed a different kind of egg among the others. She was proud to have so many eggs.

"Oh, Mrs. Paine, see what I have," she said. Then she looked down and there in her very apron a young snake had just hatched. That girl gave a scream and down went the eggs on the floor. That seemed funny to the rest of us kids, but that girl didn't laugh about it.

I spent most of my life on the farm, though we moved to Adair when I was five years old. My father never cared for the farm. What he really liked was the livestock business, but after a few years in Adair he moved the family back to the farm. Since he was in the livestock business, he was on the go all the time. He *made* money. He bought hogs, fattened them, and sold them for slaughter. Of course, he was also trading horses, cattle, and sheep, or whatever came his way, but while we lived in town it was mostly hogs. He liked Adair and its country, never wanted to move elsewhere, so kept buying more land. I never knew him to sell but one eighty-acre farm. He had the first twenty-five-dollar-an-acre land in Adair County, the old home place down south of town. He kept adding on and adding on, and when he died he had 1,100 acres of land. Part of it was pasture, part was farmed, and part was for buildings—barns, corrals, house, garden, and all that. Most of it was for growing feed grain.

My dad was a Southern Gentleman, really, though he never lived in the South. He would go in and sit in his chair—when we'd see him coming, anybody who happened to be in his chair would get right out, now, because he wanted his chair, and no other chair would do for him. At four o'clock in the morning he'd give a war whoop and everybody had to get up. But he stayed in bed until breakfast was ready.

I had problems with Dad. Seemed he and I never agreed on any one thing. If I thought this way, he was sure to think that way, one thing or another. Maybe, having three older girls, he thought I was a brazen sprout. I'd get an idea, and before he even knew it I'd put that idea into action. Guess he didn't usually know what I might do next. Guess I didn't know, either, half the time. But what's the use of an idea if you don't use it?

I never had much use for Dad. Seemed he never did care for us kids much, was more interested in making us do what he wanted than in being friends with us. Maybe he thought it was too much of a problem to have to bother with us. He'd spit in your eye as soon as look at you. I never saw him cry but twice. One of those times was when Hattie died. The other time was when he thought Mattie was dying. Nothing else ever seemed to shake him up that much.

Mattie didn't feel very well for a long time, and finally she had to have her appendix out. She didn't get along very well. When I think of it, I believe the doctor gave her too much of some painkiller and it caused depression. At the time, didn't any of us think about such things, we just were shocked because Mattie decided she was going to die and she was very certain of it. She was only about sixteen. One afternoon Mattie called us all into her bedroom—girlfriends, sisters, all the family. Oh, the folks were all a-crying, taking on something, and Dad was carrying on with them. I never saw him take on so much, but he did then. He was sitting there in an old rocking chair crying away.

Mattie said to me, "Now, Lee, before I die you must promise you'll never drink anymore." She was just going on like that. She had them all crying. Everybody had to give up what Mattie thought was their bad habits before she could leave this sad world. Well, I just kind of began to figure out for myself that I wasn't so sure about Mattie. She didn't look to me like she was going to die. She had been my little kid sister a long time, and I knew her pretty well, I thought. She kept it up, and just when everybody thought Mattie was taking her last breath, here came an old turkey gobbler, walking right through the door into her room.

"Gobble, gobble, gobble," we heard him say. I don't know how he got out of the pen or into the house, but he walked right through the door into Mattie's bedroom. He seemed to look right at Mattie when he said "gobble, gobble, gobble," or whatever it is that turkey gobblers say. Mattie looked at him for a moment as though he had just stolen her show. Then she threw back her head and began to laugh. She jumped out of bed and kicked that old gobbler clear out of the house. That was the last we heard about Mattie dying. I was sure glad I hadn't promised her anything. That's all it took, a little humor, to cure Mattie. We'd all been taking her so seriously she had about believed it herself. Suddenly we all about died laughing, just making up for all the tears we had shed. Dad laughed hardest of all.

My mother was a worker. She was the backbone of the whole business. She stayed on the farm and looked after it and supervised the hired men while Dad traveled about trading horses, cattle, whatever he traded at the time. The farms and the kids kept a-coming until finally there we were, all eight of us. I was the oldest boy. There was Hattie, born in Putnam County, Illinois; Amy and Abbie, both born in Tonica, Illinois; then me, the first born at Adair; and Lewis, Eugene, Mattie, and Arthur, all born in Adair County, Iowa. Eight of us, and Mother had her hands busy all the time. Even with the help of the girls and a hired girl, she never got everything done.

As I grew up, it came about that I was the only one who could handle Amy. When she got older she could whip Dad, and Mother too. Many a time I've seen one or the other of them have a black eye where Amy had hit them, and in those days families cared for their own, didn't shut them off in an institution. One time we were eating supper and she threw the kerosene lamp, a burning lamp, at Dad. Hit him right on top of the head. Broke the lamp all to pieces, kerosene spilled all over the floor. It's a wonder it didn't burn the house, a wonder it didn't kill Dad.

I always thought Amy's violence was because they didn't start out right with her. With Mother and Dad, everything Amy wanted, she got. From infancy they should have maintained a strict but kind discipline, but they never refused her anything. That was the worst thing they could have done. If they had corrected her and controlled her when she was little, she would have been better, but after letting her have her way until she was big, they found they were helpless. They used to call me after I left home. They called me plenty of times when I was still home, too. I'd just lock her arms behind her and hold her.

When we built the new house, we had a closet upstairs, just what I needed to discipline Amy. When she was misbehaving I'd just take her there and shut her in that closet. There wasn't any way to light it, nothing but kerosene lamps and candles those days, wouldn't have been safe to put them in there with her. So it was a dark closet. That was the only way I could control her, and Amy knew that if she behaved herself I wouldn't put her there. She could control herself. She knew how to behave. She didn't hit Mother or Dad if she thought I was around. I still felt sad about having to do that to Amy, but I couldn't have her loose with no control over her behavior. She must have had great anger because of her condition, but injuring others didn't help. I guess Mother and Dad thought they could make up to her some for the accident which caused her to be such a care and so useless to herself. It just didn't work out that way. That was just another part of my boyhood, and my manhood too, keeping an eye on Amy.

When Arthur was a baby, Amy just took him away from all of us, even Mother. Amy raised that boy herself. Nobody dared lay hands on Art or they had Amy to fight. She had a fiendish temper. Art wasn't spoiled by her treatment, though Amy was. Even after he grew to be a man nobody dared to say anything against Art. Oh, no. Artie, she called him. Arthur was one of those people who had a special personality; everybody liked him. They said he had git-up-and-go. He and I tied together several times on business and other things.

My big sister Hattie grew up to be a beautiful young lady. She wasn't much more than a girl when she married Harvey McCartney. That was in the early summer of 1894. I was very proud to have a big brother-in-law. Like all little brothers, I could be a nuisance to Hattie. She was so much older she was almost like an adult to my sisters and me, though now I can see she really was just a little teenaged kid herself. We used to give her a bad time, but we loved her too, and we depended on her for many things that we took for granted then. I guess Hattie knew how much we needed her.

Only a month after her marriage Hattie became sick. She died on July 10, 1894, a little more than a month after her wedding, just as her father had died a month after his marriage. It seems to me now that she must have been the one of us all that my father thought most of. She wasn't his real daughter, just a little stepchild, but she was a dear, sweet girl, and I can still see her long brown hair blowing in the wind.

All those years on the farm the only relatives we knew were my mother's brother Lee and his wife (they never had any children) and the families of my father's half brothers and half sisters. It seems like those Ser-Vis families who didn't live near us were often showing up for a visit for a couple of weeks or a month; they were great visitors, a close-knit family. They were the only cousins I knew as a child.

One of my father's half sisters, Lucenia, had married a man named Bazdale Ish, and they had had a large family, all older than I was. They lived in Anita, the next town west from Adair. Well, one day Lucenia up and left her husband for a doctor and took the three youngest children with her. She went to Chicago, but her plans didn't work out. After a while she wrote my father that she was destitute. Dad went to Chicago to help and took me with him. He did what was necessary to get Lucenia and her three teenagers in a livable condition; in fact, he ended up buying her a house at 6941 Normal Avenue, which her descendants held until about 1960.

While the older people worried out their concerns, Lucenia's older son, George, and I decided we'd go fishing. I was just a boy, but George must have been in his mid thirties. We hired a boat and went out on Lake Michigan. George was a very quiet fellow and we got along fine. He thought I knew how to sail a boat and I thought he knew. Didn't either one of us bother to check with the other. We got quite a way out, hit a squall, and the boat upset. I went down, down, down. I don't know how far. I came up right beside the boat, looking for George. I got hold of the edge of the boat (it had turned upside down) and I hung on, looking everywhere, but I didn't see George. I couldn't figure out what had become of him. It turned out that when he stuck his head out of the water he was inside the boat. Somebody picked us up and brought us back to shore. Boy, it was cold. That Lake Michigan water is ice cold all the time anyway, and this happened in the spring.

After that we didn't want to go boating on the lake. George said, "How about us taking in the stockyards?" Yeah, I thought I'd like to see the stockyards. We tried to see it all. You'd never believe how big it all was. I know now that the whole stockyard idea came from a man named Sherman back in 1848. Less than fifty thousand people lived in Chicago then. Nobody had heard of a market where any man could bring his animals and sell them for a reasonable price. So the old Bull's Head Stockyards was set up at Madison Avenue and Ogden Avenue, and millions of people have known it as the Chicago stockyards, and it was running at its best at the time I first saw it, about 1890. It closed in 1971, and I guess Chicago has smelled better ever since. But it affected people around the world while it was operating.

When I first saw the Chicago stockyards it was pretty busy and so was I, for it was enormous. I tried to watch all that was going on around me. I noticed that each man seemed to do just a small part of what went on, but it all fitted together to make the great big thing that I saw. They had vanloads of young men called typewritists. (Women weren't allowed to be secretaries or typists, especially in the stockyards, a wild and woolly place not fit for women.) Animals were brought in, priced, placed on the market, sold, and the owner got his cash, all in one day. Commission men were everywhere, from six o'clock in the morning till sometime after four in the afternoon, handling millions of animals and dollars every week. A commission man knew everything that was going in that stockyard every day. He carried more information in his head—why, it would take a computer to keep up with him today. He kept the place going, didn't waste time on anything.

One of the first commission men I knew was Harry McNair. He had been there on my first visit to the stockyards when I was a boy, and he was still there forty years later. I don't know how many years he put in at those yards, but others were there a long time too. McNair got to be a great friend of mine. He was a fine man, honest but full of humor, too, when he got a chance to make a laugh. He stood more than six feet tall and had a great dignity about him.

When George and I roamed around the yards we saw huge drays being drawn by the biggest horses I'd ever seen. Four- and six-horse teams and more were hitched to each wagon, and they crawled up to the loading platform of railway stations to unload and load again. Railroad cars were filled with so much I didn't see how they could put another thing in, but they did. A canal had been dug to make the Chicago River flow past the stockyards. Docks had been built and ships were loaded there, horses and men doing all the work that machines now do. George found out that about fifty miles of streets and alleys connected the stock pens with the loading and unloading chutes of the railroads. Fifty thousand cattle, two hundred thousand hogs, thirty thousand sheep, and five thousand horses were being handled all at the same time. You'd think all those animals would make a place smell awful. Well, they did, but it could have been worse, because they'd built a system of underground drainage which was working fine, and what was found out years later didn't affect them then.

Well, I saw it all, because George and I would go every day until we'd seen all we could find. It was the greatest animal market in the world at that time. Every day George would promise to take me back again the next day for a couple of weeks or more. That was one of the biggest educations I ever had. Oh, I could tell you a lot more, but there soon came a day when Dad wanted to get back to Adair, so we had to get onto the train, but it was only the first of many times I went to the Chicago stockyards.

Another wonderful memory: Old Bazdale Ish. He was the man Lucenia left behind in Anita, left him for that doctor and moved to Chicago with the younger children. He used to take me places. He stands out in my memory. I used to call him Uncle Basel, never knew his name was Bazdale. When I was a boy eight or nine years old I used to go over there quite a lot, and one thing that impressed me more than anything else was to see a man with a white apron on, cooking. My father never had an apron on in his life, but Uncle Basel did. He and his son Frank bached for years and years.

Uncle Basel was a great marksman and a great hunter, killed prairie chickens by the thousands all over the prairies. He and I would go out and get prairie chickens, and he'd bring them home nearly every day, dress them, and cook them. They tasted better to me than anything in the world. No one could cook like Uncle Basel. What a fine old gentleman he was. Just as clean as anyone you ever saw, nice white beard coming clear down to his waist. The beard and the apron just came together and you couldn't tell which was the whiter. One time he came to our farm and set up a new telegraph wire along the railroad track. He was coming along with his wagon and team, and a flock of prairie chickens flew up and hit the wire. He got out and picked them up, wrung their heads off and brought them home to my mother. She cooked them for dinner, but it wasn't near as good as what Uncle Basel cooked. I told Mother so. Oh, that made her mad! Uncle Basel got pretty old and went to California to live with his daughter, Alice Strawn, and her family. He died there. He was a great and good influence on my life.

THREE

My Early Days

When I was about ten years old my father gave me a pony and a checkbook and sent me out to buy cattle. Plenty of boys became dealers that way. I'll tell you about the first deal I made.

Because this was such an important event in my life, I fixed myself all up, boylike, with a big white hat, spurs, saddle, lariat, and I set out buying cattle. I rode all day on my pony until almost dark. I rode into the farm of an old Irish gentleman. He was milking his cow. I asked him if he had any cattle to sell.

He said, "I'll tell you, I've got this cow here I might sell. She milks so hard she's hard on me nerves. If you'll give me twenty-five dollars for her, I'll sell her to you. But I'll tell you, my boy, I don't know whether I want to take your check or not."

I was a bit chesty, so I said, "Well, twenty-five dollars is a bit too much for me. You'll have to sell her to me for twenty or I don't want her."

He sold her to me. Maybe he was just finding out what kind of a kid I was. I took my lariat off my saddle and put it around the cow's neck and got onto my pony. I tied the rope to the saddle horn and started home, six or seven miles. That old cow wouldn't lead, so I had to drive her. She was still fastened to the saddle and she wanted to go everyplace I didn't want her to go. At nine o'clock that night I got home with my first purchase.

My father came out and said, "My, what in the world has been keeping you? I've been worried to death about you."

"I bought this cow down there and I wanted to bring her home."

"What did you give for a cow like that?"

I told him. He chuckled a bit. "You're all right. You just go right ahead. You're a cattle buyer now and always will be." That made me proud of my first deal.

I pretended I didn't hear next time my girl and her parents visited, but I heard her dad and my dad talking about it. Out parents had engaged us to be married when we grew up, and they wondered could I learn to support a family. My parents' friends, the Crawfords, thought the world of all of us, and we thought the same of them and their little daughter, who was nicknamed Tad. The four parents were always afraid the two families would be separated and lose track of each other. I guess it was because of that they got their little girl and me engaged when I was about two years old. I liked my little fiancée a lot, and I guess I thought it was all right to be engaged to marry her. I know I always had lots of friends who were girls as far back as I can remember, but I never thought about getting married except to that one girl. I sort of grew up to marry her. Everybody knew about our engagement, and we were proud of it.

The parents of that girl treated me almost like their own son as far back as I can remember, and my folks were the same with that little girl. All the years I was little we used to visit my little girlfriend and her family a lot. They'd visit us too. In those days people were more sociable than they are today, seems to me they were. We'd go to their place and stay a whole day, or sometimes overnight, and they'd do the same, come to our house and be there several days, maybe a week if they could. I thought that was all right. I liked that little girl, and we used to play together, explore the farm, whichever farm it happened to be that we were at. It was a good feeling, being engaged to her, and all the parents thought so too, I suppose. They had made the bargain.

When I was old enough to work the fields, life was just one long walk. We sowed our oats and seeded by hand. We had to carry the seed on our backs and scatter it. Then, to cover the seed we used a four-shovel cultivator called a "muley" and I think it was rightly named. If you weren't careful it would fall down. I always had to take the colts for my team, especially the mule colts.

Dad always said I could work any kind of a mule that had hair. After the small grain was in, plowing for corn was next. Two or three horses were hitched to a plow and the driver had to walk all the time.

Then came haymaking. The only machine that had a seat was the mower. Nearly shook your insides out to ride a mower over a rough field all day. After mowing, the hay was raked with a horse-drawn rake, leaving long rows two to three feet high and forty feet long of raked-up hay. Couple of days later, when that was dry, the men walked by and tossed the hay into shocks with a pitchfork, shocks being piles of hay as high as a man's waist, or his shoulder. Then it had to dry some more before it could be stacked. After three or four more days of curing in the sun, finally a wagon came along and men pitched the hay into the wagon with their long three- or four-tined pitchforks. Of course, an ordinary wagon wouldn't hold much hay, so we had to take off the regular bed and put on a hayrack, high and wide, to hold a good load. The hay was hauled to the barn and again pitched with forks through the wide-open upper door into the hayloft, where it was packed properly so there'd be no hollow spaces and it would be easier to get it down for the animals during winter feeding times. I'm saying this now so young folks today can see how the work was done back in the good old days, when nobody ever thought of jogging or running for exercise.

We bound the grain by hand and threshed it with a threshing machine powered by a horse, took six teams of horses. The grain came out of the machine into the tally box and was measured with a half-bushel basket and lifted into a wagon. Sounds easy, but before night those half-bushels got pretty heavy. Straw was bucked away from the machine into a stack.

The first self-tie binder I saw was a wire binder which belonged to my dad and Uncle Lee. Everyone thought that was a great invention, but it didn't pan out too good. Cows swallowed little pieces of wire that got lost in their hay, and it killed them.

The corn planter was the next great invention. We cross-marked a field into squares with a sled like a drag that had two runners. The man on the planter drove the team, and a small boy rode the middle of the planter. When the planter crossed the intersection of the two lines, the boy jerked a lever with his hand to let the seeds fall. I would get so tired I would sometimes fall asleep and was awakened by a whip across my back. Oh, I could tell you about a lot of planters. They all did a certain kind of job better, but all had their problems, too. We picked all our corn by hand for many years, and forever before my time. We shucked it and scooped it into cribs.

Farming has changed a lot since I was a boy. One man easily does more than ten men used to, and does little walking or hand work (but ask him, he still does enough). The small farms are all gone now, families no closer than a mile apart. We enjoyed life. Now farmers have good roads, good houses, and good schools, but it all costs a lot of taxes and other fees to provide. I wonder if we're better off.

The life of a growing boy is supposed to be interesting, but when you come to follow a plow all day, or a herd of sheep, sometimes I used to wonder what was interesting about it. Just plain old slavery most of the time, but sometimes there was a break. Sometimes I made the break, and life might be very interesting at such a time. Being the oldest boy in the Daniels family, I had a lot of responsibility, but I also got to dream up a lot of the pranks we played on the girls. We boys, with our tricks and mischief, didn't make their lives any easier, but probably not much harder, either. At least we gave them a laugh now and then—and usually got our pants tanned for our trouble. But it was always worth it, the fun I had, getting their goats.

I remember one night when I watched where my mother and Hattie hid the Easter eggs. I sneaked out and took all of them and put them in my basket. Easter morning came, and the girls couldn't find any eggs. They cried and carried on, but in a little while they found I had a whole bushel basket of eggs. Oh, they were mad. Now, maybe you think I didn't get a trimming from those three girls. Amy loved to hide eggs and hunt for them, too. Mattie got so mad because I had her eggs—well, of course, Mother made me divide them up. Mattie had hers in her little apron and she got all excited. I can see her going yet, tearing off across the grass. She was running so fast her curly hair was just standing out in back of her head. Something threw her, and down she went with that apron full of eggs. She was just covered, egg all over her. Mother hadn't cooked the eggs. Boy, if you've ever seen such a mess. That was scrambled eggs for sure, and with a girl mixed in, too.

Another time, Mother and Father had gone to Adair and left Hattie to take care of us kids. I was fighting with the girls. The fight lasted quite a while. Hattie threatened to spank me. I just wasn't going to let any old Hattie spank me for fighting with any old girls. I climbed up a tree and tried to frighten Hattie by hanging myself. Oh, Hattie just begged me to come down. I was going to give her something to be really sorry for. I intended Miss Hattie to know who was boss from now on.

My plan backfired on me when the limb I was standing on broke. The rope got tight around my neck. I didn't like that choking too well. It was a pretty sad feeling when the rope got tighter and tighter. I grabbed the rope with both hands so it wouldn't choke me. I couldn't get up in the tree because I didn't dare let go of the rope, but I needed both hands to climb up and relieve the tightening rope. Oh, I was choking. Hattie got up in the tree. She had a great big butcher knife. I'll never forget that. Long as her arm, it seemed. She climbed up in that tree and she whacked that rope. I dropped to the ground. I wasn't very high up anyway. Well, I never tried to hang myself after that.

When I got down, Hattie took the rope off my neck and put me in the little pantry where Mother kept all her dishes. I was still fighting mad. I wasn't over my mad for a while yet. I went to throwing dishes at the door, and I broke every dish in that pantry. Mother and Dad came home and, boy, I had to stand at the table for a lot of meals before I could sit down again. Boy, I got a licking for that afternoon's work. But I never tried to hang myself again. That's just one of the ornery tricks I pulled off when I was a kid.

I thought of a few more, too. One involved a hired girl we had, a German girl named Lois Schmeling. Mother always had to have a hired girl, so much work to do, big family on a busy farm, and all—cooking, harvesting, canning and preserving, sewing, laundry, ironing, and all. Why, just a mountain of work for a woman. Lois came to live with us. She had been with Mother a long time, like one of the family. She was a great hand to play a joke on us kids. Sometimes her jokes were a little rough.

Once she put sandburs under the sheet in my bed, and when my brother and I got in, you know what happened? Those sandburs went right through the sheet. When I got out of there I was dragging the sheet with the sandburs sticking into me. My dad was laughing—nothing like a practical joke to make him hold his sides and rock with laughter. When I came downstairs dragging that sheet with the sandburs, that just tickled the gizzard out of him. I thought, Old girl, I'll get even with you if it takes a hundred years.

There was a porch alongside the house, and Lois' room was right above this porch. There was a window opening onto the porch. She slept with her bed pulled right up next to this window. I got my pal, Arthur Crawford, into the plot with me, and we decided we'd have some fun with the hired girl. In the afternoon we unlatched the window and fixed a way to get up onto the porch. We had a ladder and we'd planned everything. We crawled up onto the porch after Lois had gone to bed and crawled through the window and under her bed. We'd push our knees up against the mattress. Oh, she'd yell and scream. We'd push with one foot and then with the other. She'd get settled down and then we'd let her have it again. Lois was howling, "Oh, Mr. Daniels, come up here! There's a man under my bed!"

Dad came running. Arthur Crawford got out ahead of me. We had the window open just enough to get out, and he slipped through. I got halfway through and the window came down and caught me. I never heard anyone laugh so as my dad did. I was just in a good position for what he suddenly had in mind. Boy, did he ever give me a spanking, laughing all the time he was doing it. "Them darn fool kids, tormenting that girl," he said. Then he'd laugh again.

With that many kids in the house, there just had to be some pretty comical things happening most of the time. I remember one time we had a hired man, George Chapman, about the time I was twelve. He was always playing tricks on us. Mattie and I decided we'd play a trick on him. We knew he was afraid of bumblebees. He'd run like a whitehead for just one little bumblebee. We had been trying for a long time to think of some trick to play on him. We finally got this good idea when they started making hay. Boy, if he saw a bee, he'd just fly out of that field. You couldn't get him near one. Mattie and I decided that was the way to play a joke on George, even up the score for a lot of tricks he'd been playing on us.

We went out in a clover field with our straw hats. We'd knock a bumblebee down with our hats, pull his stinger out, and put him in a fruit jar. We pulled stingers enough to half fill that quart jar with bees. It didn't hurt the bees any, they were all alive. George slept at our house in a room by himself, and we took that jar of bees up and put the bees under the sheets of his bed.

Well, come night and he went to bed, took off all his clothes except his shirt. Everybody was sitting in the living room, supposed to be reading. I don't think Mattie and I read very much, only nobody noticed. We heard George walk across the floor a couple of times, and then the bedsprings creaked as he got in. We had to hold our breaths to keep from busting, but it didn't take long. George laid there a little bit and pretty soon the bees began to buzz. We knew just what they'd do. About two seconds and down the stairs comes George, hard as he could run, busted down through the wooden door and the stairway, never stopped at the living room, just ran right through the screen door, across the porch, never stopped for anything. I'll bet you could've stood on his shirttail when he went through, about fifty bees chasing him. Didn't have a thing on him but his shirt. Ran out into the yard and couldn't get rid of those bees until he went and jumped into the watering tank.

Dad and everybody first wanted to know what was wrong. Didn't take them long to figure that out, and then they all busted out laughing. Dad laughed so hard he couldn't paddle us for that one. George Chapman left right away. Came back and got his clothes and pulled out. Mattie and I, we just hid. We didn't dare show up. We didn't know what he'd do, but we had a good hiding place where we could watch. Funny part of it was, he didn't know we'd done it. He thought the hired girl was the guilty party. George Chapman. I wish he could listen now.

After he left us he started a dog and pony show. He came to Adair one time with his show. I didn't get to see him, but my sister Abbie did. He mentioned his fight with the bees, said he was never so scared in his life. Abbie told him those bees were harmless, that their stingers had been pulled out, told him it wasn't the hired girl but Mattie and me who'd done it. I'd like to have seen his face then.

At my girl's house one time, the old dog had a litter of puppies. My girl, Tad, trained one. It would get up on a chair and say its prayers and all this and that. She gave it to me for a present on my tenth birthday. I called that dog Trim. He would do anything.

There used to be lots of tramps wandering wherever the railroad tracks led. They'd drift, ride the freight trains, and beg a meal or a few days' work. Maybe they had helped build the railroad, followed it west, and now had to walk back looking for work. The railroad tracks went right through Adair. These men'd go to people's doors, sometimes just ask for food. Some would steal anything they got a chance at. There were all kinds. Some were just poor, harmless men who didn't have anyplace to go and couldn't stop going. Some would work, do a good job, stay as long as the work would last. We got that dog Trim so he wouldn't let the tramps come in the yard, and we trained him by putting a pack on our backs and running from him. We got him so he wouldn't let a tramp come near the place.

I was always wishing I had some sheep. I wanted Dad to get me some, but he thought I could grow a bit more first. There was a man lived near us who had some sheep. Dogs got into his sheep and tore one of them up. Well, this man gave this little torn-up lamb to me. Oh, I was happy. I just thought I owned the whole world because that lamb was mine. I doctored the little thing up and, of course, it followed me wherever I went. Old Trim and the lamb were always right at my heels. Trim just loved that little lamb. He'd lick those sores like he was the mother, you know. They just got along fine. They'd play together, and the dog would follow the lamb.

My father bought a lot of sheep, and I guess because of what that other dog had done, Father thought Trim would kill some of his lambs. First thing I knew he had Trim tied up in the corncrib. Poor Trim. He just cried and cried for days, because he wanted to go with me. I guess I cried too, a little, because I liked having my dog follow me around and I had to go with the herd, now that we really had sheep. There weren't any boys playing around idle when there was work to do, not in those days. We didn't have any fences then so I had to herd those sheep. They were Merinos, those curly black sheep, and they didn't know anything. They were the dumbest outfit I'd ever seen, and I sure wished I had my dog to help me.

One day I thought, Well, Trim, you've had enough; I'll just take you out even if you kill them all. I opened the door and let him out. Oh, he was so glad to be loose and with me. He jumped up and licked my face again and again, jumped higher than I stood, and he ki-yied and carried on, but I got him settled down. Talk about a sheepdog, he was one of them! We'd had trouble getting those Merinos through the gate. There were two thousand of them, and they'd get up to a gate and jam into it so nothing could get through.

The man we'd bought them from said, "I'll give you a couple of goats. They'll lead these sheep into the pen." We got the goats out there, and the billy was no good. He bothered the sheep, chased them, wouldn't let them through the gate. The little nanny goat, she'd lead them in, only finally she got scared and left, so we had only the billy, the big old nuisance. We had to break him of getting in front of the gate. He didn't know that, but old Trim did. Trim went right over the backs of the sheep and gave that old goat a good going over. Of course, the goat ran from Trim. After that, whenever the sheep jammed at the gate old Trim would go up over their backs after that old Judas goat. The goat would run through the gate and the sheep would follow him. Trim was out and around, putting them all in. He didn't need anybody to help.

You know, it's fascinating to watch a dog work sheep. He just knows all the answers, and he knows the problems before the thought, and he knows what to do in every case. A sheepdog is a natural-born psychologist. No matter what kind of dog you've got, you can make a sheep dog out of it if you've got any brains at all.

With Trim working the sheep so well, we thought we were pretty good trainers, but a few years later, when I had grown a bit taller and had bigger ideas in my head, I went to a Wild West show and there was Buffalo Bill Cody, and I believe he might have been one of the greatest animal trainers of all time. Surely he was great for those days, but he would be great today, too, such was his genius with animals. I saw all of his shows in Atlantic, and I went out to his ranch near North Platte, Nebraska, before his show failed. I couldn't keep away from horses, and he had some great ones. At one time he wanted me to go with his show. I was crazy to go, but my folks said no.

Buffalo Bill's real name was William Frederick Cody. He had hunted buffalo for the Union Pacific Railroad before he got the idea that the public might appreciate a chance to see the beauty and grandeur he had seen. He was right on target. They flocked in to see whatever he had, and he was showman enough to keep them coming wherever he set up his tents. He had a lot of old show wagons, cages, Indian relics—one thing and another. After he quit the business, many others thought they could do the same kind of show, but they couldn't. His genius could not be copied successfully. He had that certain touch. He is buried at Lookout Mountain, twenty miles from Denver, and the things from his show are in a museum at Cody, Wyoming.

Buffalo Bill was one of the greatest heroes of the nineteenth century. To me, he was a hero, a fine man, always very friendly, the greatest. He was just as common as an old shoe—at least, I thought so. He met everybody as an equal. To the public he was an ideal. To himself? I've never been able to figure that out. He was an adventurer, wanting to try everything once. He was a great showman with a wonderful show. In a way, though, Buffalo Bill was kind of a fake. He was a great marksman, but when he would ride a horse at a fast run and throw a little ball about two inches in diameter into the air, clipping it off every time with a rifle, there was a trick to it. I once asked him, "How can you do it? How do you hit that ball every time?"

Smiling, he answered quietly, "Bird shot in the shells."

FOUR

On My Own

After my experience in South Dakota and Montana, I still wasn't satisfied that I had found what I wanted to do with my life. I had been thinking about doctoring ever since my dog Trim and I had cured that little dog-chewed lamb years before. I always felt strongly about sick animals and sick people, but I didn't know what I wanted to do.

I was on my own now and needed to make some money, so while I was thinking about what to do with my life, I went out and borrowed $2,250 from a bank and bought a bunch of cattle to fatten, to feed up. When they were ready for market I went with Uncle Lee to Chicago to sell them. We put them into a boxcar like everyone else did and rode along with them until we got to Chicago. There we put them into pens to await their sale and took beds in the hotel which served stockmen. Uncle Leroy was in the commission business. He always was like a father to me. But even with his help, I didn't make a thing on those cattle. Uncle Lee felt sorry for me because it was my first try and I didn't have a profit.

He said, "Lee, I did everything I could, but it didn't help you. You're young, so don't feel too bad about losing money on those cattle. When I go back home I'll get you another bunch of cattle. You can feed them and get back the money you lost on these."

I'd had to borrow that money from the bank and I was $1,250 behind now. I owed that much to the bank and I didn't own a thing. I said so to Uncle Lee, and he looked at me and said, "Lee, I'm going to give you some advice. I believe you'll agree with it. If you lost your pocketbook here in Chicago or anyplace else, where would you go to look for it?"

"Wherever I thought I'd lost it."

"That's the way to do. If you lose money on anything, that's the place to look for it. If you make a deal and lose money, remember. That's a good lesson for you. Go back home and pick up that money where you lost it."

I did. From that time on, I was awful careful about buying cattle. The thought that's been with me all my life is, If you lose anything, don't cry about it. Go back and pick it up where you lost it.

After finding out how to buy and sell cattle, I decided to try sheep. I borrowed money to buy them with, borrowed it from another banker. I bought a thousand lambs and fed them. I made them just as good as they possibly could be made. I had bought them in the fall and turned them into a cornfield after the corn was harvested. They couldn't have had better feed. They were so fat they could hardly get up off the ground. I went to the Omaha market to sell those sheep. When I got there I thought I was going to lose my shirt. I could get a thousand dollars more than I gave for my sheep; the market wasn't in my favor. I'd lose all my feed. Takes a lot of feed for a thousand lambs. I went back home and told this banker who had loaned me the money. He said to sell the lambs, so I sold them. When I got back he said, "You told me a story about your uncle. He said if you lose money, go back and pick it up where you lost it. Didn't you tell me that?"

I said I did say it, and that banker stared at me a while. "That's the reason I let you have the money for those lambs. Now you're gonna have to pick that money up where you lost it."

"All right. But I fed up all the corn I had and all the hay."

"You didn't feed up all the water you had, did you?"

"No." I had plenty of water.

"Got shirts and everything?"

"Yeah."

"Well, why don't you borrow another thousand and take on another thousand lambs?"

"Would you furnish the money?"

"Yes." After a minute he added, "Now what are you gonna have to give for corn?"

"Twenty cents a bushel."

"Can you buy any hay?"

"No, there's no good hay out there right now."

"Some of these sheep feeders are feeding alfalfa and molasses. Did you ever try that?"

"No, I didn't."

"There's a factory up here. We're going to call that man on the phone and make a deal for enough to feed those lambs." After he talked to the feed supplier he looked at me again in that way he had.

I said, "There's a man that worked for me before, came to me with two thousand of the best lambs I've ever seen. I never saw such a bunch of lambs as they are."

"What does he want for them?"

"Just what I got for mine, four cents a pound."

He sat right up in his chair. "You go right down there and buy those lambs. I don't mean nibbling. Now you get out of here and go right down and buy those lambs."

I flew out of there, went down and bought the lambs at four cents a pound. I was weighing them five hundred at a time, two thousand of them. That's a lot of lambs. As far back in the yard as you could see were my lambs. An old sheepherder who hadn't been there in the morning stepped up to me and asked, "What'll you take for the first five hundred?"

"Nickel a pound."

"I'll take them."

He took five hundred lambs, and I got them started into the wagons which would take them home. They were too small to drive. I was weighing the last five hundred when another buyer came up with a rig. He offered me five cents a pound for them. Oh, I was just stepping high there. I'd just gotten my lambs and made part of that two thousand back. I went to the bank, and I was just feeling happy as I could be.

The banker said, "Did you get those lambs weighed?"

"Yeah."

"Well, how much was there?"

"I sold five hundred of them to an old herder and five hundred to another feeder. I'm taking a thousand home. They're on the way."

He looked unhappy. "I don't believe I'll let you have the money."

"You son of a bitch! What kind of a deal man are you? You promised to finance me on those lambs, now I expect you to do it."

"I was fixing to finance two thousand and you went and sold half of them."

I said, "Take your pencil and figure out what those thousand head cost me—just about three cents a pound. Now, these lambs will make money, and then I'll pay you off. Then I'm done. I don't need this kind of business."

He paid for the lambs, paid for the feed, gave me an account at the bank for what I needed for those lambs. I fed those lambs for six weeks. When I took them back to the sale barn the market was sky-high. I paid that banker back his $2,250 plus what I had lost on my cattle deal, and I had $2,000 profit over everything. That was a pretty good feeling for a young kid.

I wanted to buy some cattle after I paid that banker. He looked at me kind of funny and said, "I don't want anything more to do with you. I pulled you out of one hole, now you won't get me into another."

"All right," I said. I walked out of that bank and never went in again. There were other banks more willing to put up with my ideas so long as I made money for them, which I always did.

        Well, the base for all this cattle feeding and sheep feeding of mine was right there in Adair. Adair, Iowa—the place where I was born and where I lived most of my very, very long life. Just drive down Interstate 80, and about halfway between Des Moines and Omaha sits Adair, right on the highway. Take the Adair exit and you're right in town, the way it used to be. I'm told it has grown a lot since 1970. It's a typical little Middle West farm town—stores, banks, machine shop, church, little bit of a jail that nobody used to get into but that's changed now, too. You can almost see the horses and buggies parked along here and there, but now it's mostly pickup trucks and farm cars. But my story is not involved with what's there now. I only remember what was there a long time ago, and that's the part that lasted a long, long time.

Adair started in 1872. Town and county both are named for an officer who served during the War of 1812. The Rock Island Railroad put a line through the area in 1868 and 1869, and that made a little difference. Goods could be shipped that couldn't be sent so far before. All the men had to do in their spare time was pitch horseshoes out behind the barn, and the women didn't have any spare time to worry about. Now they all watch TV. Things are enough different today that nobody wants to think about it. Now the boys jump *into* their mustang or pinto instead of onto it when they go courting.

Adair is unique, because it just happens to be the only place in the United States where the tools of three generations of transcontinental telephone still stand. On the south side of town within a quarter of a mile of each other are poles erected in 1915 for the first transcontinental telephone system, nearby are poles erected in 1931 to carry all-weather phone cables, and near both of these is a radio-telephone tower put up in 1951, carrying television programs and over a thousand long-distance phone conversations all at the same time. No, there'll never be another place like Adair, not for me, not for a lot of others. That was the way the Indians felt way back when the U.S. government moved them out in big freight wagons to make room for the whites who wanted their land. I don't blame those Indians for not wanting to leave.

Adair being the quiet little town that it was for so long, you might think not much happened, but it didn't seem so to people like me who grew up around there. Why, we just thought we were right in the thick of all the activity. I went a lot of places, saw a lot of people, did a lot of things. Everything that happened, you know what? I learned something. I learned about people and places and things. And I learned about myself.

I was seventeen when I decided to finish high school at Atlantic. I hoped to study to be a doctor, but that is another story. I made a lot of friends in Atlantic, and I already had a lot of friends. We had a good time there, and I made good grades. Life was great, living there, doing my job after school hours and spending long evenings with people I enjoyed.

We were all talking about this newfangled thing they called the automobile. Great joke. Everybody knew no silly machine could ever take the place of the horse, but those engines were fascinating. The internal combustion engine was one of the greatest inventions of man. Who could imagine what the world would be like without horses? There'd never been such a time. Horses did so many jobs, you couldn't imagine being without them. Everything that needed moving was moved by horses, except for a few ox teams, but so few there was no comparison. Everybody depended on horses. People walked to spare a horse for heavy work or because they couldn't afford a horse. They had been with us from the beginning of memory. This was a way of life we never dreamed would change, it would go on like a river, forever. Growing up on the farm as I did, I have a great love for horses.

The first car that came into Iowa was a Reo, a hard-wheeled old Reo. They shipped it into Atlantic by train. The buyer of the car was staying at the Park Hotel. I knew him because I had lived at that hotel a couple of weeks before I could find a place to board. He got smallpox, and he wanted to know if I could drive that car from the depot up to his hotel. I? Oh, gosh, I was quite a hero. I could drive a car, you know, or thought I could. Kids at school would think, Oh boy, he's something, he's going to drive that automobile.

Well, it's a long street from the depot to the Park Hotel, clear up the hill. About thirteen hundred people lined up there. Uphill all the way, too, icy streets in the spring of the year, thawed just enough to make it muddy in the middle of the day. The kids all had to go see that wonderful automobile, so they let them out of school. I got it started, got it pretty near halfway up the hill, and I got stuck. Rigg Stafford got behind the Reo and pushed, pushed it clear up to the Park Hotel. Well, that wasn't enough for us kids, we had to see more of that car. Coming back, the mud was so deep the boys had to push it downhill. The horses? Boy, they just reared and plunged, snorted and blew steam, they were just scared to death of that thing. It was a one-cylinder concern, went "too too too," those old iron wheels plowing through the mud.

Within a week others thought they had to have cars too. Cars began to show up in Atlantic sometime around the Fourth of July. They charged twenty-five cents to ride you around the block. Everybody had to have a ride in an automobile. They had a Reo in Fontanelle one time. I think every Dutchman there gave a quarter to ride around the square. Why, in those days a lot of people didn't earn a dollar a day. Twenty-five cents was a lot of money. I got the highest wages of any hired farmhand in the county feeding cattle. They paid me twenty dollars a month. I had to pick corn, feed cattle, do housework, deliver the baby, and do everything else, make love to the girls, I guess. I even got paid for that, all that. Then they go spend a quarter to ride around the block.

I was about eighteen when I went to work for a neighbor. By and by the county fair opened in Greenfield, the county seat. At that time everybody went to the fair. You'd get up early, do all the chores—feed the animals, milk the cows, slop the hogs—then hitch the team to the old wagon so's to have room for the entire family and drive fifteen or more miles to the fair. You'd stay all day and come home after night had fallen to do all those chores over again. Well, someone had to stay home this time, because the boss' wife was pregnant and couldn't go.

The boss said to me, "Now, Lee, we want to go to the fair. My kids are showing their projects, and we just have to be there. This is a pretty big family, but we all have to be there." I didn't mind staying home. I'd seen the fair before and I'd see it again. He gave me instructions. "Now, Lee, don't get too far from the house, so if my wife gets sick you can call our married daughter across the road, or you can call one of the neighbors. Anyway, it probably won't happen for another week. If I thought it would, of course, I wouldn't go to the fair myself."

Off they all went. I worked around the yard all morning. There were plenty of things to attend to—mend the fence, feed the stock, odds and ends of jobs. After three or four hours, I heard the boss' wife calling me. I thought she sounded kind of desperate. I hurried up the path to the house. I could see she needed help. I said, "I'll get your daughter right away," and I jumped onto a pony and hurried across the road. The daughter had gone to the fair. So had all her family. The only thing there was livestock. Well, I'd get the neighbors. The neighbors were all gone too. Boy, I began to sweat a little and I hurried back across the road and up to the house. My boss' wife was standing on the porch holding onto a post, and she didn't look very good to me. I told her what I had found out.

She said, "Lee, I hate to ask you, but will you help me? This baby is ready to be born."

She was right. I could tell. I'd delivered calves, colts, sheep, and other animals. I didn't argue. It had to be done, so I did it. There wasn't time to think about anything else. I just delivered that baby. I tied its navel, washed the mother, and cleaned her all up, washed the baby. All the time the mother was telling me what to do and I was doing it. Way after dark the family came home. This nice little boy baby was lying there nursing when the father walked in.

"My God, I didn't expect this to happen!" my boss yelled.

His wife smiled and said, "If it hadn't been for Lee, I don't know *what* would have happened."

You know, babies seem to have a genius for being born just when they can scare up a little excitement. I had tried to call everybody in the country and they were all gone. No phones then, I had to go to the houses. Do you think that baby could've picked any other time in the world to be born? Not a chance, had to be right now. Even the doctor was gone, and my dad, too.

Now they all flocked to the little show they had missed, to comment on the fine delivery. The mother wanted to name the baby after me. I put up such a fuss they decided not to do that. They named it Bert. Of course, in a day or so all the neighbors knew what had happened. I went by the name of Dr. Daniels for years. Every time they wanted to tease me a little they'd call me that. Doc! Glad I wasn't bashful.

Doesn't seem to me there was any connection between me delivering that baby and wanting to be a doctor, but the two did happen fairly close together, when I think of it. I'd wanted to be a doctor for a long time. I was a good scholar back at high school in Atlantic, and I thought a lot about an education. I came to be stronger and stronger for an education in medicine, I wanted to help people, and to my knowledge still, there's no better way than to be a doctor and either cure them or teach them how to take better care of themselves, or both. I talked to some of my teachers, and they thought I could make it at the university medical school. By the time I finished high school I was ready to become a doctor. The only problem was how to get the money and be able to go to school too. Not enough time in a man's life for both of these, unless he has something special he can do for money.

My girl, that I'd been engaged to since I was two years old, she and her parents had lived with her family in Oklahoma for a long time, but we'd seen each other once or twice, and we'd never even thought of changing our plans to marry. I didn't worry about her. My first concern was to get myself in shape to support a family. We loved each other, and I knew she'd be willing to wait for me while I got myself ready for a long and useful life helping other people as well as myself and the family I expected we'd have. My dad wasn't keen about my wanting to be a doctor, but I didn't intend to let him stand in my way. Mother didn't say much, but she seemed to think it was a good idea. She'd have been behind me whatever I did if she thought it was what I really wanted to do with my life. I was just past eighteen when I moved onto a farm up past Dad's farm and rented some land from him. But that wasn't enough; it wasn't the way I wanted my life to be.

When I had a little money I went to Iowa City. In 1898, the university there was just a small place, nothing like it is now. But I went straight to the biggest and the best medical school in the state, the University of Iowa. I took courses necessary to prepare myself for the study of medicine, and I enjoyed the life of a student who was serious and determined to be something in this world. I spent about three months in medical school. I wanted to go on, but I ran out of money. Turning it all over in my mind, I decided to go home and put in another crop and then go back to medical school.

Oh, my crop turned out wonderful, but it took a whole year, or nearly so. Everything I turned my hand to came in good—had lots of corn. When it came time to go back to school in January, I was tied up with a lot of corn and a lot of livestock. I tried to borrow money for school from my father, but he wouldn't give it to me. He had me. I couldn't go to school without money. He could just as well have loaned it to me as to somebody else, he knew I'd pay it back. He wouldn't.

Dad said, "You're a farmer. I don't want you to be a doctor. If you want to go to college, I'll pay your way at agricultural college, all the way through." He wanted me to be what he chose, not what I chose, for my own life.

I said, "No, I don't want that. I can make a living on the farm without going to agricultural school. The fellows I've seen who did go haven't got along very well. I don't want to be like them. I don't want to develop my theories and then have to pack them away and never see if they really work. I want to really do things, not live in a cage protected from everything I might not like." Didn't seem like there was any way I could go back to medical school. I had seen some of the old doctors of that time, and they didn't know much. Seemed to me I could do a lot better for the folks in Iowa if I could just get the training I needed, but it didn't work out.

FIVE

The Chicago Stockyards

I was back and forth between Adair and the Chicago stockyards a few times while I tried to solve my problems about medical school and, you know, I just kept getting more and more fascinated with that place. Carl Sandburg wrote a very interesting poem about Chicago. He told it the way I knew that city, but you have to imagine a lot that he didn't tell. Now, I went there a lot, but I didn't very often go anywhere but the stockyards, so I won't try to tell you about the rest of it. But those stockyards were big enough to keep me busy a long time if I tried to tell you all about them, which I won't.

The Union Stockyard stretched from Thirty-ninth Street clear south to Fifty-first. It went from Kedzie to State Street, and the actual size is said to have been something like nineteen or twenty square miles. Imagine that much space filled with nothing but baaing sheep, mooing cows, hee-hawing donkeys, squealing pigs, horses making all the noise they could, grunting steam engines, hollering men, and everything else that might happen in that much space filled with thousands upon thousands of men and animals. People came there to work from all over Europe and a lot of other places, too, and all over this country. I just wouldn't know where they all came from. And the animals came from all over this country, too.

Can you imagine how those stockyards smelled? On a windy day they said even the millionaires clear on the other side of town could smell it—good and strong. Gave them a chance to realize where all their money came from. Poor people, why they just smelled that— worse than any barn— all the time, and the poorer they were the nearer they lived to the stockyards. Fierce. Just disgusting for families, and many a time I thought how glad I was my own family didn't live near that stinking place. Of course, for us men it was just a part of the job, and we got away when our work was done, but those poor families, I don't see how they could stand it. Noise and stink. Anywhere you went in Chicago you usually smelled and heard that yard. But if that's where your support was coming from it wouldn't be very good business to say much about it. Why, those men in the packinghouses were just covered all day with blood, filth, dirt unimaginable, all over them most of the time. Enough to drive a man to drink, or worse. But that was how they supported their families and I supported my family by taking animals there both to sell and to be butchered.

Think of the amount of business that took place there. Why, a man just can't imagine that much. The Chicago stockyards never had a rival. There never was anything to compare with them in the world in volume of sales and related business. About the mid nineties, an average sale day in the horse market was three hundred, including private sales. There was stabling for four thousand horses, and each commission man gave a bond of twenty thousand dollars as proof of his good faith to those consigning their animals to him. They held an auction every day but Sunday, and people were there from all over the world. Auctioneers made a pretty good salary for those days—three to six thousand dollars a year.

Sitting around the horse market in Chicago used to be kind of boring, so the boys tried to keep something going. Told each other their opinions about everything you could think of, including southerners. At the turn of the century the War between the States was only thirty-five years back, and there still were bad feelings about it, on both sides, whole families divided, and there wasn't another war for over fifty years to help people to forget. Though most of us didn't like Negroes, we didn't like the people who had held them as slaves, either. Maybe we would as soon the whole affair had never happened, but we couldn't sweep it under the rug. There it was, every day of our lives.

You never knew what might happen next when you caught the train for Chicago. It was rough in town those days and isn't any better yet, but no rough stuff was tolerated around that horse market. You saw more rough behavior and heard more rough talk in the cattle yards. Farmers shipped their cattle in there, and the first thing they'd want to do was to go out into the town and get drunk, and then you can guess the rest.

One spring I shipped a lot of good horses into Chicago. A potato grower came in with a friend to buy from me. I looked twice at that friend and I could see he was Henry Ford. Oh, that was a long time ago, must have been 1903 or 1904. I thought I was a pretty good horseman at that time. Ford's first car hadn't been out very long. You know, he had a buggy and put a motor in it, geared it up, that was his first car. Ford called his car a Quadricycle because it had four wheels. Awful-sounding name for anything a man's gotta depend on. He had a great dream about making a car for the middle-class people, one they could afford to buy. I asked Mr. Ford, "What do you think this car you've got will do? A horse can do anything a man needs, and everybody knows what to expect of him. This contraption you've got—I wouldn't know what it would do."

Henry Ford said, "This car is going to be a success. I'll make a car cheap enough so everybody can have one." He did. I didn't get a car, not for years afterward, but he told me all about his Ford that day. He had taken the running gear of a buggy and put his own motor in it. No time to fool around building a body, the motor was what had to be invented. That was all they knew about making a car then, and Henry Ford was the only one who knew that. Anyway, I thought so. Others were trying, too, but he got there first, or at least cheapest. He tried it out, and he knew what he had when he talked to me. But I wasn't so sure.

"It's a success. You won't need horses anymore," he said.

To myself I said, "I'll keep right on with my horses."

We had a long talk that day. In the period 1903 to 1904 alone, I found out later, Ford sold 1,700 cars. That doesn't seem like very many cars today, but then it was more than you could imagine. Like selling 3,400 horses, and wagons to go with those two-horse teams. Amounted to way over a million dollars, but I don't know how much it cost to build them. You'd have to figure it all in to see how much profit he made. But with the horse, you only figure what he cost when you bought him and what you might've had to feed him when you fattened him and rested him, or gentled him if he'd been wild before.

It gave a man something to consider, but the more I considered, the less I believed. "How about that gasoline engine?" I asked. "All that smoke's enough to kill a man. Get into the barn with the door shut and it'd kill you sure."

"Oh, no," he laughed. "But you remind me of something. You know, I've worked out a number of different engines trying to get just the right one for my car. I got a neat little one-cylinder motor, funny little thing, more like a toy, wanted to try it out, middle of the night, so I took it into my wife's kitchen and clamped it onto the sink. I was all set to start it up, but my wife wouldn't let me. She had our baby boy asleep in the next room, and she thought the exhaust from that engine would kill him, and the fumes would poison him."

Ford laughed, but I wasn't so sure. "What if all those fumes, after a few years, stay in the air, fill the air with that gasoline smoke?"

"Oh, can't hurt anybody," he said. "Just blows away in the wind. Man's been burning campfires for thousands of years—railroad engines, steamboats, factories—all kinds of fires for a good many years, and nothing's happened. Why would this little engine make any difference?"

I didn't know why. "How about the steam engine?" I asked. "Wouldn't that be cleaner?"

Ford didn't think they were practical. "If it stinks up the air, we'll cross that bridge when we come to it. I hope it won't be a problem." He looked thoughtful as he said all these things, and I felt better. At least he wasn't just doing whatever would bring him money. He wasn't forgetting about all the things that might happen. He was quite a bit older than I was, and he should have known what he was doing, he'd had time to figure it out. He explained how gasoline was refined and produced from the petroleum that was so abundant throughout the world, what a lot of jobs that would make, aside from all the jobs making automobiles and even making the wheels with rubber tires instead of the old iron ones.

"Besides," he said, "speaking of dirt, how about all that manure from horses that dries up and blows into everybody's faces? How about the muddy streets that we have to wade through so many months of each year? How about the flies and other insects that crawl everywhere?"

I could admire Ford, but my best thing was the horse, and I stayed with him. I wasn't so sure, not at all, and a lot of other people felt the same as I did, though a lot of others were buying cars as fast as they were produced. Didn't affect my business at all, not for a long time, a very long time. But there came a day . . . but now I'm getting ahead of my story, way ahead.

I had a lot of good horses there, and the man Ford was with bought about half of them. Maybe Ford hadn't convinced his friend either. That all happened a long time ago. I was just a young fellow trying to start my life, and I was glad for that sale. But I often think of what Henry Ford said that day: "Mr. Daniels, the days of horses are over. They're coming to an end. Sometime, maybe not soon, but not too long, machines will take the place of the horse. Automobiles first will take the driving horses away. Other machines will appear after that and do the work the horse does today cleaner, safer, don't have to feed them when they don't work." I guess I grinned a little too wide when he said that, but he was right, to a certain extent. He knew what he was talking about, he had vision and instinct—to a point. I couldn't prove he was wrong, I only thought so, and I thought about it a lot, for a long time after that day.

Henry Ford was a tall man and not very good looking. He was dressed neat, but his hands were black. He was sort of a blacksmith to start with. He made that engine, kept making it a little better and a little better. Finally got a car that everybody could afford and no trouble with them wearing out, they lasted. First cars he put out you could buy for three hundred fifty dollars! A few years later Ford cars came out with brass all over them, covered with it! You could hardly look at a Ford, it was so bright. I bought my first car before that bright one showed up. Bought it from Rowley Thomas. Quite a thing to own a car those days.

SIX

Girl Business

Because I was the oldest boy in the family, I decided it was my job to oversee the boyfriends who showed up to see my sisters. If I didn't like them, I chased them off the place. If my sister wanted to marry a fellow, I'd chase him off. I had leased acreage from Dad, and I lived in a house on the property. Mattie usually stayed with me, kept house for me. I saw her with the same fellow a couple of times. I said, "If you're going to marry that fellow, I'll have to chase him off the place." Mattie didn't like that, but she couldn't do anything about it except get mad.

Next time that fellow came I'd meet him. "Now, my little sister is not going to marry you. I know you. There's just no ifs or ands about it."

There was one fellow in particular who came to see Mattie for a while. I told her several days before I spoke to him, "Mattie, he's not fit to live with a dog, let alone with you. He's rotten with disease and he's mean. You'll just live a life of misery. Say what you please, leave here if you want, but when you live here . . . Well, I'm just going to kick that fellow off the place."

Mattie was mad. I was digging into her business. She said, "Well, I'll just go with him if I want." She wouldn't believe what I told her about disease.

I said, "All right, but he can't come here, he can't come in my house." Couple days later he drove up, jumped out of his buggy, a big, brawny fellow.

I said, "I believe you'd better get back in the rig, mister."

He said, "Why?"

I said, "You're not going to go with my sister anymore. You're just

50

rotten clear to the core, and she's under my care. Now, get in that buggy or I'll make it so hot for you, you'll be glad to get in. I want you to get out of here and never stick your foot on this place again. I'll break your head if I can, and I believe I can."

He didn't ask any questions, and he never showed up again. Mattie bawled around. She was just brokenhearted, but she got over it.

Next thing I knew she was about to marry Fletcher Hunt. Fletcher was a pretty good fellow and I figured she had to have somebody, so I didn't say anything. They lived much of their life in Colorado. They were married something like sixty-five years before Fletcher died, so I guess it wasn't a mistake. They never had any children.

Abbie was a good girl, one of the best. Dad always was suspicious of Abbie, but I knew she was doing all right. She'd go with one of the young fellows around there, go to church or something like that, and Dad would send the hired man over to get her. I don't know why he didn't trust Abbie.

One thing happened and then another. The girl I had been engaged to since I was two years old had made up her mind. She said it was time to marry and I could get my life in shape after the ceremony as well as before. She had come up from Oklahoma because for her it was time for us to marry. I didn't think so, but there was all the clatter and slam-bang of listening to the fireworks, along with all the other facts to be considered, and my dad putting in his two cents' worth whenever he could make an excuse to do so, and half the time in between. I never could make Dad listen when I talked about medical school. Finally my girl got mad. I guess she thought if she wanted to get married, I ought to jump at the chance.

"I'll just marry the first man who asks me," she said. "That's what I'll do."

I knew she meant it, but I hoped she'd cool off a little in a week or so and think it over. We had been engaged all those years, and I really hoped she would wait a few years more so I could be as ready for marriage as she was. A man has a different set of problems than a girl has when marriage is considered. I hoped she would realize that.

There was a fellow we both knew, my girl and I. He was a nice-appearing man but one of the lowest dogs that ever hit that whole country. He had plenty of money, a nice house; his folks had died and left him their home. He started courting my girl, and nobody could tell her what he really was. She just thought I was jealous. She thought she had the laugh on me, and she wouldn't listen to a thing. She married that no-good, and she just lived one hell of a life.

It all kind of took some of the medical school idea out of me. I couldn't feel so sure I really wanted to go to school after that. I was a little more willing to settle for less, because somehow I didn't have as much reason to be a doctor as I'd had before.

I went out with several girls right after my girl married, but none of them appealed to me. Then I got myself a reputation which cost me plenty, and it wasn't my fault I got it, either.

I had a team of little black broomtails, which is what we called wild horses. One Sunday afternoon I thought it would be a good time to break them in as a team, so I hitched them to the buggy. They had never been hitched up together, so I tried them out, to see what kind of team they'd make. The mud was deep, they couldn't run very far. I figured that mud would wear them out and sober them down. They wouldn't be skittish and playful very long. I drove that little black team a mile or two and came alongside this Wiley girl walking beside the road. Her family had moved to Adair from Chicago, and she was a real nice-looking girl, pretty as a picture. I stopped and asked if she wanted a ride. I was going right past their place.

She said, "Why, yes, I'd like a ride." She got into the buggy, and then she said, "Let's turn around and not go past the farm," meaning her family farm.

I said, "What difference would it make? Won't they let you go with anyone?"

"They don't want me to go with you."

We drove around and went for a ride downtown. I picked up my younger brother Gene. The horses were feeling pretty tired, it being their first time in harness and the mud so deep. I'd go a little way and then stop and let the team rest a while. We finally got to the Wiley home about ten o'clock that night.

Wiley, her old man, came to the door and said, "Lallie? Who is that out there?"

She told him.

"Now, you get in this house. That feller ain't gonna come here."

I saw I was in trouble, so I tried to turn my darn team around. I heard Wiley a-yelling. He scared my horses, so they leaped and started to run. In the dark the horses ran between two trees they couldn't see and got the buggy stuck. I couldn't get them out. There I was, helpless. I made up my mind I wasn't going to take any yap from that old man if he came out there. Wiley's hired man came out, and we kind of worked on the horses. Then Wiley came out and he was going to do this and that and the other thing. When he saw I was in trouble with my horses he came and helped get my rig loose from between those trees. I thanked him and the hired man and started home to where I was living on my rented farm just past the old home place. As I passed, my mother came out.

She called to me, "Lee, you'll have to go back and get Lallie. Her father beat her up."

"No, I'm not going back to get Lallie. A person can't go over there, they act strange. I don't want to get mixed up in their family affairs." I just didn't feel responsible. I had asked the girl if she wanted a ride home, and when she accepted she then changed all the plans and made something entirely different from what it had been. We came in late mostly because of my horses but also because I had gone out of my way for her. I didn't want anything more to do with the Wiley family or their troubles. Lallie had got into the buggy with me, but it was her, not me, who knew that her folks had said she couldn't go out with me. But she did it. I had not known. Right then I already had enough of Lallie. My mother thought differently. Nothing would do but I'd have to get Lallie.

"All right, Mother, I'll go get her, but I won't take her down to my house, because I'm baching there. If she wants to stay here tonight, that's fine. Tomorrow, if she wants to go someplace, I'll take her there. I just don't think anything else is necessary."

Mother said, "I don't know about tomorrow, but she can stay here tonight."

Next morning Lallie and Mattie came to my house and stayed a while. I said, "Now, Mattie wants to go home and, Lallie, you know I can't keep you here. What are you going to do?"

"Oh, it wouldn't make any difference. I'll stay here with you."

"No, you won't stay here with me. If you've got someplace to go, I'll take you there." I took her down south to Fontanelle, she knew some people there. I wore an opal ring my sisters had given me for Christmas, opal being my birthstone. Birthstones are supposed to bring good luck, but that one didn't, not that time. I always wore it on my finger, and this Lallie kept saying she liked it. Suddenly she said, "Let me see your ring. It is a beautiful ring."

I took it off so she could see it. She stuck it on her finger. I tried to get it away from her, but she wouldn't let me have it. I left her in Fontanelle, my ring still on her finger, though I hadn't put it there. I came home and she kept phoning me. I was going with another girl, and Lallie found out about that. She came over there with the idea she was going to sue me for breach of promise. That came pretty near breaking me up with my girl before we even got started. I had an awful time for a while. I didn't know the whole story.

I had a lot of corn to haul. Dad and some neighbors were hauling corn. We had to haul it through this little valley to Fontanelle, Adair, and Casey, wherever we wanted to sell it or store it—corn, hogs, one thing and another. I had to move my corn, but every man in the place was already working, so I phoned a fellow I knew and told him I'd like to have him send his children over to help me a little. Kids would like to earn a little money, and they'd be a big help when I couldn't get older people. Those kids didn't come until about ten o'clock, and when they did come they brought some of the Wiley kids with them. They no more than got there when up came a blizzard and I figured I'd as well stay home.

The kids no sooner got home than the man Wiley called me up. He was just carrying on. The idea, he said, of him having to hire a man to haul corn when his own kids could be doing it, and on and on.

I said, "What's the matter with you anyway? You crazy or something? Why, I wouldn't ask a dog to go out in this storm."

Wiley said, "Well, it doesn't make any difference, I don't want my kids working away from home. Plenty of work for them home. I feed the whole damn bunch and they can work for me."

Dad had bought some corn with Wiley and another neighbor, and I was helping shell. I was hauling corn when I could, along with all the rest of the work. We had to weigh every load we took to market on Dad's scales. Wiley kept throwing himself around and I ignored it. But one time when I had my wagon ready to go on the scales I made up my mind, I had as well have it out with this Wiley man. I let him get through weighing, and I drove my team onto the scales.

I said, "Wiley, I want to talk with you. Wait a minute."

I weighed my load of corn and tied my team beside Dad's team. "Now, Wiley, I want to ask you something, and I want you to tell me the truth. Do you know anything that would cause people to talk the way they have been talking about me? They've got it figured I'm not fit to live with decent people."

"Well, I don't think you are," he said.

"I don't think you are, either. You go to church. Well, they always told me that a Christian was against anyone going down the wrong road. I don't like a hypocrite and I don't like you. Now, get off that wagon. I'm going to make you swallow what you've been saying about me or I'm going to beat the living daylights right out of you."

"Maybe you can do it," he said.

"I know I can. At least I'm going to try." He was a man about thirty-five years old and a lot bigger than I was. He got down off the wagon. I had a big fur coat on.

Wiley said, "Take off that coat."

"I don't need to take my coat off to handle a hound like you." I made for him and got him. I hit him as hard as I could, hit him right on the chin and knocked him over. I got hold of his throat. I just choked the daylights out of him. Dad came over and tried to pull me off, the hired man came, but I wouldn't let loose. I just hung onto Wiley's throat.

Pretty soon I got up. "Now, I want you to tell these folks that you've lied and you're nothing but the worst kind of man. Tell them you've even run your stepdaughter away, tell them everything. Tell them that everything you've said and done is nothing but a lie."

Wiley said, "Don't hit me again. I'll tell 'em."

I was twenty-two or twenty-three at that time, a bit husky. I was mad at all the trouble Wiley had caused with no purpose but to do dirt to someone trying to be decent. I wasn't very big, never weighed more than 140 to 155 pounds and was about five feet eight. I'm still that tall. I never shrank when I grew older. I wasn't a bad boy. I treated girls like a gentleman should. I behaved myself and never misused anybody. Parents would put their girls in the buggy with me and know very well I'd take care of them. I never stepped out of line. Sometimes it looked like it, but wasn't. I'd have been going with girls yet if I hadn't found the one I wanted, that I would. I went with all of them.

This Wiley, he just thought he was going to eat me up, but I still had my fur coat on. I never heard much more about the Wiley family. And I never got my opal ring back.

As a kid, a young man, I was popular, always have been. I never ran away from anybody, always met them like I was a human being and I expected them to be too. I've had very little grief with people I've known in my more than one hundred years, nor will I ever. I treat them right and they treat me right. Most people will do that. I didn't always have my way or win, by any means, but I always got out of the problem without losing my whole skin and sometimes came out pretty well.

After my girl married that no-good, I took a long time to get married. I carried memories with me until I was twenty-three years old or more. I went with all the girls. I never refused to go with any, but I didn't think very much about any of them. I didn't think about having a family of my own. My brother Lewis married Edna Giles. That didn't bother me, I guessed I'd stay single the rest of my life. Gosh, had I known how old I'd be someday . . .

I bached after Mattie married and moved away. Of course, Amy never married. She wouldn't have been able to keep house for me or anybody else, even herself. She had to have our mother's constant supervision. I lived by myself quite a lot for a few years. I fed stock, bought young animals and fed them to butchering shape, shipped them to Chicago or some other auction, came home and sowed my crops, and went to parties with others my age, but it all seemed kind of artificial after that engagement broke up.

One night I was having a date, this big, fleshy girl and I. I used to go with her mostly to devil Mattie and the rest of the family. They'd all say I ought to have a nice-looking girl. But this fat girl was a lot of fun, and I went with her a time or two. One time Dad happened to meet us on the road.

I got home that night, and when he got a chance Dad said, "Have you fallen in love with that sort of girl?"

"No, Dad."

"Well, I'll tell you something, young man. By God, I don't want a bull around here. I don't want her for one of my family."

"All right. I hadn't figured on anything like that."

"Well, by God, they'll just worm you into that, and you'll be marrying that big fat slob, and I just will not have her for a daughter-in-law."

"I just go with her for the fun of it, Dad. She's fun and it makes Mattie mad. I just do it to tease Mattie."

"Fun, is it?" He went off muttering to himself.

After a couple of years, my girl saw her mistake and was sorry for what she had done. She came to my place and begged me to marry her, said she'd get a divorce. After some thought I agreed to it. I said, "We don't have to stay here. We'll go out to California and live there." I'd been reading about California and it seemed I might like it there. Besides, no long, snowy winters, less cold when you couldn't raise anything. I asked several people who had come from there how it was, living in California. I don't know what happened, but her husband got wise to our plan. I suppose he was jealous. He tried to kill me.

I was driving a herd of cattle along the public road in front of his place. He shot at me, put a hole through my hat and took a nickel's worth of hair off the top of my head.

About that time the woman's father came up from Oklahoma to visit his daughter and her new husband. The husband told him he intended to kill me and told him why. Maybe he didn't know it, but the great friendship between her father and my father had started the entire thing. Her father came right over to my father and told my folks what he had heard.

"You warn Lee to be on the lookout," he said. "I'd never forgive myself if that boy was killed." He and Dad came to my place and told me what the husband had said.

"Now Lee," he said, "you better pull out, leave before it's too late. Go off somewhere else. Protect yourself or you'll get killed."

I said, "I'm not going to run from anybody, and you go right back and tell this man that if he ever tries it, he wants to be damn quick, 'cause from now on I carry a gun and I'll shoot first and ask questions afterwards."

About a month later I took a horse to the blacksmith to be shod. I didn't know this fellow was around, but he was in the blacksmith shop.

"Are you ready to kill me now?" I asked him.

He didn't say anything.

I said, "Because any time you're ready, mister. If you ever lay your hand on your gun, and I know you've got one, I'll kill you just as sure as you stand there."

The blacksmith had a hammer in his hand. He jumped in and grabbed the fellow, raised his hammer up, and said, "If you ever pull that gun out, Lee won't have to kill you. I will."

That stopped him right there. I heard he had a terrible row about that with his wife, but she never left him. She put up with him. She lived a life of hell, but she stayed. I was near her place in 1967 and I went to see her. She was just a little old frustrated woman. Little? She was fleshy and big. Her husband had died years back, and his brother died and left her a quarter of a million dollars, but she said, "Lee, I wouldn't go through what I did again for ten times that much."

Yes, I always had girlfriends in school, I had girlfriends after I left school, I had girlfriends all my life, nice ones. I still have girlfriends. I just like girls. Maybe they like me, too. But it wasn't so easy to be serious about any of those girls. Maybe this is what they liked about me. I know that if any of them started getting serious about me, I wasn't interested in going out with them again. I just wasn't ready for marriage yet. I didn't even know how I'd support a family if I did have one. I still had to go places and find things out. Better to get this finished than to tie myself down when I wasn't ready. Besides, I didn't really like any of those girls I was going with. That's pretty important too, you know. I wasn't serious about girls except that one, and she wasn't for me anymore. But I kind of think some of those girls were a bit serious. It just happens that I married two of those old sweethearts of mine. I'll have to tell you about that. Two? Well, yes, I married two, but not at the same time, not quite.

I was about twenty-three years old when the Bennett family lived about four miles from my place. I knew the brothers well. Roy and I worked in a coal mine together once, and the youngest brother, Oscar, and I were pals. They had a young sister named Lena. She had a girlfriend named Mina Armstrong. For some reason, the two girls went with one crowd and Oscar and I went with another, the Adair crowd. The girls had their lives and we boys had ours.

I met Lena at a dance one night, and I kind of liked the looks of her. She was a cute little thing. She'd just tickle a bug's ear. I tried everything to get to go with her. Lena's father, Mr. Bennett, worked in the coal bank too. I asked him if I could come to see his daughter.

He said, "You can't see my little girl. You're just altogether too wild for her."

I guess I might have married Lena Bennett, but her father stopped it, just like that. What really stopped it, a couple of months later Lena married Frank Patrick. Frank was a nice fellow, worked hard, was good to her. I didn't try too hard after that. I've found everything's fair in love and war, but I let it go.

I needed a good man to work for me, so I hired Frank. Then I got to thinking about it. Oh, oh, I thought, there could be another deal with a gun. Maybe he won't just clip the hair off my head. I told Frank I didn't believe it would work out. Why, that just broke Lena's heart. She didn't think there could be any trouble between me and Frank. She had tried to ditch him even before they were married. Her folks touched off . . . Oh well, that's my love life.

Lena and Frank Patrick moved away, and I didn't know where they'd gone. They went out in the sandhills of Nebraska and later to several other places. I lost all track of them. I didn't know that they always got the Adair paper. They had two children, a girl and then a boy. The boy died as a young man. Years later, Frank died. Their girl grew up, became a nurse, and married. Now she is dead too. Lena never had any grandchildren. She worked as a nurse to support herself. One of her patients died and left an only daughter. Lena agreed to be a foster mother to this girl, Daisy Melick. They were together many years. My children all grew up . . . But there I go, ahead of my story again.

SEVEN

Lessons in Poker and Mining

About the time I had all this girl business on my mind as a young man, I went into the cattle business in a big way. I was making money and putting it right back into my farm and stock. I was still a bachelor, and I was pretty hard up, really. I was sure glad I didn't have a family now.

I shipped to market every week, bouncing along in an old caboose with every shipment. I had hired a man and his wife to live in my house or I couldn't have done that. It took a day and a couple of nights. Time usually dragged along. I remember this time there weren't many in the caboose where the shippers usually rode. We stopped to pick up some more cattle cars. A big German got on with his load of cattle. The summer was hot and he wore a white shirt. He had money, a roll that would choke a cow, had it tucked into the breast pocket of that white shirt. He walked into the car and sat down right beside me.

Pretty soon I said, "If I were you I'd put that roll of bills somewhere else. Somebody's liable to tap you for that. We'll go into some railroad yard at night and have to change cabooses. Somebody'll get that."

"Oh, nobody'll get that away from me. I've been around before."

I thought, Maybe you've been around, but so have I. I know what will happen if you go into Chicago with those bills in your pocket that way.

We hadn't much more than settled down before he wanted to play cards. I wouldn't play with him, so he went from one man to another. Nobody'd play with him.

"Oh, come on, play cards with me. I want to play cards. Play cards with me, we'll play just for fun." He came round to me each trip he

61

made through the cars. When he had made two or three trips to the caboose where I was sitting he said, "Come on and play cards with me just for fun. Penny ante or something like that."

I said, "Well, I don't know how to play poker. I never played a game of poker in my life. That ain't all. I don't want to play. But, you know, if I was playing poker with a man, I'd play with him just like I buy cattle. When I name a price, that man's got to take it, and I take the cattle." Then in a joking way I said, "If that roll of bills finds its way from your pocket into my pocket, now don't you feel bad about it. I always play for keeps. But I've never played a game like this. I don't play poker."

He said, "I'll show you how."

Well, this wasn't my first game of poker by any means, and I had always been lucky with cards. We sat down playing penny ante and that worked pretty fair. He'd win a little, then I'd win a little.

After a while he said, "This is too slow. Let's try it for a dollar."

"All right," I said.

We played for a dollar ante, and it went about the same way. Then we got to making the ceiling the limit. All the time he was showing me how to play. We played all night, and by the next morning I had won the roll of bills that he had, and he wanted to bet me his load of cattle.

I said, "No, I don't want to play poker anymore, but I'll tell you what I'll do. I'll match you heads or tails to see which one takes all."

He thought that would be great. I took heads and it turned up heads. I got his cattle, his roll of bills, and all. We got to Chicago and he didn't have money enough to buy his breakfast. We went over to the stockyards and I made him write out a bill of sale. I sold my own cattle and his, went over to the office and settled up.

He was standing there. He said, "You ain't gonna take all that money away from me, are you?"

I said, "Now, I'll tell you, mister. I gave you a fair chance on the whole thing. I didn't cheat you in any way. I told you when we started playing that when I play, it is for keeps. There is no backing out. If I lost that money, you wouldn't give it back. It happens you lost it, and I don't expect to give any of it back. But so long as you haven't got any money to buy your dinner with, I'll buy it and give you fifty dollars to pay your way back home."

He never waited for his dinner. He took that fifty dollars and started for home. That was the last I saw of him. I didn't hear a word about it. Didn't expect to. I stayed in Chicago overnight and next evening took the train for home.

The next morning I got to Des Moines. I played cards a little at a place there. I never won much, but I decided this was a good way to pass the time until the local train came which would take me home. I sent all my money home but a couple of hundred dollars. That's the way I always played poker or made any bets, horse races or anything else. I always played my winnings, never played anything out of my pocket. If I lost my winnings, I didn't lose anything. If I won, I'd put what I wanted back in and play my winnings again.

There were four of us playing at the table, I was getting my share of the winnings . . . and I woke up a couple of days later in Cheyenne, Wyoming. I was broke, dirty, had a big cut on my head, how in the world I ever got there I didn't know. Those men I was playing with must have hit me, knocked me out, and sent me up there, because I was on a passenger train.

When I got off that train I didn't know where I was, didn't know anything, it was just like dropping out of nowhere. I went over to the hotel, washed up the best I could, and was sitting in the lobby. I didn't have a dime in my pockets. They had taken every cent I had. A rancher came into the lobby looking for hay hands. I heard him ask a fellow if he wanted a job making hay.

I listened and then said, "I might go out and make hay with you, but I haven't any clothes with me except what I've got on. I'll have to have some work clothes if I go with you."

He said, "Can you stack hay?"

"Yes, I can stack hay."

"A dollar and a half a day."

"Oh, no, I've been a farmer all my life, and I know what it is to stack hay. What kind of rig would I have to stack after?"

"A lift rake, and three buck rakes to haul hay in."

"That's more than I ever have done, but I've stacked from one of those overhead stackers before, with two rakes. But here it don't look like the hay would be too heavy, and if you want to give me two fifty a day for a few days, I'll go out and stack."

He said all right, went out and bought me a pair of gloves, some overalls, and a hat (I had even lost my hat). I went out there and worked until I had enough money to come home. I had been gone two or three weeks. My folks didn't know what had happened to me, didn't know where I was. The man and wife working for me, living in my house, were all excited, didn't know if they had a job or no job. The sheriff, police, and everybody else were hunting all over Chicago and all the way down to Des Moines, but I wasn't in Des Moines and I wasn't in Chicago. I was pitching hay outside Cheyenne.

That's just another experience I'd hate to go through again, but two things came out of that experience. This usually happens after you get your head knocked in a time or two, to bring you some sense. I've never played a game of poker since, with but one exception, which I'll tell you about later. Nor do I intend to as long as I live. The other thing: three or four years later I received a letter from the German who had lost his money and his cattle to me. He thanked me for giving him fifty dollars to get home with. He sent a letter with fifty dollars in it and interest from the day he got it. I wasn't the only one who stopped playing poker. He told me in his letter that he never played another game of poker and never would.

The money I'd sent home before I got into that friendly little card game in Des Moines helped out some, but things were still pretty tight. I knew I'd still have trouble coming out even, so to make some money I got involved again in something that I'd done earlier and that was pretty far removed from the cattle business.

I knew someone who had a coal mine that was 365 feet deep, and the coal was only about a twenty-four-inch vein. You had to lie on your side and take the slate out from under it to get the coal out. I had not worked coal for quite a while when I started working that mine. They gave me a room by myself that hadn't been developed, and it lay under a creekbed. I worked in there, crept along, now and then finding water here and there. The room was about a hundred feet long, maybe fifty feet mined one day and fifty feet the next day. You didn't take all the coal down in one day. You had to throw water on the face of the coal to break it down and to keep the coal dust down. Another way to do this was to use explosives. Either way breaks the coal, loosens it from the slate above. You throw that slate back all the time, but there's never enough to fill up the hole that you're leaving when the coal is hauled away and taken to the surface. We always had to use props to keep the ceiling from collapsing, had to set these props in good and tight to keep the ceiling solid for our own safety.

When they opened that coal mine everybody was interested in it. A newspaper reporter was sent out from Greenfield for the occasion. He came down there with a white shirt, white suit of clothes—pants, coat, the works. Oh, he was all dressed up. My friend Roy Bennett and I were working in the mine. Roy was pushing. They had cars inside the mine that held nearly a ton of coal. When these cars were loaded, a man had to push each one. They headed downhill, but someone had to guide the car into the elevator cage. Then they'd hoist the cage to the surface and the other cage would come down. Roy was pushing coal and I was mining.

The reporter came down into the mine, and he was going to write a big story about the new mine. He said, "Oh, my, I can't walk up through there." So he asked Roy to let him ride the car when Roy pushed it up into the tunnel for the next load. He had to see how the boys were mining coal. Roy pushed him up on the empty car and put on a load of coal. Then the reporter wanted Roy to push him back; he didn't want to walk. It was only about two hundred feet. Under the elevator cage there was a sump. Black coal-water would drain into the sump and was pumped to the surface, where it ran off down the hillside below the mine. There'd usually be six or seven feet of water in the sump.

Well, Roy got to pushing the car with this dude on top. All of a sudden, accidentally on purpose, Roy fell down and let the car go.

Well, Roy thought the elevator cage would be sitting right down there over the sump waiting for the car, but it wasn't. Car, coal, reporter, and all went into the sump. You never saw such a comical sight in your life as that reporter when we got him out of there.

I never did see any article that newspaperman wrote about our mine, but over fifty years later I went to see Roy. He was sick in bed. I hadn't seen him in all those years. I was married to his sister Lena by then, and she and I went to see him. He wasn't himself half the time, but when I walked into his room he knew me right away. I said, "Roy, do you remember when you gave that reporter a ride in the coal car?"

Poor old Roy just laughed fit to kill. He said, "Really, I didn't mean to dump him into that sump. I thought the cage was there. But it wasn't, and the whole outfit got dunked. Somehow, I always thought the water in that sump was a little blacker that day than I'd ever seen it before."

We worked hard mining, all of us men, but we had some great times down there too. It was warm, we could work down there in the middle of the coldest winter and be just as comfortable as you please. Wet and damp when you were lying on your side swinging that pick, but you'd get used to it, like anything else. Visitors came down in the cage, walked around through the tunnels, talked to the miners. Some of them would wander around, get lost, finally find a worker, and we'd have to guide them out. Some of those rooms had been mined back almost to the county road, about sixty rods, I imagine, up under some other man's land, and he wouldn't allow us to go any farther. Air got bad down there too. They forced air in, but it was still bad, so much gas in there. We were always afraid of an explosion.

Of course we all had to use electric lights to get in there. When we first started mining we used an old oil lamp with a cover on it. If you raised your head, out went your lamp with the breeze. It got so bad we had to use electric batteries in our caps. The cap fit your head with creases in front that you just slipped the light and battery into.

There used to be a lot of whiskey agents come to that mine. Nearly every week there'd be two or three come down into the mine with their samples. They'd have a whole case of little bottles about three inches high. Of course, every miner would have a sample now and then, a little specimen, to see which was best. We'd drink up all their samples and not give them any orders, poor cusses. But that didn't stop the salesmen from coming back again in a month or so with another case of samples. Maybe they thought "poor cusses" about us.

One day I was working my room, had it just ready. I'd taken some coal out, but not very much. I had the whole thing in shape so I could work there that day, and I was down a-lying on my side, picking away and picking away with my pick. The air was awful bad. We were mining back so far from the opening, didn't much air circulate. Didn't dare light a match or anything like that, and after you're in there a while you didn't notice the bad air and the darkness so much. You got used to it. But you kept in mind that there could be an explosion with that gas. It helped you get along the way you had to. I was working away there, and I thought, I have the best room, the best place in this coal mine to work. I was sure because it wasn't so far into the pit.

All at once a slab flake fell down that five men couldn't lift. Fell right on my back, mashed me down, but *there* was a chunk of coal. We'd taken out some big chunks—thick, long, and wide. The end of this flake landed on one corner of this huge chunk of coal, and I was pinned under. I wasn't hurt, but I couldn't get out, I just couldn't wiggle out from under that flake. But the chunk of coal had saved my life. An old Scotsman was working nearby, and I hollered to him. He got all the others to come, and they lifted that flake up and I walked out. They had blasted out the main artery in that coal bank. It was as high as an ordinary house door.

Another day, I crawled down into my cubbyhole to crack some more coal loose with my pick. Couldn't swing very high down there, but I gave it all the space I could and sunk my pick into it, and there was a stream of water! Came right in. Just a small stream, but it shot clear back all over the piles of coal I had got loose. I knew I'd hit an underground body of water. There'd be an ocean in that mine and it wouldn't take long to arrive. I gave a war whoop and told everybody to get out of the mine as quick as they could, water was coming in fast. I got out. My old pick was still down there in that hole, water pouring out all around it. Water filled up my room. By the time I got out of there the entire level of the mine was full of water, lots of water. The whole outfit came near filling up. Everybody got out. They closed that mine, and it has never been opened to this day. Guess my old pick's still hanging there in the slate. I didn't make any money there.

EIGHT

Indians

One adventure I had in 1908 and 1909 was at the Tripp County drawing on the Rosebud Indian reservation in South Dakota. My wife's father, William Henry Armstrong, and I decided we'd go down and put our names into the lottery and see if we could draw a good piece of land. We went to Omaha. From there they made up a special train to take the interested men up to look over some of the vast acreage the federal government had gotten away from the Indians. There would be a drawing after we'd filed our names.

Now, I've been in a lot of wild crowds in my time, but I've never seen one as bad as that one was. It started in the saloon. Of course, nearly everybody drank beer at that time, and we were all in the saloon. Among us was a great big fellow, he weighed 230 pounds or so. He got drunk and, oh, he was going to ship everybody he could see. A little consumptive-looking fellow was working there in the saloon cleaning spittoons, sweeping floors, and one thing and another. He looked like you could push him over with a feather. He passed this big fellow with a spittoon in his hand, and the fat man kicked the spittoon out of the little fellow's hand, knocked it onto the floor, the stuff in it was spilled around.

The little fellow said, "Now, Mister, I don't want any trouble, so don't do that again. You'll wish you hadn't."

The big fellow laughed, shook all over, to think that little wart would call his hand, talk to him like that. When the little man passed him the second time the fat one kicked at the spittoon but didn't hit it. Instead of him kicking the spittoon, the little one landed on him. I never saw anyone get such a thrashing! That little fellow was so quick! He just batted the big boy, batted him all over that saloon, and every time he hit him the blood would just fly. Finally the big fellow broke and ran to get away from the little one.

Came time to leave for South Dakota, and we all got on the train. Everybody was kidding this big guy about the little fellow beating him. We were all in the parlor car. Some were playing cards, some drinking beer, and some this and that and the other. This big fellow came in, smarting off a little, and we all got to roasting him. He didn't like it. He picked up a beer bottle and threw it at one of those who were tormenting him. He missed his aim and hit the arm of the seat I was sitting in. It threw beer all over me. That wasn't a very good time to start anything, and I didn't. I laughed about it and let it go. Only a little while later two fellows got into a jangle with the fat boy, and if I hadn't caught him by the leg they would have thrown him out the window of that moving train. He was all out, but I grabbed him by the leg and pulled him back in.

The next morning we were in Dallas, South Dakota, and went over to register our names and stand around for a while. Several of my Iowa neighbors had come on that trip too—four of them, I believe—so we just went together, hired a livery team, and went up to see the land in question, which was not far from the White River. We thought we'd like to know something about the country. Oh, that land looked wonderful. Tall grass and lots of hay, the land looked fertile, and it was level. I thought I sure would like to have a piece of it. Took quite a while to drive up there. We stayed for a while and finally started back. We hadn't thought to take any lunch with us and it was getting along in the middle of the afternoon, not a house in sight and you could see for miles. Someone said, "I wonder if there isn't some rancher nearby would give us something to eat."

I was driving the team, and a little later I saw a small wooden building off half a mile or so. I drove up there, and an Indian woman came to the door. We asked could we have a sandwich.

"Oh, yes, you can get something to eat here," she said, agreeably enough. "We have soup, if you like soup."

We all went into the house (I think they call it a hogan), and she dished the soup out of a big kettle. Everybody was hungry and they started to eat, but I just didn't like the looks of things too well, so I took a couple of crackers while the rest of them batted into the soup.

My father-in-law said, "My, lady, that is the best soup I ever ate. What's it made of?"

She smiled a bit. "Soup made from coyote. Him make very good soup, you think so?"

Mr. Armstrong lost his soup then and there. He made a dive for the door, but he wasn't fast enough. He lost his coyote soup, and I don't think he ever wanted any more. I'll bet when we got out of sight that Indian woman had a good laugh about the white men who wanted Indian land but couldn't eat Indian food because they were too squeamish.

We started for Dallas. After a while, driving along, we noticed something in back of us. It was a prairie fire, and in that tall, lush grass it was moving fast, right toward us. I ran the team all the rest of the way to town trying to keep ahead of the fire. At Dallas they had a big artesian well. It would spray about an acre of ground when the wind was right and blew the spray around. Everybody ran toward that well to keep from getting burned up. That fire flattened the whole country, burned everything for miles. Every man had to be ready to fight the fire to keep it from burning all of Dallas. Only it didn't get that far. The wind shifted, sent it right back where it had already burned everything, and it died. It was close for a time, we wondered if we could hold it off. That time it didn't get any part of the town, but they had such fires there many times.

Later each man in our crowd drew a claim. Then we went back home and waited to be notified about our claim number so we could go back and file our claims. I was sick and couldn't go when we were notified in the spring. Mr. Armstrong went up. He found the claims we had been assigned were no good, rocky, and the soil was semidesert, sandy. He decided it wasn't any good, so we never proved up, we let our homesteads go. Sometime later the government sent up payment to the Sioux Indians in Tripp County.

One of the settlers had made a deal with the Indians when the government took over their reservation. The government decided it was a deal. Every Indian over sixteen or eighteen got 160 acres of their own choice. They also got twenty head of horses, twenty head of cattle, implements of all kinds to farm with, and a new wagon. (These were Studebaker wagons, the government had shipped a trainload of them.) The Indians had to round up all the horses on the reservation to get them in and sort them. They could take any horses they wanted. The rest of the horses were shipped out to different places to be sold.

I was there when they were rounding those horses up. They rounded somewhere about five thousand, herded them up into the enclosure. Cowboys, both whites and Indians, ran the horses into a corral and they had a ring—oh, it must have been a quarter of a mile or more—made of barbed wire. Those horses, wild as they could be, were crowded into that corral. They'd get crowding in toward the gate, it had to be narrow so it could be closed. They'd hit that barbed wire and, oh, it was the bloodiest mess! Those horses would run and hit that barbed wire and cut a great gash in their hide. They'd never seen a fence before; there were no fences whatever on Indian land. Of all the cruelty! It just made me sick when I saw some of those horses. The federal agents and others responsible for putting up those fences should have fixed some better kind of fence. There must have been a better way than barbed wire—board fence, poles, even brush. There's a kind of wash on barbed wire to prevent rust. When that wash gets into cuts, it prevents them from healing. It's very poisonous; cuts heal slowly if at all, and they get infected easily. Many a beautiful horse was sacrificed at that roundup to somebody's ignorance.

I sat there and watched what went on. The Indians would take their horses out and away they'd go as fast as the horses could run, out to their farms, which the white man said the Indian should have, all for his own, out of his own land. I suppose they turned those horses loose once they got them there. Cattle the same way. The government put Hereford cattle out there, twenty cows and a bull and a wagon to each family. If the white man lived that way, then so must the Indian, that's the way the whites thought.

At Dallas, white men came to buy land left over after each Indian got what it was decided he should have, his 160 acres. Those whites took along lots of whiskey and beer, everything intoxicating, up there with them. Wide open. They weren't supposed to give liquor to the Indians. Those Indians would come in and crawl down on the floor under the table. The white men brought their liquor, slipped it off the table and down to the Indian, pretending to be his friend. Some of those Indians got awful drunk. The whites were not any better.

One Indian in particular had been issued a new Studebaker wagon with a spring seat and an end gate you could let down to unload— many a farmer'd like one of those. He had a pair of spotted ponies hitched to that wagon. He started for home on the run. The first thing he lost was that end gate. He never stopped, went right on. Hit a ditch and off went the wagon box. Never stopped. Last I saw of him he was going across the prairie standing on the hind running axle just a-hooting and yelling.

Do you want to know what they'd do? Those Indians would get drunk and take those wagons out. Next morning they'd bring them back and get another wagon—good new wagons. That fool giving out wagons thought he was doing somebody a favor. When the settlers got there they gathered up all the pieces, mended them, and put them back together. Then the whites had the good new wagons. The Indians got wagons, machinery, whatever they wanted. But there were other Indians in the same band who were raising corn, potatoes, grain, doing pretty well, too, weren't poor by any chance. But that's the way the whites got the reservation property away from those Indians.

Of course, Iowa has its own Indians, too. The Mesquakie Indians live in Tama County. I have always heard them called the Tamas. Like all Indians originally, before being ruined by the white man, they are industrious, clean, and upright, a people to be admired and respected. The story I have to tell you I cannot find in any books, but it is the story I have known all my life about the Tamas, and I believe it is true. I don't know why it has not got into the books by this time.

At one time there were a lot of Indians in what we now call Iowa. Then the white man came into this wonderful land where the Indians lived. The white man wanted the land, so the United States government moved the Indians down to Kansas.

The Indians didn't like Kansas at all, wasn't like they were used to, couldn't live as they always had. They couldn't do anything else about it, so they started out, some riding, some walking. They started toward the only home they had ever known, or ever wanted to know. They traveled days, maybe weeks. Only a few of the Indians ever got back to Tama. Most of them died on the way, but they died trying. They did not accept defeat. Seems to me twenty-four was all that returned home to central Iowa.

But they stayed. They settled, and the whites couldn't get them off the land again. They wouldn't get out. Stayed. And stayed. They earned a little money here and there in different ways, and they pooled it and bought a little land. The whites were being beaten at their own game. They couldn't get the Indians off the land they had bought and paid for the white man's way. They couldn't kill them, either, at that time. They'd done too spectacular a thing, coming all the way back home and buying back the land that really was theirs anyway. Those whites couldn't do a darn thing but leave those Indians alone, and I don't know how good a job they did of that.

Today there are more Indians up there than there were before they were driven off. The Indians built up their population by affiliating with other tribes. They added to their land, a few acres here and a few acres there, then larger and larger acreage until they had their old territory back. Later they sued the federal government for several million dollars. The case was under litigation for I don't know how long. In 1969 a decision was made in favor of the Indians. In the meantime, they built their schools, one of the finest school systems anywhere, at Tama, and they have their own hospitals.

The government has taken great pride in taking care of these Indians. Taking care? Seems to me they did a great job of taking care of themselves. The government seems to ignore the fact that the Indian would rather care for himself than be a ward. Now they're free. They're just like any citizen. The government hasn't any rule over them, any more than over any other citizen of this country. This land belongs to the Tamas. That's how the dispute was settled.

I'll have to tell you about an experience I had with the Tama Indians.

I was buying horses there about 1934. I had an order for some spotted ponies. I knew there were a lot of Indian ponies on the reservation, so I went up there to see what I could do. I got in touch with the Indian agent, and we went out where these ponies were, on the range. The ponies were all running loose along the Iowa River. Oh, my, I never saw so many cockleburs in my life, even at my own farm when I had all those sandburs, which are the same thing, for all practical purposes. Not only were burs all over the land, they were sticking to all the horses. Their tails and manes were just matted. I remembered what a time I had getting sandburs off my farm. This is a coarse plant, native to the land, a weed, for it has no use to man. It bears prickly burs which may be as long as an inch, but no longer, that's enough. Every bur is just coated with fairly long stickers, and they hold, they never let go if they can help it. They stick to everything that comes near them. They stuck to every horse on that reservation.

I bought a few horses from the agent, and while I was out there I saw this beautiful spotted mare. I wanted her in just the worst way. She belonged to an Indian woman whose husband was a chief of the tribe. The agent and I went up to this place and eventually went into the house. Oh, their houses were just like those of the white families in the area at that time. Everything was clean and there were long shelves along the walls. They lived up off the ground a couple of feet, about like most of the farmers who could afford a good home. Well, I went up there.

When I was going anyplace like that—buying or just meeting family people—I always put some candy or something in my pocket for the children. We arrived at the house just at noon. Not a child in sight. The man wanted to know if we'd eat dinner with them. Of course, we had to eat dinner, they are a very hospitable people, and you should not insult them by refusing to eat. I had to eat dinner. I wanted that spotted mare, and I knew that was the only chance to get it. The Indian woman got a box of crackers and one of those fifteen- to twenty-pound cheeses. She took a big butcher knife, and she came along past the family and guests and sliced off the cheese and handed it to each person. Wasn't any plate, didn't need one. Just take it in your hand.

She passed around crackers, and that was the meal. Neat, quick, gracious. I thanked her very much for it. It was good cheese and genuine hospitality.

All this time I had kept my eye on the four little black shiny eyes peering out from under the bed. I thought one child must be about four years old and the other about two. They had gone under there to hide when strangers came. I took a piece of candy from my pocket, dropped my hand down like I was just hanging it beside me while I talked. I was looking the other way on purpose, and here one of these little fellows slipped out and, quick as a wink, he got the candy and back under the bed he went. It wasn't long until the other one slipped out. I had candy in the other hand. While I looked the other way he slipped out from under the bed and grabbed his bounty. Well, they just kept a-doing that until finally they were both standing at my knees.

We visited for a while with the Indian woman and her husband. She was telling some stories about the chief, some of the legends about the tribe. I kept asking her about different things. Finally I came to asking her about this horse. Oh, no, no, she wouldn't sell that horse, no, sir.

I said, "Would you take a hundred dollars for it?"

"No, sir!"

"A hundred and fifty?"

"No, sir! No, sir!"

"What will you take?"

"Not for sale, not for sale!"

I could see there was no use to go any farther. The agent started to talk to her about the horse, but she told him the same thing. We thanked her for the meal and went outside.

I didn't have enough horses to make a truckload, so the agent said, "We'll go down where they're cutting wood, and maybe you can buy some of the teams off them. There's this one team especially, a team of buckskin horses. I know you'll like them." We got in our rig and rode toward the pasture and met an Indian coming up. I stopped him, got out, and looked at his horses.

He kept saying, "Nice mares, nice mares."

I said, "Yes, they are. Would you sell them?"

"No, me not selling."

The more I talked to him the more he said, "No, me not sell them." I had to leave there with part of a load of horses.

The government had appropriated money for the Indians to develop their land, especially the forests. The Tamas planted part of their land with pine trees. Their rows are just as straight as an arrow, up the hills and crossways, just like a cornfield, a beautiful sight. Their timber was getting quite big when I was there.

I often think about those Indians, how they walked back to Iowa, clear from Kansas. They were still under government supervision when I was there, had their Indian agent there all the time. I was talking to a nurse who worked in the hospital at the Tama reservation, been there several years, and she said, "This is the worst place to find anything out. A child can have a sore, and some of those sores can be cancerous. He can have tuberculosis, but we can't find him." They used to have an awful lot of tuberculosis when I was there, but these Indians would take their sick children and hide them from the nurses. They were afraid their children would be taken away. Maybe the Indians thought they had a reason to distrust the whites. I met three or four nurses there, and each one told me some experience about how they'd try to help the children, get reports about them so they wouldn't miss being treated. The parents were afraid they'd lose their children. Maybe they wanted the Great Spirit to heal them. Why shouldn't anyone treat their sick the way they believe is best? You get into awful deep water when you get into that question. Anyway, that was a long time ago, and I suppose it has all changed by now. What I remember most of all about the Tamas is the four little eyes peeking out from under that bed, to find candy. After I coaxed them out, boy, did they ever. Oh, they just leaned up against me, one on one leg, the other against the other knee. That amused their mother too. When I thanked her and said I wanted to pay for the meal she said, "Oh, no, no, no. Cheese and crackers?"

I remember, too, a time years before then, one winter when I was busting from a boy to a man, I went into an Indian camp at Tama looking for horses, and they sold me some. While I was there I went down to the Iowa River, where they were fishing. I was especially interested in learning what they did to feed themselves. They cut a hole in the ice about four feet wide and eight or nine feet long, crosswise of the river. The women, old men, and kids would go, one group, up the river, another group downstream. They'd all come together dragging buckets, tin tubs, anything that made a noise, and they'd drive those fish up to the hole. The Indian fishermen stood there beside that big hole with spears, and they'd spear the fish and just throw them out on the ice, where they froze. Got modern frozen-food processing all beat out. No chemicals, either.

I stood there and watched. "Let me try it," I said.

"No, no. White man, he fall in. Water deep. White man fall in. No, chief, we not going to let you."

That's the way they catch their fish—scare them. But they wouldn't let me have a spear, and they were busy. There were lots of carp and other kinds of fish in there. They were spearing anything big enough to use. Catch a little one, they'd throw him back. How they were dragging those fish up there! Why, that water was just boiling with fish in that opening, because they came there from fright. Then the Indians decided they had enough. They left the foaming mass of fish and water to freeze over again, gathered up the catch, and returned home. Indians always took just what they needed and left the rest. I never did know them to waste food. They knew how to keep a never-ending supply available. They were the first students of ecology, but the rest of us just didn't have enough sense to know the value of their ways.

NINE

Mina and Me, and the Kids

Mina Armstrong, remember, was Lena Bennett's best friend. After Lena left town I dated Mina a few times. Mina was a good girl, as innocent as a baby. She didn't know the first thing about life. I asked her to marry me, but I had to ask her parents first. Mrs. Armstrong said yes and was set to have the wedding service over in Greenfield, in the county seat, Mina being her oldest daughter. But we set it all up for June 6, 1906, in Atlantic instead.

On June fifth I called the hotel in Atlantic and had them pick me up a wedding gift. I arranged a wedding dinner for four—Mina and me, my sister Abbie, and her boyfriend, Pat Calloway. Abbie and Pat stood up with Mina and me. Come the sixth, Pat and I took the team and went over to the Armstrong house to get Mina. We drove to Anita and had to wait for the train. Also had to wait for Abbie. She was working in Anita and had to meet us. We waited in the lobby of a hotel, just sat there. Everybody was whispering, "They're gonna get married." Then they'd look away if they thought we'd heard them. We sat there until Abbie came, then we caught the train for Atlantic.

The time came, we went up to the preacher, and he tied the knot. He did a pretty good job, it lasted more than fifty years. I was all excited, but, of course, I would be, the first time I was ever married. (I was excited the second time, too, and the third. Luckily, that was enough.) So I took Mina by the arm and we started to walk out of the church.

The preacher said, "Say, didn't you forget something?"

I began to look around, thought maybe I'd lost something. I said, "I don't know."

79

He said, "You forgot to pay me."

"How much do I owe you?"

"Ten dollars."

"All right. Here's ten dollars." We all giggled and left.

We went to the hotel to eat, took a taxi—we had to have a taxi, you know, it was the style. A fellow came with his taxi and took us to the Park Hotel. They had a dinner all fixed and we sat down at the table. What do you suppose they served us? You wouldn't believe it! Corned beef and horseradish greens! I guess it was good food for a horsetrader. No wedding cake, nothing. The only thing they did do, the waiters all got around our table and congratulated us and sang a song. Then we took the train back to Anita.

Some friends of Mina and me had heard about our wedding, a married couple. They wanted to have a reception for us. It was held in a nightclub. Nice crowd of young people. None of them are alive today, just me. I was so busy we didn't have time for a wedding trip, so we went home. It may sound funny today, but that is the way a good many people got married then. Nothing unusual about it at all.

We drove a rig home long after dark. I took my bride by the hand and started for the house after I put the horse away for the night. All at once I remembered something I should never have forgot. I'd been living alone in that house for several months. Those days, men just didn't do any housekeeping, that was women's work. You never could imagine how it looked. I had never thought to have my sisters come in and clean the place up. I felt pretty bad about that. The old house had seen better days even before I moved in. It was a shame to take a nice little girl like Mina in there, but this late at night there wasn't any place else to go. Anyway, she must've known what she was getting into before she married me. If I forgot, I'll bet she had some idea what a mess it would all be.

No, now that I think of it, she wasn't ready for it. I had never paid any attention, but owls had got into the attic. When we went in, a darn owl flew right down and landed in Mina's hair. Darned near scared that girl to death.

She screamed, "I'm getting out! I'm not going in that house." I should have told her it was a good-luck omen, but I was kind of frustrated myself. I coaxed and I begged. Finally I got her to go back into the house, but I had to pick her up and carry her, and that's how my wife got carried over the doorsill.

I had two men working for me, and it was just the season to cultivate corn. I had to get up and go to work next morning. A week went by, two weeks. We made a lot of plans for a honeymoon, but every time we were about ready to go, something else turned up. After a month we decided we couldn't go until September. Time wore on and no honeymoon. Pretty soon we had a little boy. By and by we had a girl, and five years later another girl. About ten years later we had the third girl and still no honeymoon, but we had a honey of a family. God gave me the kind of a family that I could be proud of. They were all farmers, not rich but comfortably fixed. Mina and I raised a nice family. I am proud of them, and I love them all. I couldn't have better kids.

Our son was born March 23, 1907. We named him Kenneth. He was always a good child, never needed much correction and always wanted to please us, to do what was right. I think once was all I ever spanked Kenneth, and afterward I thought that was a mistake. I suppose he began to feel like the man of the house pretty early because I was gone so much. The birth of my son was about the happiest occasion of my life. He was the first child born into the Daniels family in the third generation. Of course, each member of the family had its own plans for his welfare. We lived in that old shack of a house where I had lived long before Mina and I were married. Dad said, "We will build you a new house." He was afraid his grandson would freeze when winter came. We started to build at once.

We had a hired girl working for us, Rina Carry. One day I came home and Mina and Rina were crying. I asked what the trouble was. I was really scared, thought someone had died. Well, those two girls, silly girls, they thought Kenneth was so smart he wouldn't live long. I told them I never knew of anyone being so smart it killed them. At eighty he is still very much alive and going strong, so they had nothing to worry about.

Kenneth was nearly two years old when Esther was born. I named her for my father's mother, the grandmother I never saw. Oh, that tickled Dad.

By 1911, with our family getting bigger, we needed a home of our own. I'd been looking around for a couple of years, not saying much about it but checking out this one and that one. I bought my farm in 1912, and I thought it was a good farm, but I was awful deceived about it. When I bought it you couldn't raise over twenty-five bushels of corn to the acre. I bought the farm in the spring, but I was busy and didn't want to do anything with it until fall. Later I went back up to see what I needed for fall plowing. The sandburs were so thick you could hardly walk through the fields.

A little Irishman was working for me. I sent him up there with his fine team of Clydesdales to clear out the burs. Clydesdales have woolly legs, long tails and manes, and I ought to have known better than to send them there, but I was busy with other things and just didn't think about it. They made two runs through that field, and their owner couldn't get them to go through those sandburs again. He phoned me down at the old farm. "Lee, you'll have to come up. Those burs are killing my horses. You come up."

I went, took one look at the Clydesdales, and went back and got my clippers. I clipped their legs clear up as far as the sandburs went. I clipped their necks and trimmed their manes, because I didn't want those burs taken back where I lived. They'd seed the whole place in no time.

I plowed enough around there so I figured we could burn the dry plants in the fall, burn 'em off and get rid of the whole sandbur problem. My hired man did a good job of burning them off; it didn't look like there was one left. Next year they were just as thick as ever, all through the corn I had planted. I hired two men, took them up there, and we just hoed all summer, cultivated three, four, five times. I didn't think there was a sandbur left on the place. Along in August I went out to the field. Lord, you couldn't walk through it for sandburs, hip high. The fertilizer I'd put in for corn had done those sandburs a lot of good.

A few days later I went down to Omaha, got some cattle, and went over to the sheep barns. Don't know why I went over there, because I didn't have any idea of buying sheep. I just stood there staring into a sheep pen thinking about those sandburs. A man walked up and stood there. We got to talking and he asked how I was getting along on my new farm.

"Not too good. I got too many sandburs, and I don't know how to get rid of them. We just hoed all summer, and that's expensive business."

"I'll tell you how to get rid of them. The right kind of sheep are here today, a corral full of them. They have long wool clear down to their knees, different from western sheep. You get yourself a bunch of those sheep and take 'em home. Let the sandburs get good and ripe, turn the sheep in, and let 'em get all the burs they will hold onto them. They won't be in there long."

I did. I bought three hundred sheep and took them home and turned them into this cornfield. A week later you couldn't tell they were sheep. They looked like enlarged sandburs, just as full of burs as they could be.

The man had said, "Now, when they get as full as they can, get a shearer and shear them. Shear them mighty close. If you can't do anything with that wool, just burn it."

I'll have to tell you about shearing those sheep. When we started shearing, we hired a fellow from down in Greenfield. He came down and he had a pair of overalls on, sleeves cut off clear up to his shoulders.

I said, "You've got to get some other clothes on."

"Oh, I don't need them."

I thought, You will need them. I said, "Got any gloves?"

"Nope."

"I don't believe you're going to get any shearing done."

This man had his own special gasoline-engine shearing machine. The first sheep he got he did pretty well. He said, "See, I don't have any trouble with them."

The next sheep he began to feel the sandburs and he quit. He had sheared two sheep. I thought I'd have to get somebody else, then I thought, no.

I said, "I'll go into town and get you some stuff so you can shear sheep." I bought him a pair of leather boots and a pair of gauntlet gloves, and I went to the blacksmith shop and got him a blacksmith's leather apron made to fit around his legs. He went out and sheared about a hundred sheep by noon with his gasoline-engine shearer, but he was having a little trouble with his machine.

As I went to eat he said, "While you're eating I'll see if I can fix that gasoline engine." He got to work trying to fix that engine.

I went out after eating and penned another bunch of sheep to shear in the afternoon. I drove them up just a little above the big house, and I saw smoke blowing out of the shed. We had been shearing in the shed, and that's where this man was working on his machine. I rushed back into the shed. Everything was afire, gasoline all over the floor, and it had run down through the floor cracks into the corncrib. He got excited. I had a new tractor too near the fire, and this man jumped on it so hard he broke the crank on it. I ran to the house and nobody was there but Esther, just a little girl. I don't remember where Mina was, or Kenneth. Here was a little girl about four years old, but she phoned town for help to put that fire out.

That man went down to the pump house and broke the handle on the water pump. Why, there was a tank full of water within forty feet of the fire. He never thought of getting water there. He was just jumping up and down in that fire trying to save his machine. I fought the fire out myself. There was an old carpet I had been shearing on, and that was on fire. I got that and swept it off, but there was fire underneath. I had a new ax I had bought the day before, and I had left it sitting in the corner for some reason or other. I took that ax and cut a hole in that two-inch floor, went down under it. I didn't have a shovel or anything else, so I scooped out the burning corn with my hands and got it out. Well, we got the machine all fixed up and went ahead shearing the rest of the sheep. We put the sheared ones out in the feed yard. As soon as we got them sheared and the wool sold, I bought three hundred more of the same sheep. That was the end of the sandburs on my place.

Now, back when I bought my first sheep to clear out the burs I had been told to burn that woolly, bur-filled stuff that we sheared off the sheep. I tried. It didn't burn very good. My parents were going down to Shenandoah, a fellow there was buying wool. My folks took a big sack of this stuff down to see what they could get for it. Now, a woolsack is big; it holds two hundred pounds of wool. It is about six feet high and three feet wide. I put all this burry wool—or woolly burs, whatever you'd call it—in those big sacks. One sack is what went to the market with my parents. I put a sack on my little trailer and hooked it on behind their car. I bet it weighed three hundred pounds. I said, "See if they'll buy it. If you can get anything for it, sell it." Wool was cheap at that time. Good wool was bringing ten to eleven cents a pound.

A buyer has something like a crochet hook to test the wool with. He sticks that hook through the woolsack and pulls it out, and a little wool stays on the hook. But by pulling it through the burlap bag, all the burs would stay inside the sack, and he must not have guessed they were there. I hadn't thought of that. What that buyer pulled out was a nice sample of long-staple wool.

He said, "That's good wool. I'll give you ten cents a pound for it any day. Have you any more?"

"Altogether, three hundred fleeces," said my dad.

Dad sold all those sandburs for ten cents a pound. Never heard anything about it at all. They sold it to somebody else, I suppose, never looked inside the bag. Next buyer was taken the same way, and the next. But, boy, I bet somebody somewhere got a bad sting on that wool, because you never saw anything like it.

After I got the sandburs cleaned out, Mina and I lived a long and happy life on that farm. We had lots of ups and downs, like all other folks, but Mina was a wonderful mother and a good woman. She was always good to me, she always understood that making a living was not easy. It was hard on her to have me away from home as much as I was, all that farm work to be done. That was the worst trouble with our marriage. After we'd been married several years, there were times when I'd be gone three months.

When World War I was going on, I got into the army-horse business, and it kept me away from home for long periods at a time. When I think back on it, I wonder how Mina got along. Besides horsetrading, I was up to my ears in the business of raising, buying, and selling the meat that the people of the United States of America and many other countries have on their tables every day, and also for their festive occasions. It was just a business, and my family went along with it. It was our way of life, and it lasted more than half a century, like with thousands of other families.

When Esther and Ken had grown a little, I often gave them money to spend. Oh, a dollar wouldn't buy very much, let alone a quarter or a half-dollar, but once in a while I'd give them five dollars to spend, so they'd have some money left when they came home. Just as I took it out of my pocket, whatever it was, I gave it to them. One time I was a little short, so I gave my boy a dollar. He took it and looked at it, then he said, "Dad, what the hell can a man do with a dollar?"

Another time he wanted a pair of boots. He didn't need them any more than he needed four hands, but he got it into his head he had to have a pair of rubber boots. Well, I'd bought him a Shetland pony, and he could ride her anyplace, but he still wanted rubber boots. I said sometime I would get him a pair. On a certain day he decided he had gone barefoot long enough, though it was warm and he had shoes. He only went barefoot because he wanted to. He got on his pony and I missed him. When he came home from town he was wearing a pair of new rubber boots.

I said, "Where did you get them, Kenneth?"

"Oh, Kelsey and Wegner's."

"How did you pay for them?"

"Why, I gave them a check."

"You don't mean to tell me they'd take a check from you?"

"Yes, they said it was all right."

"You get right on your pony, young man, and come with me to town. Those boots are going back." Oh, he cried all the way to town.

I went into Kelsey and Wegner's, and I was pretty angry about this. I said, "What in the world are you men thinking about? Sell a little boy a pair of boots and take a check for them! It would have been all right if he had had the money, I wouldn't have said anything about it, but the idea of you men taking a check from a ten-year-old boy surprises me. You know he doesn't have a checking account. Have you got that check here?"

They gave me the check and I said, "He even signed my name, and you let him do it, and took the check! Well, now I've got the check and you can take your darn boots."

They said, "Oh, we didn't mean anything by it. We knew you'd pay for the boots when you came in, and we knew the banker would cash the check."

"The banker better not cash any check I didn't put my own name on. And I know you'd get your money, but I don't want this ten-year-old boy or anybody else to get the idea they can write checks on my account. I want to know how much I've got, and I don't want somebody else to fool with it. And I don't like people who will take a check from a child that way." I walked out of the store, to another store, bought Kenneth a pair of boots, and let him come home.

When I got home I said, "Now, Kenneth, I should punish you for this, but I won't do it. But I don't want you ever to write a check against my account again." Of course, he never did.

The Iowa farmer of those days was somebody special, and my son Kenneth was fast growing to be one of that class. He wasn't very big when he first held the state prize for the best corn. They tell me that's a lot of corn. I see what they mean. Great joke. But it was also a great joke helping little Kenneth get that prize for the first time. Of course, any kid under eighteen is going to have a lot of help one way or another to take the state prize in any state. Kenneth was no exception. Yeah, that was a lot of corn.

His entering came about accidentally. Well, not accidentally, either. Maybe we better say there was some shenanigans mixed up in it. But I won't say whose shenanigans. There used to be little county fairs—still are—all over Iowa, all over other states too, so far as I know. Each fair gave out a set of prizes—first, second, and so on. My dad got interested in the little corn shows around. It got to be quite a thing. Mattie's husband, Fletcher Hunt, got interested too. He and Dad got to showing corn all over the state, and they were always crowing about the prizes they won and how good their corn was. Sounded like a couple of bantam roosters, if you'd listen. "That's the best corn anybody had," I'd hear them say. "Nobody could beat it."

They had a show one year, and corn, colts, and candy was about all that was shown. Everybody kind of got interested in it, you know, word got around, and people were talking about it everywhere I went. I kind of began to have an idea, and I said to Kenneth, "I'd like to beat Fletcher and Dad. I've got some awful good corn. I don't want to show it against them myself, but I'd like you to show it against them."

Kenneth was pleased. We hunted our fields over until we had ten ears of the prettiest corn I ever saw. Nobody knew anything about it but Mina and Ken and me. When the show came along, Ken exhibited our corn. He won first prize. I never saw two fellows as beat in my life as those were. Dad told me, "You never raised that corn."

I said, "Well, I did, and without any special care. What do you think I am? I aimed to beat you. You and Fletcher don't know anything about corn, and I don't either. This boy knows more about corn than any of us."

"You bought that corn someplace."

"No, we picked that right out of our own fields."

Some of them got real huffy about it. I did too when they accused me of lying.

Later there was a grand show at Ames. That was the big one, had all the prizes, even had one for the best half-bushel of shelled corn, a prize for twelve ears, twenty-five ears, a seed-corn prize, everything. I was buying a lot of corn, was thinking of my seed corn for the spring. Thought I'd just have a field of seed corn next year myself. Kenneth and I picked out the best and hung it up to dry.

I said, "Ken, if you've got patience enough, I believe we can beat them out next year on that type of corn. I know we can, because I saw the kind of corn Dad and Fletcher had, and I know we can beat them all. We can beat every one of these growers."

Ken thought he'd like that. We took a bushel of corn, maybe two bushels, took it to the fair, and beat everybody in the state. Got all the first-place prizes but one, and that got second place. I went all over the state showing, and Kenneth went along most of the time. He was proud. He grew corn with a real determination after that. He just knew, like a boy will, that the big cup was his. He was the proudest kid I've ever seen when he came back home with that cup.

When Kenneth was only eight or nine years old, I was running the farm as usual and buying horses when I had to or when I could. I had two men working for me. At this time everybody seemed to have money. Esther, my second child, was a sickly child. Seemed she was sick all the time. She was a dear, sweet little girl, but like all parents we were concerned about her because she was shy and sickly. I had a nice saddle horse, gentle as could be. I had a hired girl who liked to ride. She'd take Esther in front of her on that saddle horse and every day take her for a ride. Esther got so she was quite a good rider.

I also had a roan horse, an awful good saddle horse, but the man I bought him from thought he was an outlaw, so he traded him to me. Soon he was one of the nicest, gentlest horses I ever had around. Esther was riding the roan to school, and Kenneth was riding another horse we were just breaking. One day they started racing, like kids will do, and Esther's horse ran away with her. We never could get Esther on a horse after that, afraid to death of them, just scared to think about it.

Esther had a teacher who abused her when she was small, when she first started to school. She was afraid of that teacher, and the teacher just seemed to pick on Esther. She just worried that little girl until we had to take her out of school. When she was old enough, we got her into high school, where she graduated with her class.

Opal was born several years after Kenneth and Esther. She was just the opposite of the children I already had. From the time she could walk she wanted to ride something. Believe me, I'll bet that today she could ride any bronco any man ever rode. She was a tomboy from A to Z. She was with me all the time. Whenever she could get away from school and housework she was with me. She went wherever I went. She knows more about the horse business today than most traders ever dreamed. From the beginning, Opal was my Benjy, just like I was Benjy to Uncle Leroy Paine. She's just like me in a good many ways. When she was little, seemed like everything I did, Opal had to do it too. She thinks like me, acts like me.

Opal wanted to go with me one day. She was about ten years old. We drove along, worked many miles of busy farms that day, coming along as best we could, driving blind horses, cripples, and one thing and another, buying as we went. That was during the years I was buying horses to be shipped to Europe for food or butchered in this country for dog food and such things. We called them killer horses. I'll tell you about them later when I get to it. Well, Opal and I stopped to get dinner. She was hungry, like all kids are. I said, "Opal, what do you want?"

"That beefsteak looks awful good to me."

She got her beefsteak and she was chewing away at it. Suddenly she asked me, "Daddy, what do they do with those old, crippled horses?"

"They butcher them and send them across the ocean to Europe. People eat them."

She looked at me as if it was a joke and she was wondering what there was to laugh about. Then she just pushed her plate away from her, and she has never taken a bite of meat since. She'll eat fish, but she won't even eat chicken.

It's a long time now since Opal was married. She and her husband raised calves for years, bought them in Wisconsin. Didn't do too well for a while, calves got to dying, and Opal adopted the sick ones, doctored them. Some were very gentle, a breed called Charolais, nice big eyes. One calf was looking at Opal over the fence one day, and she said, "You know, I look at that calf and I just feel bad. Think of it, we feed it and pet it and care for it just to get it murdered. When they leave for market I just can hardly stand it. I know they're going to be murdered."

I'm a great deal that way myself, but you know, God put cattle on this earth for man to use for feed. That's what we believed in my day. They're all here for some cause or other. Why people won't kill them I can't understand. Now, take the people of India, they have those sacred cows, let them run in the rice fields and tramp the rice down because they think they are sacred cattle. I said something to Opal about that. She asked me, wouldn't I like the job of being a sacred cow? I'd rather be a wild Brahma, I told her.

TEN

War Talk and Gold Mines

Back about 1914 I got a call from Des Moines for a load of cowboy horses to go to Mexico. They were having a war down there, and some general had to have these horses the next morning. They had to be on the train and ready to go. The army called to see if I could get the horses.

I said, "No, I can't get them. That's impossible. Give me a little more time."

"No, they've got to go tomorrow morning. See what you can do. You've got to get them for us. We want twenty-two head—twenty-three, one to be an officer's fancy horse."

"I can get that one, but he's going to cost a lot of money."

"Go ahead and get him if you think he's the right kind. Oh, and they want them all shod." He hung up.

I started out and traveled as far as I could go. I'd just stop for a minute anyplace. Soon as I'd buy a horse, I'd send it right in to the blacksmith and he'd send it to the shipper. That way I'd get them all to the blacksmith, and I wouldn't have to do anything more with them. I could go right on buying more horses. The train came at twelve-thirty. I just had time to go out and get that officer's horse. I had a hard time buying that one. I heard the train whistle when I was still two miles out. I gave that horse a whack with the reins and he got us in. My boys had the other horses all ready in the boxcar. There was an officer prancing back and forth. The train was ready to pull out.

I rode up and he said, "This my horse?"

"Yes, sir."

"Well, get off him and get him into the car." Didn't ask me anything about this horse or any of the others. I knew what the price was, so it didn't make any difference. In two or three days I got a check for those horses. I got a good price for them, made money on that deal. That was the way with the horse business at that time.

In addition to the war in Mexico, there was a war on in Europe. It was pretty close to all of us, but it was closer to me because I bought many horses that were involved, even lost their lives, in these wars. The United States was standing on the sidelines, but I was buying horses for the Italians, English, Belgians, and French, as well as the Mexicans. I shipped thousands of horses, thousands of them.

Right in the midst of all the war talk, we had trouble with wolves. At one time there were lots of wolves here. They got to bothering sheep. We had sheep on my farm, and a neighbor had sheep. Wolves got into the sheep, and we sent for the professional wolf hunters to come with their hounds and try to catch them. One morning here they came, all excited, on their saddle horses. One said, "Get on your horse and let's go catch those wolves."

I got on my horse and we went out. We started to follow the hounds. We ran two wolves until the horses were about given out. We finally got one in the back section of the old home place. He ran west about four miles, turned around, and followed the creek back. The dogs headed him and then he took off across the country. My youngest brother, Arthur, was a young man by that time. He heard the commotion and got on his horse. We were right in back of the old home place. Art took out, and he was quite a way ahead of the rest of us. He ran his horse into a cornfield at Dad's place. The wolf was so tired out that Art rode right up alongside him, jumped off his horse, grabbed that wolf by the throat with his hands, and choked him to death. That was an awful chance to take. He might have been badly gashed by the teeth of that desperate animal, but I guess the wolf was just too tired to fight by that time.

The other wolf had taken off in another direction and we followed her. We had run this wolf so far we knew she was tired out. As soon as the dogs caught sight of that wolf they just took after her. Why, it wasn't any time till we got her. Two wolves in one day. That stopped the timber wolves, but every few days we had to have a coyote hunt. We finally quit. I sold my sheep and so did my neighbor.

We went on for several years and then some of my neighbors got some sheep. One day one of my neighbors and I were going over to the pasture to look for some cattle. I had been sick with pneumonia and couldn't walk yet. My neighbor wanted me to go with him and look at his cattle, so I did. We got over there and saw a coyote kill a sheep. We phoned for the dogs to come, for the professional hunters to bring their hounds. They got lost and drove way off someplace else, way off out of the way, but finally they came. The trail got cold, and I wasn't feeling like I should stay out. Then one of the dogs picked up the trail and followed the coyote over to my pasture, about two miles and a half from my house. There was some timber over there, and we were all satisfied that was where this coyote would go. It looked like a female, and it looked like she had pups. The hunters congregated over there, dogs and men.

We had the trail hounds, and someone had brought some greyhounds to help catch those coyotes. Now, the trail hound follows by scenting the tracks, but the greyhound follows by sight. The greyhounds were chained, and a young boy held the ends of the chains. He had been told, "You hold them, and when you see the coyote and the trail hounds come out of the timber, turn the greyhounds loose."

All the other men took the trail hounds and went into the timber to see what they could find. They even drove me over there in a car. I was sitting on high ground, so I could see everything. This little boy was sitting there beside me holding the two greyhounds. The male came out of the timber first and ran right up to me. I couldn't get out of the way, and he just stood there and snarled at me. The greyhounds got excited, got the little boy all tangled up in the chains. All the men had guns, but they were all at the wrong place. Then the female coyote came out of the timber, and both of these coyotes ran together. We could see them for a couple of miles. The coyotes turned into the timber again, but they soon turned back. Their feet were so sore from running that they didn't want any more timber country.

By that time there were about fifteen men present. They crossed through the timber and chased the coyotes out. When they came up I was close enough that I saw several half-grown coyotes come out of the timber clear on the other side of the men. I didn't have a gun, so I just sat there and watched nine coyotes come right out into the open. Just sat there. Well, those hunters didn't get any of them; they all got away.

One was a wolf, a killer. Somebody had caught him in a trap, one of his toes was off. I could tell it was the same wolf that had got into my sheep a couple of years before and killed thirteen sheep in one morning, the same wolf. He didn't eat them, just ran through the herd and would catch a sheep by the throat, cut the throat, and away he'd go. I had trailed him all day at the time and finally lost him completely. This wolf had the same toe off the same foot.

I had been satisfied that the coyotes had some young there in one place, but I hadn't found them. I couldn't find the den, either. One of my neighbors was plowing that day, and the little coyotes were out playing. They came out of the den and were playing in the plowed ground. I guess they could find a lot of insects in that turned turf. They say coyotes eat insects. Well, if they just didn't eat sheep too! This man had no gun with him, but he took his whip and killed all of them, nine of them.

Still, it seemed like every day that old wolf would get into some-body's young pigs or into the calves or chase cattle in the field, or something, every day or so. I hired a government man, told him I'd give him a hundred dollars if he'd catch that wolf. He couldn't catch it. Said it was the first time he had failed on an assignment, and he was there a month. Those government men would find wolf tracks right up to their traps, but that old boy was smart enough he wouldn't go in. That agent camped in the pasture for a month trying to get that wolf, then he finally left.

One night one of the neighbor boys heard a racket. He was upstairs in a big house. The racket seemed to come from about fifty to a hundred yards from the house. He had a .22-caliber rifle with him and could see this old wolf in the hog pen. He thought it was the three-toed one. It jumped out of the hog pen with a little pig in his mouth and sat down to eat it. This boy up with his rifle and killed that wolf. The pig was already half eaten, but a lot of others were saved. We haven't been bothered with any such visitors since. There's only one way to keep them away. If you've got enough yard light, a wolf won't come near.

This same old gray wolf once palled up with a female coyote. My grandsons were staying overnight with me one night, and they heard our dog barking. I went out with the shotgun. That wolf and his coyote friend were sitting right near my barn, and my dog was raising the dickens. Just as I went out, here came that old gray wolf right over the top of the fence into the yard. I blazed away, knocked him end over end but didn't kill him.

I saw that female a lot of times afterward. She had her den over in the timber of my pasture. Someone found her cubs and killed them. Killed her too, I guess, wasn't any wolves here for a long time. I heard one a couple of times, though, the last year I was on my farm.

The boys formed a gun club. Fifty or sixty men with shotguns, not rifles. They'd surround a section and work toward the center. They got a lot of coyotes. For a couple of years they'd have a hunt every Sunday. They cleaned the foxes out of here. Foxes had been as bad as wolves to kill young lambs, steal chickens, and everything they could find that suited their appetite. Even so, I didn't mind what they ate, it was what they killed for fun and left laying on the ground.

War at home, war away. What can a man do but fight? At that time it seemed to be the only answer.

Even with all the war talk going on, though, people still managed to come up with new schemes for making a lot of money. It must've been in the year 1916 that a business company was formed in Adair and nearby towns to develop a Colorado mine. The mine was way up the side of a mountain nine miles outside Denver. They set up all the machinery and equipment needed, put in a concentrator, and got it all set to develop this mine on a big scale. The prospects were awful good. They sent experts to the mine and had good reports, good ores showing up. They opened up several veins to get the mine in operation so they could say truthfully that there was ore. Then they could sell their interests honestly. That ore had to be carried to the smelter in Denver. It was smelted to separate gold and silver from lead and whatever else was in the ore. Then they'd smelt again to separate the gold and silver.

All the interested parties put up the money to bring in the machinery needed. They called it the Red Oak Mine. They hired an overseer and a crew. Everything went along smooth and everybody was well pleased. Then all at once they got a report that the mine had played out, the ore was gone and it wasn't worth taking out, such poor grade. The owners were duly alarmed about this report. They called another meeting and decided to send someone out to the mine, someone who wasn't in the company, someone who might be looking for a job. They sent me to Denver.

I had never done any ore mining. I had mined coal in Iowa, as I told you earlier, but never in a place like this Colorado setup. Now I was going out there as a spy, a detective, to see if the owners were getting a square deal. I showed up in Denver looking for a job. The first job I had was on a drill, and at that time they were run by a motor. I worked that drill. That hard ore would just shake the teeth out of you. I stuck to it, but I didn't find out much. Didn't know enough about ore to know if what was going out of the Red Oak Mine was good.

I had quit gambling, as I told you before, but now I had to seem like one of the boys, so I started out in bars and other places where I could gamble. Yes, I did quit gambling, but maybe I had a special reason to put away my good resolutions for a while. I had a relapse, for a reason. I was getting paid to do this job. I'd get a couple of paydays and go in town and gamble a little with some of the boys.

I was afraid they'd start noticing that I didn't live like they did, start asking questions. I didn't feel safe at night. I might get shot, you know, if they found out I was a spy. I was there for a purpose, so I had to be careful how I looked to the others. I was an undercover man, so I had to do things that made them think I was just another miner. That was the only time I ever did undercover work. They didn't need anything like that regularly where I lived. That was quite an experience, mining in Colorado.

I finally smuggled a piece of ore out of that mine and took it down to Denver to be assayed. The report came back that it was worth so much a ton, more than the assay they had when they first opened the mine. Then I knew something was wrong.

Every Saturday the miners got off work at noon and everybody would go to Denver. They had a lot of things to do. I played cards, always lucky at cards, so I got into a game one Saturday with a fellow named Patrick and some other fellows. Pat had a burro packtrain running from the Red Oak Mine to Denver. I got into this game with these men. The others dropped out after a while, but Pat and I, we kept gambling. When daylight came I owned a burro packtrain and what little money Pat had, and a whole lot of other things. Instead of feeling sorry about his bad gambling luck, Pat said, "I'm glad you got it, because you're going to get some experience."

I said, "All right." But I wondered what he meant.

He said, "There's a load of groceries got to go up to the mine this morning, and you gotta pack them so's them Rocky Mountain canaries can't shake them loads off."

I had never packed a burro in my life, and I learned you gotta pack them pretty secure. Those little animals may carry lots of loads and go where few others can go, but they don't do it because they like to. You put those sacks on their sides, and they have to be packed just right. They can rub off a pack on a tree or a rock. Those packs can be got rid of pretty fast.

I said, "Well, you gotta help me."

No, he wouldn't help me, but I got ahold of another fellow, who helped me pack those mules. Then I drove them nine miles that seemed like ninety back to the Red Oak Mine. Those burros were pretty ornery that first trip. Next morning I had to take a load of ore down to Denver.

That turned out to be the regular pattern—groceries up to the mine one day, ore down to Denver the next. It was kind of fun, because those burros were pretty well trained. They'd keep the trail well. I had also won a collie dog. He would keep the mules in line, and they'd get down the mountain. I'd unload them, and next morning I'd load them up again with groceries, start back that long nine miles to camp.

I kept that up for two weeks, but I couldn't get any trace on where that ore was going. I knew they were getting it out of the mine. I knew they were doing something with the good ore, but what they were doing and how, I didn't know. I couldn't find out a thing.

I had a little black burro that was mean. He was awful hard to do anything with. He'd break away and I'd have to run after him and catch him to put that pack on him. He didn't like to be loaded in the morning. He didn't want to carry a load. It was quite a load, 280 pounds, for a little fellow like that. All the others carried the same, but they didn't make all this fuss about it. This little black, he'd fight me every time I tried to get that pack on him. I pretty near had to tie him down to get a load on him.

One morning I had the burros all packed and ready, all but this little black one. I went to put the saddlebags on him. He broke away and ran up on top of a ridge a good quarter of a mile away, maybe more, off up where the miners took the slag out of the mountain, ore and everything. That black burro ran up there, and I went up and caught him.

When he was coming down he chipped up a piece of what at first looked like slag, a chunk about as big as your head. I just happened to notice it and I thought, Where'd that come from? Of course, I knew what it was. I took that piece down to the assay office. Sure enough, it was good ore. I went back up there looking around at night to see if I could find any more of that ore. The slag pile was full of it, great hunks of that good ore. They were dumping the good ore out and sending the poor stuff down to the assay office.

When I got the proof, I had to get out of there. I got a train and came back to Adair. I told the stockholders and officers all about what I had found, and I wrote a report for the assay office. The mine company fired the foreman, and shortly after he was fired the concentrator burned down. That discouraged the stockholders. It would cost a lot of money to put up another one. They got in touch with a syndicate in England and managed to sell them their interest in the mine. They paid out all the stockholders that were in the business. Then the United States got involved in World War I, and they couldn't mine the Red Oak. The English owners couldn't do anything with it for several years. But after the war was over they went to work on it, and that mine proved to be one of the best in Colorado. They got millions of dollars' worth of ore out of it. I don't know whether it's still running, but I imagine it is. There was a lot of ore in there. Not much gold, more silver and quite a lot of lead.

Like Patrick said when I won the poker game, I had the experience.

I had the experience. But that isn't quite all the story. What could I do with the burros? I thought of Uncle Lee Paine. Turn his advice around to work the other way, and it just about hits this problem. Now I wanted to lose something. I went down to Denver to the card rooms and I tried every way in the world to lose those burros, but I couldn't lose them. Finally I got ahold of an old fellow one night, and I got playing poker with him. He thought he was just beating the socks off me. I had a little money with me. I put it all up and lost it. Then I said, "I'll tell you what I'll do. I'll put up this burro train and everything that goes with it, saddles, collie, everything. If you win, you go right ahead with my job. We'll match to see which one gets it. Either I get to keep the money and the burros or you get everything."

He said, "All right."

I think he already felt like a victor. I flipped the coin and he won. I got rid of those burros. I said, "I'm glad you won, because you're going to get some experience." I got out of there on the fastest train for Adair.

Sometimes you have to be a good loser as well as a generous winner. You sure do. That's one card game I got into that I was happy to lose. To think that I got rid of those burros, a bunch of burros, fifteen or sixteen of them, and lifting all those heavy sacks, two for each burro, every time you load them. You'd have to lift every one up and put it on the saddle. I was getting about enough of that.

ELEVEN

The Army-Horse Business

Time went along, and the United States kept getting more and more involved in the European war. Woodrow Wilson, the president, had a lot to say, and everybody thought we ought to go whip those Germans. We were in it up to here, and finally in April 1917 we officially declared war.

I tried to enlist four times. I was one of the first to show up at the draft board at Adair. I was with the first bunch. I had a bad leg, had been kicked by a horse. They turned me down, wouldn't let me in the army. The last time I tried I pretty near got in. Seemed like they just didn't want me. I felt like a reject, especially because the army did take my youngest brother, Arthur. Gene was exempted because he was taking care of my parents and Amy. Lewis had tuberculosis and a family too. They decided I would be more useful inspecting the horses the government bought to send to France and other Allied countries and also those horses bought for our own army.

When the army finally decided to let me in as a horse inspector I didn't pay much attention to details. I wanted to help out in this war. They called it The War to End Wars. That was my kind of war. They gave me this job inspecting horses. I didn't realize it, but I was signed up for eight years. Well, I found that out soon enough.

I got to Camp Dodge pretty fast. It was near Des Moines and only about forty miles away from my farm. It was quite a job, but somebody had to do it, and I figured it might as well be me. At least it was something not too many could do and do right. They'd ship the horses in from everywhere buyers could find them. I'd stand in one place, and I had the horses led up to me on the walk. I could see them pretty good from where I stood. They'd lead the horses up and walk them past me. Then they brought them back on a trot. I looked at the eyes and the mouth, and the ones I didn't want I'd just motion out with my hand. I never said a word to anyone. Usually, I'd have three or four hundred horses to inspect each day.

There were a lot of people in that place buying the horses I turned down. They'd buy a lot of them, get them cheap, take them out somewhere they weren't known, and make pretty good money selling them. Those horsetraders were not from our part of the country. They were people who came there to make dishonest money buying cheaply from the government and selling high to the farmers and others who needed and used these animals. Of course, farms needed horses and mules worse now than they ever had before. They had to produce all the food they could, now that a war was going, and their best stock was being taken by the government. Other countries depended on our food. Some of these foreign buyers even carried briefcases. I thought that was funny. A horsetrader keeps his information in his head, not in a briefcase. Only European-born traders would think of such a thing.

Some buyers would gather several carloads of horses and come to Camp Dodge with these loads. When they came to the inspection station they would say, "Here's a bill for my horses." I was taken aback when that happened to me the first time. The owner had brought a load of horses to me to inspect, and he was handing me a hundred dollars.

I said, "Now, just take the horses out."

Next one, he did the same thing. I waved him off.

He said, "Oh, my goodness. Ain't you gonna look at them?"

I said, "No. I don't want to get in prison. If I were to take that money, I would never get away from here without a ball and chain on my leg. Now, don't bring any more of your horses for me to inspect. You can't bribe me, nor can anyone else. I'm here working for the federal government. My brother and a lot of my friends are over there fighting for their country and their lives. If I was to take one of these horses, one of these snides, and one of the boys got on it and was killed, I'd feel like I was the cause of it. No money could in any way be worth that to me." I never sent one bad horse over there for the boys who were fighting.

The government at one time put Morgan stallions onto some of their contract ranches. The stock raisers, the ranchers, were under contract to raise those horses, and they could do whatever they wanted with them—work them, use them—but they couldn't sell them to anybody but the government, and there was a fixed price on them. All the United States government had to do was order their horses in. The contract horsemen had to bring in the government stock on their farms.

They'd bring them. Some would be broken. I got 101 head of, oh, the most beautiful bay horses! Morgan horses they surely were, with a short back. I liked them and took them to Omaha to be broken to ride. I hired a little fellow to help me. He didn't weigh much more than 125 pounds. He and I would ride every one of those horses once each day. How else was I going to know if these horses were ready to go to war? He rode with his feet out of the stirrups and never had a horse throw him. We got through with them and sent them on to the boys in Europe. Next thing we knew the government had another bunch sent in. I had to leave, but I got another man to take my place.

I showed the boys how to gentle those horses. We'd get the horses into the stall and shake an old oilskin raincoat. Two men would go into the stall and just shake those raincoats over the horses. Scare the living daylights out of them the first time we did that. They'd just fight that raincoat! Kick up their feet, raise a fuss. But they'd get used to it, and when they came out of there they'd stand still. We could saddle them up and ride them. They weren't afraid of men's ways anymore after that.

Then they were put back in the pen and we rode them continually. My brother Arthur was in the First Cavalry, and the horses I trained were sent down to the boys he was with. Art and all the boys I saw from there said those were the best-broken outfit of horses they ever received. Tough Morgan horses. The boys remembered them.

When a mule or horse goes into the service, after they pass inspection, the stable boys bob their tails off right to the end of the bone, cut their manes down, roach them so the mane stands up—dress them all up. When they'd get all fixed up, those animals would act like little kids with new clothes. They wanted to show off. They felt good about themselves and would want you to see how good they looked.

Well, they didn't just roach them, they clipped them. Then they'd brand "U.S." on the neck and on the hoof. It takes a long time for a brand to wear off the hoof, because a hoof doesn't grow like a fingernail, or not much like one. Some brands I know were visible for four or five years. The brand never wears off the body where they burn it on. The scar stays there forever. A horse carries his owner's brand to his death. I guess he's as much a slave as you could imagine.

I didn't get home very much after I went in army service. My wife was alone with the three children, and I couldn't always be sure she even had a hired man to help her. Kenneth was ten years old or more by that time, but a boy that age, though he can do a lot, can't really run a whole farm and go to school too. Mina had the two little girls, and it wasn't easy for her. But I had to do what I could, too. A war was on, and they needed every able-bodied man in the place where he could do the most good. Seemed like I was that man in that place. After they decided what I could do, they never seemed to have much doubt about how much they needed me. They seemed to think I was suddenly indispensable.

I would have been working a month or two with no time off, and I would maybe get home for a couple of days, take my hat off, and the phone would ring. I got awful tired of working away from home. A lot of times I didn't have time even for a shave. Just start to talk with my wife and kids, and the phone would ring. "Get over to that place and inspect horses," they'd say, some new lot somebody'd bought.

I'll never forget August 1917. We were getting the Eighty-second Division ready to ship out. These horses were all sheared, tails all bobbed, everything. But they called me up at home to inspect for glanders.

Glanders is a disease among horses, always fatal, and if a man gets it, he better get to a doctor fast or it can be fatal to him too. In animals we still can't cure glanders. The only cure is to kill and bury every animal that has it, then disinfect every bit of barn or yard they have used. This treatment is why the disease is now rare. If your animal gets glanders, there is no hope. Just notify the authorities to come and do their job.

Almost all the horses in that shipment had that sickness. We had to get them out of there some way. Soldiers were dying, and they didn't even know what was the matter. I told them that the reason was they'd got glanders from the horses. Well, they called me at home and I went down there the tenth or eleventh day of August 1917. Hot? Oh, it was stinking hot. Those stinking horses, I could smell them before I left Des Moines. The horses were at Camp Dodge, which is five miles outside of Des Moines.

They began to lead out the diseased animals. A big pit had been dug, and they'd bring the horses and, oh, it was a stinking mess. In that hot sun you couldn't smell anything else, and it was horrible. I was awful careful not to touch any of those horses or men. We killed fifteen hundred horses that first day and let them fall into the pit and put lime on them. Shot 'em. Shot some myself. Altogether I guess there were seventeen hundred horses to be destroyed. When they came in from the farms they had never been near that disease. Somehow the infection had got into the pens, and the fresh, good horses just in from the farms had got that filthy disease.

After all the infected horses were shot and buried we had to disinfect all those pens in the whole Camp Dodge stables. Working in a place like that, standing in the hot sun all day long, I couldn't eat anything if I wanted to—stink, stink, *stink*, that's all you could think of. It's all I can think of yet when I remember. What an awful stink. There were watering troughs a foot deep and three feet wide, some were six feet long, and they were kept full of water. I've seen those horses standing there, and they'd fill that tank half full, just with the pus coming out of their noses. We had a terrible spell there at Camp Dodge.

After the war was over a lot of horses had to be killed, because glanders had sprung up all over. People carried it on their clothes—soldiers coming back from Europe, maybe. I hope I never see such a sight again.

They had other inspectors, but it always seemed they put the big load onto me. I guess that was because

I was willing, and whatever the job seemed to demand, I did it. When you're willing to work, people depend on you, they know you'll do things and not shirk out of them, they pile more onto you. If I wanted to get off for a few days at home and put in for some time, they'd say, "Well, you got to go down to Kansas City," or St. Jo, or someplace else, "and inspect horses," or they'd say, "Another man's got a leave."

Some of the inspectors got tired of it and went into regular service. Some of them weren't competent and got fired. Some of them accepted those one-hundred-dollar tips. A lot got caught at that. A couple of fellows in Des Moines got caught. I was glad I didn't have to stand in their shoes. I got a lot more work to do than some of the rest, and until that job was finished I sure didn't see anything of my family. But I had the satisfaction of seeing a job well done, which is a pretty nice reward.

TWELVE

Almost out of the Army

After the Armistice was signed in November 1918, the boys started coming home, and everybody felt that a new life was ahead. That awful war certainly had changed our lives. We would never be the same as before. Of course, everybody was glad the war was over, that War to End Wars, glad we had ended the wars which had plagued every country since the beginning of human history. We all felt good, like we had just done a very necessary dirty job and had done it well. Through all the ages of man, wars had come and had left the land and the people in a sad fix. Now we had ended wars. We thought we must be somebody special, and we were ready to shine as the greatest people the world had known. What was left was ours. We had conquered the unconquerable. We were the ultimate product. Man was the greatest thing on earth; there wasn't any doubt of that. Families were back together, young men were back home making eyes at their girls, everybody had a little money, and they were spending it, even though prices were higher than ever before. We looked out on what seemed to be a bright new world, a world such as man had not seen before. People didn't sing "Over There" much anymore, they sang "Beautiful Ohio" and the "Missouri Waltz," "A Long, Long Trail A-Winding" and "K-K-K-Katy, Beautiful Katy." About the time the boys started coming home, I came to fully realize that I had enlisted for eight years and I had four more long years to serve. I wasn't happy about that. I was pretty sick of being in the service, there was no longer any war, and I wanted to be with my family. Four more years. A very long time. A hell of a long time, especially for a married man, especially for one with a big farm and a lot of stock and a family growing up. I wanted to be with them. I hoped that after this last four years my kids still knew who their father was. I pulled every string I could get hold of to get out of that enlistment. The army even wanted to send me to Spain to inspect mules for the Spanish government. I'd have to be there my entire four years which I still had to serve.

I said, "No, sir, I'm not going."

They said, "You are going."

I started with the people I knew at home who had some authority and I worked clear up to the governor of the state of Iowa. I talked with anyone who had influence in the state of Iowa. I pulled pretty hard on some of those strings. They petitioned the president, and the president let me off.

He let me off!

That was great, but they still had their pound of flesh. I had to lose all my rights, pensions, insurance, everything. Of course, I did well enough financially, but I gave good service during that four years, too. As much or more than any other man. But now I could go home—I thought.

Before I could finally get out, I had to sign an agreement that I would dispose of the horses that were sent to Des Moines as they returned from service in Europe. They'd send a trainload at a time. I had to be there to see that they were auctioned off. That was part of it all; those horses and mules they sent back were valuable United States government property, and they had to have someone to sell them back to the farmers and others who needed them. Of course, like everything else, lots of people had made the old mules and horses do when they really needed new ones, young and strong ones. That kind of sacrifice helps win a war. Now the war was over and the old ones could be turned out to pasture because the government was selling the new ones cheap, and everybody rushed to buy them. I guess even the horses were glad to get back to Iowa after such a war. Maybe they even hoped to get back to where they had been in life. If so, they were mistaken. With the help of one man, that war had changed the whole world. It would never be the same again, and horses would never be as valuable to the farmer as they once were.

The man named Henry Ford worked that change. The war had

offered the opportunity for fantastic developments in machinery to do many jobs better than horses could. I could see pretty clearly now what Ford had told me back in the Chicago stockyards. He had known what he was talking about. The days of the horse *were* numbered. The numbers might have been pretty high once, but they were running out fast now, so many changes were happening.

I had full control of the animals shipped back to Des Moines. I had a couple of good men with me, and I'd have them go through each shipment in the morning, when stock was unloaded. All those good, young horses that I could, I bought for myself and sent out to my farm. I paid the government price, just like anybody else, but I got the pick. Seems to me I had to get sixty dollars a head. That's the price the government wanted. Had a lot of them I got a hundred seventy-five for, sometimes two hundred. Mules weren't so high. The U.S. price had to be thirty-five dollars a head. I bought a lot of them that never had been in the war at all, never been in battle. I wonder what a horse thinks of the man who rides him into battle.

I'll have to tell you about an Irishman who had a pair of little buckskin mules. Before the war, every day this Irishman had driven through Adair with these mules hitched to a wagon, because part of his farm was way down on the other side of town, and the only way he could get from one farm to the other was down Main Street. Every day as soon as he got to the edge of town the mules would run away with him, and they'd run all the way through town. This little old Irishman, he'd stand there in the wagon pulling on those mules. They must have had the toughest mouths in the country, they never stopped running. And nearly every day he'd lose his hat. But he went, every day, on down to work his farm. He had a son who was of military age when World War I broke out, and the boy enlisted.

I asked him, "How come you enlisted and left your dad out there alone?"

He answered me, "Well, we have to work those darn mules, and I just hate 'em. I joined the army so I'd never see them again." They sent him to Camp Dodge at Des Moines.

After the son was gone, the father decided he didn't feel like working those pesky little mules anymore either, so he and I struck a deal on the mules and I bought them from him for the federal government. I had lots of orders from the government at that time. I put these mules, never thinking about it, into a shipment to go to Camp Dodge at Des Moines.

There was one surprised Irish lad when he went out to drive a span of mules and found himself assigned to drive those little old buckskins. They put him on the provision wagon and gave him those same little buckskin mules.

After a time he got a chance to go to England, but that didn't accomplish what he'd hoped. About that time the mules went to England too, and again they were assigned to their Irish boy. In France the same thing happened, and in Germany he still had the buckskin mules. That was one happy Irish lad the day they sent him back to the good old U.S.A. and he could leave the buckskin mules behind in Germany.

Well, he wasn't through with those mules yet! As I said earlier, the federal government sent back a good many mules after the war was over. I bought a lot of them back to sell to the farm people I knew. I had a bunch of mules come in one day, and with my hired hands I drove them out to my farm and put them in my pasture. As I leaned my elbows on the fence and looked the bunch over, I thought a couple of buckskins looked familiar. Sure enough, there they were.

A couple of days later the little Irishman came to my place, and he wanted to buy a team. He said, "I'd like to have a nice little span of mules. I like mules."

I said, "Well, I've got several pair of mules in the pasture. You can have any pair you want, and they won't cost you too much. I bought them cheap."

I took him down to the pasture, and the first mules he saw were those little buckskins, and that's what he had to have. He took them home, and the boy had to work them on the farm. He wished he was back in the war. That boy had gone all through the war without a scratch, and so had the mules. They came back, and they looked just as they had when they left the farm. And they were just about as mean. The old man said to me, "You know, I'll tell you. If I didn't know them mules went to the war, I'd swear that's the same pair as used to run away with me."

My kids used to go around singing that old song, "Horses, horses, horses, crazy over horses, horses, horses." All the kids used to sing that, but mine had a special reason. Well, if I was crazy over horses, I didn't feel any bad effects from it, like some do who are crazy over something less healthy.

We kept getting a few cases of glanders now and then. Every so often we'd have to destroy horses that had become infected. I felt like maybe I really was crazy over horses the day I found I had glanders myself. I found it out in time to cure it, though. How I got rid of it I don't know. It is bad to see a fine, big sixteen-hundred-pound horse die from that awful disease. But it was worse to think I might go because of it myself. That was one time I never want to live over again. I don't know how I got it or how I got rid of it, but I sure did.

When I finally was completely finished with horses for the federal government the first thing I did was go home and plant a crop. Maybe I wanted some roots to hold me at home for a while. But I don't think I needed roots. I'd been away enough to last me for a long while. I thought.

THIRTEEN

Back on the Farm

I've always been a farmer, and I've farmed a lot of land in my time. I never went to agricultural college, but I always liked to experiment. Something new interested me every time. I think I was the first man to start growing soybeans in Adair County. There might have been one earlier, but not more than that. I bought the seed from the Henry Field Seed Company early in 1920. I gave fifty cents a bushel for it and put in twenty acres. People just were shocked—all those beans! Well, my twenty acres brought me a bigger yield than anyone in that whole country had ever heard of. That was a good crop of soybeans, but I didn't know what to do with them.

My brother Arthur and I had bought a big bunch of Arkansas pigs, a couple of hundred of them. They looked like pigs, but they must have been yearling material, little fellows about fifty to sixty pounds. I thought, I don't know what to do with those soybeans, so why not feed them to those pigs? The pigs, it turned out, loved soybeans, got fat. Their little legs weren't over four inches long, and they were the prettiest pigs you've ever seen. I enjoyed looking at them. I called Iowa Pack and wanted to know if they would like to buy a hundred pigs. No, they said, we better bring about fifty. We took fifty pigs to the packer, and everybody stood around admiring those young hogs.

The buyer representative said, "This is the best bunch of pigs I've ever seen. Where'd you get them? What'd you feed them?"

I said I'd fed them soybeans.

"What's soybeans?"

"It's a bean that I raise out there. Seems to me like it's a natural for hog feed." They all agreed.

After they paid me for the pigs, I went home feeling pretty good. The neighbors and everybody knew what I was feeding those pigs. About nine o'clock the next morning I got a call from the packing house. The buyer asked, "Have you got any more of those pretty pigs down there?"

I said, "Oh, yes."

He told me, "Their lard won't harden. They're just greasy. Don't bring any more of them down here. We can't handle them."

That upset the business. Now to get rid of the other pigs, one hundred fifty of them. I didn't dare send them to Omaha, because the factory I'd sold these to had a plant in Omaha too. I loaded them up and sent them down to St. Jo. Never heard a word from them, but I got paid for them. That taught me about soybeans.

I kept my seed, and next year, I figured, they'd make awful nice hay. I planted ten acres to soybeans. That didn't cut me short of acreage for any other crop; I had a big farm. I cut it all for hay and put it in with the cattle. They just loved it. Then everybody, all the neighbors around, went to planting soybeans for hay, hundreds and hundreds of acres, soybeans all around. I just sold the seeds and got everybody enthused about the new crop. But I warned them not to let the pigs have it.

The Chicago Board of Trade put soybeans on the market, on the board, like they did wheat. I've seen a bushel of soybeans bring all the way from two and a quarter to three dollars, and I imagine they've been higher since I retired. Everybody soon was raising soybeans, it became a main crop. Instead of sowing oats, like we used to, they were sowing soybeans. I farmed a lot of my land to beans, too.

One year I was farming eight hundred acres of land, and I'd have from two to three hundred acres of corn, besides oats, wheat, barley, and other things, too. Of course, some of the acreage went into pasture, but I was farming in a big way. Had a lot of hired help, thirty head of workhorses, raised my own horses too. Had a bunch of mares and raised the colts every year. That's a job itself, raising colts. I started them to work at two years old, and by the time they got to be five they were ready for the feed line, ready for market.

The last years I was on the farm I had about 550 acres, most of it in pasture. If you raise enough corn and hay to feed about three hundred hogs, eight hundred cattle, and four thousand sheep, that keeps you pretty full.

In 1925 Mina and I had our fourth and last child, June. We had three girls and an older boy, a great family, one any man could be proud of, and I have had every reason to be proud of them all. Now they're all grandparents themselves, and great-grandparents, some of them, and I'm a great-great-grandfather. It all seems to happen so slow at the time, but when it's in the past it seems to have whirled by in just a short span of time.

Of course, even with all the work to do on the farm, I didn't give up horsetrading, not by any means. After I finished selling off all the returning horses and mules for the army, I got to selling back at the stockyards again, just as I had before the war. Pretty soon I got an order from England for two thousand mine ponies. A shipload of them. Two thousand! Took me over a year to buy them. Oh, they just lost a barrel of money on them, and I lost, too, more than I could afford. To get the ones I wanted I had to buy so many others that were too big. Had to take a loss on them, a big loss. I bought all the ponies that came into the Chicago stockyards for a while there. I told everybody I knew to buy all the ponies they could, didn't make any difference what color they were but they had to be forty-two inches high; that's the size of a mine pony. Had to be low-headed ponies, too, because they were going into the mines to work underground in the tunnels and couldn't have their heads higher than the mine shafts were made.

My contract with the British government was for two thousand animals at eighty-five dollars a head. I traveled a lot looking for these ponies. I would go to a farm and talk to the owner about his business. We would have a bargain all worked out, I would be writing a check, hear a big noise, look up, and here would come all the kids yelling, crying, "We don't want to sell our pony!" Then I'd have to take other horses along with the bunch of ponies to get the man to ignore the kids. I never got into such a mess in my life.

I rented a big pasture just outside of Chicago and bought all the feed I could buy around there. Came wintertime, I had expected to ship these animals before winter, but I couldn't buy them up fast enough to get the shipment together. I had to keep them clear until next spring. I had to build sheds for them to keep them from freezing to death. It was an awful lot of work and expense, cut my profits way down.

I have often wished I had taken a picture of those ponies when I finally got them to the boat. When they went up the gangplank they were just like a bunch of sheep. Each followed the one ahead, and they were docile about it, but they knew this was something that had never happened to them before.

Two thousand is a lot of ponies. Harry McNair was my partner in that deal and, boy, what we lost on that pony deal with England.

The next contract I had was for three hundred big, heavy horses for the Germans. I was sitting around the auction yard in Chicago one day when some Germans came up to me. This was on a Sunday, and I was the only one around the yard. It just happened that way. They had an interpreter with them, and they told me what they wanted through him. They also had their own veterinarians with them and everything they needed to care for the horses they bought. I happened to have a few of those good, big horses, and I figured this might be a pretty good deal so I priced my stock pretty high. I quoted them four hundred twenty-five dollars apiece. Horses were awful high at that time.

The Germans said, "Well, if you let us take them and have our own veterinarian examine them, keep them overnight. If we like them, we'd like to make a contract with you to buy three hundred of those big horses."

I said, "All right, but now if I go to work and buy those three hundred horses, I want the money left right here. I want a deposit big enough so I won't get caught, big enough so you'll have to take them. I'll guarantee every one of them to be sound, to pass the examination you will give them, but if some don't pass your inspection, you are not under obligation to take them. Every horse that passes, you just take them for four hundred twenty-five dollars each." You know, they just fell for that, they just fell for it. We went up to the office to make out the contract, and I got it all signed before witnesses.

Then I set to work buying horses. I could get a horse for two hundred or a little over, but I also got a lot of them under that, a lot for a hundred seventy-five dollars. I took all the horses I could buy for that. Whenever a big horse came in that was in good shape or could be quickly got into shape, I bought him. I was the only one working out of that stockyard that had a contract. If any of the buyers found a good horse, they'd buy it for me. Of course, they got a bit for it. Even Harry McNair remembered me if he found the kind of horse I needed. They all had a hint that I was doing pretty good on that contract. I made up some of my losses on the British pony contract with this German horse contract. A lot of times that's just the way horsetrading works out.

FOURTEEN

Daniels and McNair, Commission Men

I was shipping horses to Chicago in the summer of 1920, and I had a load of horses that just were not the right kind. They were too tall. They didn't cost me much, and I figured I could sell them, make a dollar. I got to the stockyards on a Sunday morning and unloaded them. They looked taller than ever when I got them there, but I had the boys work them over—clean them up and curry them. By and by, they didn't look so bad anymore.

Harry McNair came down. He looked at them as if he would fall over backwards and said, "Where did you get those cherry pickers?"

"I call them submarines," I told him, and we chuckled.

He said, "Lee, I don't know where I can sell that kind of horse. They're just too tall. I don't know anybody that'll buy them. I don't want to make you feel bad, but I didn't think you'd come in here with a bunch of horses like that."

I said, "Well, they're good horses, and you'd just be surprised what I can do with them. I'll just show you what a salesman I am." It was just a joke, I didn't mean it. Really, I was just so sick of those horses I could almost throw up, but I didn't let anyone know it.

Since it was Sunday morning, everyone went home but me. I was sitting on a bale of hay figuring out how much I was going to lose on those submarines. It looked like at least five hundred dollars for those old boats, maybe more. I looked up and here came an old rattletrap of a Ford car with no top, a lot of kids in it, and a great big old lady. It was driven by a little bit of an Italian man. He jumped out just as spry as you please and came over.

"Where could I buy a team of horses?"

"You have come to the right place, mister. I'll show you mine. What do you want?" I was sure glad to see him.

"I'm working down here in an excavation with an outfit, and my horses are played out. I've got to have a team of horses to go to work Monday morning. But before I look at your horses I want you to know that I want to trade my old team in on the new one."

"Oh, I'll always trade, if you'll trade my way." We walked to a big pair of brown horses weighing sixteen, seventeen hundred each, pretty tall.

The old man says, "What would you take for them?"

"I was gonna ask five hundred dollars for them," I said. I kept in mind that I'd have to trade for his worn-out horses. "I ought to get that much, but, you know, I always sell the first a little cheaper just to get started. It usually is a pretty good sale."

He says, "Well, all right, I'll buy them. Would you hitch 'em up?"

Everybody, including my own men, had gone home, so I hunted up some harness, put it on the horses, and put them to a wagon. Down the wide street he went as fast as those horses could run. Then he came back.

"All right?" I shouted.

He wrapped the reins around the brake and said, "Yes, they're all right. Now, I've got these two horses . . . I've got a roan horse that's just played out."

"How much do you want for it?"

He spit tobacco juice and said, "I gave a hundred seventy-five for him. If I could get that much for him, I'd trade him in on this team."

I said, "I bet he's a good horse, but a horse that's played out, you know, I'd have to keep him here and feed him for a month or so before I could sell him. How would twenty-five dollars suit you? We'll trade. I'll take off twenty-five dollars, you bring the roan in to me and give me four hundred twenty-five dollars for the team."

He just went for that right away. "Will you have these shod?"

"Yes, but that will cost you ten dollars more."

"All right, have them ready to go Monday morning."

"They'll be here ready to go. All you have to do is just pay me now and your horses will be here."

He pulled out a roll of bills as big around as a sauce dish and said, "Now, you come with us and bring that roan back with you. I won't have time for him in the morning."

I looked at that car. The back seat was full of kids of all ages and sizes. Didn't see how I could get in there. The front seat was so full of this old fat lady I didn't see how I could get in there, either, but this man wouldn't trade unless I went to see that roan horse. The way it ended up, I had to sit on the old lady's lap. I don't know how many kids they had, but the seats were all full, and the only place for me to sit was on her lap. I sure didn't want her sitting on my lap. I wasn't about to suggest that. There we went through the streets of Chicago to where they lived. I traded with them, and the next day he came for his horses. He went off very happy with his trade, and I thought that was the end of it. I went back to my hotel and was only there a little bit when here came a fellow.

He says to me, "Are you the fellow who sold that man the team of high horses?"

I said I was, and he said he wanted to see them. So I got up out of my chair and we went to the yards, across the street, and I showed him the team.

"Will you sell me a team? I heard you traded."

"Yes."

"I'd like to trade with you, too."

Before I left that barn that Sunday night I'd sold five pair of horses, all for the same price, four hundred fifty dollars a pair.

On Monday morning a fellow walked in and said, "Have you been to the auction yet?"

"No, I'm gonna go right away, though. I'll be right after a couple of loads ahead of me."

He said, "I'm the contractor at an excavation, and several of my men bought teams from you yesterday. I'd like to make a deal with you. I'd like to hire them—"

I interrupted him there. "No, I wouldn't hire them. You'll take them and put them into those pits. It gets hot here in Chicago, and it might kill some of them. I'll sell them to you."

He says, "Nope, I can't buy them, but I'll tell you what I'll do. I'll give you two and a half per day per horse, and I'll pay for a man you choose to take care of them. If a horse gets hurt or killed, I'll pay for him the price you're asking for them now."

I got out my paper and pencil and I went to figuring. If a horse stayed out there a month, and considering what they had cost me, and if he was to pay the man I sent to care for the horses, . . . When I added it all up I decided to take him up on his offer.

After I finished up there I went down to the auction, and McNair was in the auctioneer's box. I went up to the box to tell him I had sold out.

McNair said, "Sold out? What do you mean?"

"I've sold half of those big cherry pickers and rented the other half out."

He looked right at me for a minute. Then he said, "You'll do, I guess. I don't think there's another man in the United States who could've got rid of that load of cherry pickers and got his money back." Well, that was just luck. I happened to be in the right place at the right time.

The man I picked to keep an eye on my horses was my barn man, a young fellow who had worked for me several years. He went out there and took charge of those horses and I came on home.

I didn't ship any more horses for several weeks, waiting for the weather to cool off in the fall. But I was back in the commission office one day, and here was the man who had hired my horses. He came right over to me and said, "I've been looking for you. I didn't know where you live and I couldn't do business with you anyway. You know, every one of those horses was in good shape. If you want them back, you can have them, but I don't want to let them go. I'll give you four hundred fifty dollars a span for them, like you were asking."

Well, it didn't take much figuring that time. I accepted his offer without a second thought. Maybe those horses weren't too tall after all.

Working down in an excavation pit isn't the only thing a too-tall horse is good for, as I found out when I started out to buy those three hundred horses for the Germans I told you about. One of the first places I went to was Bedford, Missouri. After a while, I had eighteen of those big horses, but I needed twenty to load a car, because if you load them light, they'll just kick each other, tear each other to pieces.

One day a man from Bedford came into the barn where I had my horses. He had two horses. One was a great big, tall gray horse that looked like a plow horse. I don't know what was the matter with him, but I wouldn't have given anything for him. This man hung around there all day, and I tried to get another big horse or two, but I couldn't. I had to get my shipment on the road, so I bought these two horses. I gave him a hundred dollars for the two. I loaded up the twenty and sent them in. This was about on a Thursday. There was some sickness in my family, and I didn't get to Chicago until late Monday. I went right into the barn to see where my horses were, and it was just auction time. One horse was missing. One of those tall horses I had bought in Bedford.

I asked my boy, "Where did that horse go to? One horse isn't here."

He said, "Oh, that horse is sold."

"Sold? What did you get for it?"

"McNair sold him, and he didn't tell me exactly what he got. I think he got two thousand seven hundred fifty." Which he did.

The Germans took the other eighteen, but I went on into September with the smaller one of that pair I'd bought at Bedford. Then came a day when that was the only horse I had in the auction.

At the auction you have to describe your horse when they bring it out. I said, "Here's a big gray horse that I think would jump over the moon if you gave him a chance." Everybody laughed. It was a tall horse.

Harry McNair nudged me and said, "Can that horse jump?"

I said, "There isn't a stockyard in this country but what he'd jump out of. I've had an awful time keeping him in the stockyard long enough to get him in the auction. He just hops right over fences without any trouble."

Harry said, "Lee, I'm going to take a chance." He turned to the man who had just bought the horse and said, "I'll give you a hundred dollars for him."

After he had bought the horse and everything had quieted down, he said, "Now, Lee, I've never had you lie to me, and I don't think you would lie, but I want to see that horse jump." He motioned toward an

Englishman who had been around training some horses for one thing and another and said, "Get ahold of that rider and we'll see what can happen."

I didn't think any horse could jump much with that kind of a trainer. That Englishman would weigh two hundred pounds. But it was McNair's horse.

We took that horse into the pavilion and put him over the bars a few times—you know how they do, rate him every time he jumps over, then raise the bar for another jump. Why, that horse could jump way up there over my head with a two-hundred-pound man on him. Was no effort at all.

McNair said, "I'm going to see just how high that horse will jump."

I said, "I don't like to have you do that. He might kick one of those poles off when he goes over and maybe hurt himself, maybe hurt the rider. It's pretty high. He's done all right, he's jumped enough for one day."

McNair said, "Oh, I want to see what he's good for. Hey, boy, raise that pole another notch."

McNair got on the horse himself. When the horse went over he kicked the pole with his hind leg, knocked the bar off, took a fall, and broke Harry McNair's leg.

There Harry was, screaming with pain, and everybody had gone. He had a Cadillac car, but I had never driven a Cadillac. I'd never driven in the city. I tried to get him to call an ambulance and get a doctor, but he wouldn't do it, he wanted to get home.

"You've just got to get me home, Lee," he said, and he just wouldn't take no for an answer.

Well, I never sweated so in my life. Put him in the back seat and drove through Chicago traffic just bumper to bumper. I wished I'd never seen a Cadillac or the downtown Chicago streets. I didn't know exactly where I was going, and he hurt so bad he could hardly tell me. Finally I made it. I got him up there to his home. That was in the fall.

Next Easter Sunday I was in the Chicago stockyards and Harry was there. Harry had decided he didn't want the jumper horse. He said, "I'll take a twenty-dollar loss to get rid of him. Every time I look at him my leg hurts all over again." So I bought it back for eighty dollars.

Later that day I was sitting there at the Transit House, the big hotel for all those doing business at the stockyards. A couple of fellows came in and wanted to know where McNair was.

I said, "He's gone home, they've all gone home. I was about to go myself."

They said, "The ice is breaking up out on Lake Michigan, and we want to buy a couple of jumpers. How can we find McNair?" There was a park on an island on Lake Michigan, and these men wanted jumping horses for the fox hunt to be held there.

I said, "You don't have to get ahold of McNair. He's got a jumper and I've got one." I took those fellows out and I hunted up the English trainer. He got on top of that horse and trotted him, then I showed them the other horse. Well, they took the two horses to the pavilion. They liked them both. That was just what they wanted. I priced the one at thirty-five hundred and the gray at three thousand. I knew I didn't dare price them cheap. If I did, they'd walk away and leave them.

The Englishman put the brown horse over the hurdles, and the buyer kept saying, "I just don't know about that horse. He don't go over there very easy. I don't know about that. Let's see the gray go over." That gray did a hurdle seven feet high. He cleared it with that big two-hundred-pound Englishman, cleared it light, like a feather, just settling down easy.

The buyers said, "What do you mean by that, asking so much for that brown horse? I thought you were a horseman. You're asking so much for that one and the gray is the best of the two."

I said, "Well, it's just a matter of opinion. The other horse belongs to my friend, and this one to me. It takes three thousand dollars to buy him. If you want him, I'll sell him to you. You don't have to take the other one."

They said, "All right, we'll buy this horse, and we'll give you twenty-seven hundred for the brown."

I told them, "You're pretty good buyers, so I'll just let you have them."

I had to deliver the two horses up to the lake, they had a place up there on some island. It was quite a way up there, so I got a boy and put him on one of the horses and had him lead the other. I went up with a car to bring the boy back.

When Harry came down Monday morning he said, "Say, I saw an account in the stockyard's books this morning that you'd sold a couple of horses."

"Yeah. Gave 'em away. I gave one of your horses away."

"You did? What'd you do that for?"

"Well, Harry, I heard you price him at two fifty in the morning, and I thought that was a little bit high, but I guess I'll just take him at two fifty now. He'll make a little." I was kidding him.

Harry looked at me out of the corner of his eye and said, "Well, you've got a gleam in your eye. I don't believe I want to take your offer. How much did you get for him?"

"Twenty-seven hundred."

"Holy crawfish!" Harry said. "What did you do with that gray plug?"

"I sold him for three thousand." Harry just about fell off his chair. "If I hadn't made so much on the gray, I'd let you pay me a commission on the brown," I told him. Harry couldn't say a word. I think his leg quit hurting right then.

I had bought the gray for eighty dollars in the morning, and I sold him for three thousand dollars before noon. Nothing in the world affects the price of a horse as much as the people involved in his sale. There is nothing under the sun that people won't buy if you strike the right person at the right time with the right goods. They'll give you a good price for an item if they want it. There's no use to try to sell people something they don't want. They won't give you anything for it, and they won't be happy with it after they've got it. You've got to use a lot of psychology, especially in the horse business. You've got to size up your man before you can make a deal, and that's easy to do. A few friendly questions in a nice friendly way and people will talk. They'll tell you what they want. If they're in trouble, they'll tell you that, very likely. They always did me. I don't know if they told everybody.

Harry said, "I'm going to quit the saddle horse business."

"You are?"

"Unless you go in it with me."

Harry McNair and I went into the horse business. We set up a beautiful establishment in Aurora, Illinois, handled all saddle horses for Western Shows, an organization that sent shows all over the country, show horses. We handled every kind of horse, but usually not work horses.

We had a hired girl who was about nineteen years old and was going to college up there. That's the way she put herself through college, training horses, high school, too. She taught a horse just like you'd teach a little kid in kindergarten. She'd start with the ABCs, and when she'd get through with him, he was a horse! He could read, and he was a gentleman. My word, she'd handle that horse! She could send him a hundred feet or more. With just an easy word she could make him turn, kneel down, anything she wanted him to do. When she got through, he was a horse a man could be proud of. I went in one day and sold three horses to this girl. McNair wanted to know how I could do it. I don't know. Just knew the horses could be trained and that she would get something out of them. Just seemed to happen.

I'd be there and I'd sell to whoever came along. I'd be in the Chicago stockyards alone, everybody else had gone home, and I couldn't go home to my family in Iowa until I'd sold out. People'd come in there. Why, I even took my meals there. People would come into the lobby and I'd be sitting there. I'd have a nice gold cane standing beside my knee, and we'd commence to talk. That gold cane was the sign; it marked a horsetrader wherever he went. They all knew when they saw my cane that I was in the horse business. They'd come to me because the rest of the traders would all be gone for the weekend. That's one reason why I did so well trading and selling horses. I made myself available, though I never forced anybody to buy anything.

Now, you may think this next thing is crazy. I *am* a little bit crazy at times; I guess we all are. Anyway, sometimes I get overenthusiastic, like the time they shipped a bunch of horses in from Carnation Farms in California to a combination sale, colts and saddle horses. In the bunch was a black mare, the most beautiful thing I think I've ever seen. I asked the company foreman what he would take for her.

He said, "I want five thousand dollars for her."

"Do you think you can get that?"

"I've got orders. If I can't get that for her, I bring her back to California. Here's a whole trunk full of ribbons that mare has won. Everyplace she goes she wins a ribbon, and they're not all red ribbons, either." From his face I figured they were all blue. I hustled around with two of my friends, and we pooled to buy this mare for five thousand dollars. I went to get her from this fellow, told him I'd take her, and he backed out, wouldn't take my offer.

He said, "It's too near the sale. It might spoil my sale."

I said, "All right. It doesn't make any difference anyway. I'll buy her at the sale, and I bet you I don't give you five thousand dollars for her there."

He said, "Well, that's up to you. No matter if she only brings three thousand in the auction, when she goes in she has to be sold."

While I was standing there beside the mare a man and woman came up, dressed like millionaires, and I figured that's what they were. I was standing there beside them watching the ring. The trainer took the mare into the ring. We had been talking and this man said to me, "What do you think of that one?"

I said, "Why, I think she's the best I ever saw. That mare's a prizewinner."

These people didn't say much about her when she came up for auction, but the first bid was for five thousand dollars. I rubbed the top of my head and put my hat on all over again.

Oh-oh, I thought, I don't know where we're going from here.

Some other people jumped into the bidding, but this woman near me just wouldn't let that mare go. She said, "I just want that mare, and we'll just buy her."

They ran that mare up to $15,500. That just knocked the wind all out of me.

After the sale had been completed I said, "What kind of business are you in, anyway, that you'd buy a horse at that price? Here are thousands of little kids running around starving and you . . . A man is foolish to give fifteen thousand dollars for a plaything! There are hungry kids almost within arm's reach of here."

He said, "You're right, but I'll tell you. This is the only wife I've got, haven't got any children, got more money than I know what to do with. She wanted the horse, and anything she wants, I buy."

I asked, "What kind of business do you have?"

"I make croup medicine," he said and named a patent medicine.

I was surprised when I heard the name of that medicine. I said, "Why, I gave some of that to my little boy. He had croup so bad. I gave it to him, and it cured him."

"I guarantee it to cure."

"How do you make it? Tastes more like milk than anything else."

"It's a very simple remedy. Of course, I won't tell you all of it, but the base is burro's milk." We both chuckled at that and he added, "You know, my business is getting big, and my burros are getting old, don't give as much milk as they used to. You're a horseman. Do you suppose you could buy me four or five fresh young burros? 'Cause when they start to milk, if you keep milking them, they'll milk for years. But some of these I have are so old it's hard to get enough milk for my business."

I said, "Yes, I know where I can get 'em. I think I do."

He said, "You get me six. Just write your own check on them."

"Well, I wouldn't do that. When they come, if they're satisfactory, you just give me what you think they're worth."

I phoned down to Las Vegas, New Mexico, to a man I knew down there. He was in the real estate business. I asked him if he knew where I could buy a good load of burros. The spring, you know, is the best time to get them; they come fresh then. My real estate friend said, "Sure, I can buy them. What do you want to give for them?"

"Oh, I don't know. Can you get them for five dollars a head?"

"Sure I can. I'll buy you six. I'll put them on the train now, and you'll have to pay the freight on them at that end of the trip."

Well, the burros got to the buyer in Chicago before I did, so I went up to his laboratory. It was as clean as a hospital. He stabled his burros nearby.

I asked, "How are the new ones? Do you like them?"

He smiled wide and said, "Yes, just fine."

"What do you think they're worth?"

"I suppose you bought them for little or nothing. I hope you did. How would two hundred fifty dollars a head suit you?"

"Why, fine," I said. "You'd pay the freight on them, wouldn't you?"

"Oh, I've already paid the freight on them."

Just such things as that kept me alive. There's one thing about a horseman, and I've known a lot of them: he's always buying horses, but he never has much of a bank account. That's a fact.

In the next few years that medicine manufacturer bought a lot of burros from me. Finally he got sick and had to close up his business. Besides that, the government had been after him, trying to get his medicine off the market. But I had already bought quite a lot of burro mares for him, all fresh.

I was already in the saddle-horse business with Harry McNair, we were commission men. It was a great deal. It's hard to believe how much I got for some of those little horses, seven or eight thousand dollars apiece sometimes. Of course, even then the day was past when people rode a horse out of necessity. It had become a hobby, a pleasure, and people are usually willing to pay for a pleasure. They are even more willing to pay for something that sets them up, gives them prestige among their friends. A good-looking, fancy-stepping horse can give a man quite a show when you think of prestige. Or give him a fancy idea of himself if he feels a little less important than he wants to feel. Or a woman. A man can even show himself off to great advantage by just sitting around smoking a cigar, having his very handsome wife togged out, riding a fancy-looking, high-stepping horse. I find this a very interesting fact, and I found it put nice little sums of money in my pocket pretty often. It felt pretty good, and I just kept my mouth shut and let them show off their wives and their horses from time to time and let them pay me for what they wanted the world to think of them. Same thing is true with cars today.

This was around 1920, and there was quite a bit of money floating around in those days. World War I was over, the Depression hadn't even been heard of yet, and people felt nice and secure. They'd spend money they might not have let go of if they had known what was to happen. But from what I saw a few years later, a dead horse (they all die someday) is worth just about as much as worthless stocks and bonds in a dead market. At least you can sometimes salvage the hide of the horse.

I didn't know what was to happen either. We were all in it together no matter what was to come. That was the time, there, one of the best times we have known, most carefree, when everything went wild, you know. Everybody believed all their troubles were behind them, and they were ready to enjoy life and try to make up for all the bad they had lived with, and to make a better world for those to come after us. A great new world was supposed to be smiling at us all.

I bought feeding horses for a man in South Dakota in 1920. Feeding horses are the ones probably not quite full-grown yet, or maybe overworked. You buy them and feed them, get them into shape. Then you match them up—team them—and sell them off. You make yourself some money on the deal. You do the work nobody else wants to bother with, but you get paid for your trouble. The horses I bought cost four hundred apiece way down in Chicago, and the man took them and still made money. At that time you could just about get what you asked for them.

FIFTEEN

Horsetrading

At the stockyards and at my home we had horse buyers even through the mail. People would write, "Mr. Daniels, please send me a family horse," or a team to work, plowing or some other particular need. They'd send the money right along, and I'd get their horses and ship them out. But usually they came in person to make such purchases.

Of course, there were sharpers and sharks in the business. That's why everyone laughs at the term horsetrader. But by far the greatest number of dealers were honest. Sometimes they took a good beating when things didn't go just right. They often lost money and had to learn to judge horses, men, and deals just as a salesman has to know his business. These crooked dealers often didn't really know much about horses, so any smart person could see through their story. But those who were innocent and didn't know about horses were the ones who were cheated. If you traded with a dealer you didn't know well enough to trust, you better *not* trade. Fact of the matter is that in some ways buying a horse is like buying a suit of clothes, the one that is right for one man is not right for another. Doesn't make any difference what someone else wants, or thinks you want, you and that horse will belong together for a long time, and if you don't like him or he doesn't like you, then it's no good.

Sharp dealers not even connected with any legitimate market used what was called "widow of the deceased," a ploy, advertising that a trotting mare or some other expensive horse was to be sold by a widow whose husband had been a horse fancier. The horse was said to be worth three thousand or more, but the widow was concerned with getting the horse a good home and so had decided to let it go for three hundred fifty. Any fool ought to recognize that game, it's been around so long, but even today slickers pull this on those who don't stop to think, or who trust others too much. After a meeting to discuss the horse, and a little maneuvering with what appeared to be a fancy establishment and elaborate papers, money changed hands. When the horse didn't come up to standards (and he was sure not to), the buyer would return to the same address to get his money back. Nobody lived there anymore. The neighbors hadn't even heard the name. Oh, there were all kinds of tricks to be played.

In the horsetrading business we always judged a horse on several points. These points show how much training the animal had and what its limitations might be. To be sold as sound, it had to be perfectly sound in every way. If found lacking in any way, the animal could be returned within a certain number of days, and the seller had to make good the buyer's money. Wind and work had to be good if the horse was represented as perfectly sound—no lameness, sores, no blemishes of any kind—and it could not have a brand. Legs could not stand over at the knees or ankles.

Oh, many points are included for judging an animal, and if you say he's one class, you better see that he meets all the qualifications of that class. A horse sold to wind and work must have good wind and be a good worker. A horse sold at the halter is sold just as he stands without any recommendation. The buyer must take him as he is and do what he can with him. This could be a horse that has been on pasture and never gentled properly, or a very young horse.

To show you how this system worked out in practice, I want to tell you about one time when I was the judge of a colt show. They had fifty, sixty, maybe seventy-five draft-horse colts, had them all lined up. This kind of judging is done by eliminating one and then another. You just keep moving them ahead until finally you get to the last ones. I got to the last two, and they happened to be stud colts from two breeders who lived right close to each other. One of these colts was near perfect, and the other colt was better than the run of colts. I gave one first prize and the other third. I had already had one colt picked out, and I decided to give him second prize. It wasn't easy to make such a decision. Every one of those colts had appeared to its owner to be a pretty fine horse, else he would never have been entered in that show. And every owner who had entered a colt knew a lot about horses. Those two colts looked so much alike you could hardly tell them apart. When I got through judging the colts, I put the ribbons on them and, boy, this man blew his top.

"That's the greatest colt I've ever had and you only gave him third. Not even second. You gave him *third.*"

I told him, "I was employed to use my judgment here, and that's what I've done. That's the way it's got to stand."

"Well, you gave your friend there first prize on his colt."

I said, "I didn't know one colt from the other. You fellows brought them in here, and you were standing around talking. Nobody was near anybody's colt. I wasn't supposed to know anybody's colt, and I didn't. This is my judgment, men, and this is the way it has got to stand."

After the show was over, that man was still talking about how his horse should have won top money. I decided to show him how I judged each horse. I said, "Now, this horse is a wonderful colt, but he's got one fault. Sometimes they'll grow out of it, but a lot of times they won't. If you look carefully, you'll see this colt stands back a little on his knees."

They all came and looked. "Well now, yes, I see what you mean."

I went on to the sorrel colt, a beautiful colt, as sound as they make them. Showed how truly perfect it was. Well, this man had set his sights too high. He was very mad and made a big fuss. His colt looked fine, but when you give first prize, the horse has to be perfect. These two colts were registered and in a class by themselves.

I had confidence in my own judgment, so I said, "Now, I've handled thousands of horses, and I have to know. I've bought horses for people, and I have to know how they would work out. It is my business to know if a horse is not good for the work he would have to do if I sold him to a certain man. This horse would not be able to work hard. His knees would buckle."

When those horses were two years old I went over to this man's place. I wanted to see for myself. I went to the two owners, the winners of the first and third prizes. The third-prize horse was sturdy and strong, performed well, but his knees buckled.

I said, "Now, Frank, we'll go on down to Dunbar's to see that sorrel horse I gave first prize to. I want to know for myself, and I want to convince you, that I gave an honest, well-founded judgment." We went down to Dunbar's, and they had the stallion in the barn. The horse I had given first prize to was easily worth two thousand dollars. It was sound as a bullet, had developed into a real good draft horse, felt tight and solid. Everything you could want in that kind of horse.

Frank said, "I admit that I was awful mad at the time of that show. I couldn't see why my horse wasn't as good—better—than those others, but now I see what you were talking about. Now, I want to ask you one question. What can I do with that horse?"

I said, "What *will* you do with that horse?"

"I could use him for service."

"Man, you're making a terrible mistake. We don't want any calf-kneed colts on the market."

"Oh, his knees aren't that bad. Anyway, what will happen?"

"Why, you just hook one of those horses to a wagon and he wouldn't be able to pull it."

I went on to show him that the more that affliction was spread around in the hereditary qualities of the horses he bred, the less value he could claim for each one. Word would get around after a few years, and his business would be ruined because he had sold those colts with calf knees. It didn't look like a very good picture. We didn't like to do it, but next time I took a load of horses to the butcher, we took that one along. He was no good for a workhorse, or a buggy or saddle horse, just good for nothing. Legs just bent like your fingers would if you bent them back as far as you could without dislocating the joints, not like the natural legs of a horse at all.

You remember that I told you that a horse, to be judged sound, had to have good wind. Well, a strange thing happened to me one day when I went to check that very thing. I went out to Bridgewater, a little town in the southern part of the county, and a man there had a big black horse he wanted to sell. I went ahead and bought him. We agreed on the price, but I didn't think about the wind of the horse. Some of those big horses don't have enough wind to do the work you might expect of them. A winded horse is worth half the regular price. Some of them aren't worth that. He was a nice horse, weighed a ton, and they had him tied off to the side of the barn quite a little ways from the door. I got ahold of his halter, and I just came into him with my fist. (You get them by the halter, pull them around, then hit them, not hard, then run them until they're winded.) I don't know that I hit this horse that hard, but I knocked him down on his knees.

The man said, "Oh, my God, you killed my horse."

Well, I thought I had. That horse just lay there and quivered. I had hit him over the heart and hit him too hard. We worked with him and finally got him up. He was all right.

The owner of the horse looked at me and said, "Say, Daniels, you ain't very big and I'm a big man, but for God's sake, don't ever hit me."

I got kidded a lot about knocking that horse out, but that was just an accident. You've got to hit such a horse just right. I'd done that to hundreds of horses and never had one show any bad signs. This horse, like the rest, was all right after that, no sign of bad wind.

Right after the war I got into the most surprising and confusing thing that ever happened to me, and it involved a bunch of mules. I took a load of mules down to Atlanta, Georgia. Among them was a nice gray mare mule. I had her in the barn. Here came an old Negro and his wife with a broken-down wagon. They had a mule that was supposed to be pulling that load, but the man was behind pushing and the woman was leading the mule. They put him up in front of the barn and he looked about dead.

Their daughter, a girl of about fifteen, got up in front of the barn and saw my mules standing there. She said, "Say, boss, have you got a smart mule to sell?"

"Well, I think so. I think you might be smart to get a new mule. I've got some mules here, I don't know how smart they are, but they're here for sale."

"That gray mule there, I'd just like to have that mule. Would you trade me?"

"Yes, I'd trade anybody. What have you got to trade?"

"I'd like to trade that old mule I got out there."

"I don't think that'd be a very good trade for me. That mule is worth about five or ten dollars. Most of my mules are worth two hundred fifty dollars, maybe three hundred. I'd trade for him if you want to pay the difference."

She had a wise look about her as she said, "The grocery man was there, the milk man was there, and I just spent the last dollar I had, but tell you what I'll do. I'll give you that bale of cotton on that wagon if you'll sell me that mule."

I didn't dig cotton. The farther I am from cotton the better. But here it was, right after World War I. She had a wise look, and I thought, Even though the rest of the country was better off after the war, sharecroppers in Georgia had not seen better times; their lot had not improved. I decided to look at the cotton. It looked like good cotton. I said, "All right, I'll trade with you, but I don't know what that cotton's worth."

She said, "I don't either. I don't know what it's worth."

"They tell me that down here you have a landlord who takes your cotton to pay your rent bill and things. I'm an honest man. I don't want to get you into trouble by taking what that man is going to want from you. That would get you into trouble, bad trouble."

"I paid the rent here, this is the last bale of cotton I've got. I'd sure like to get that mule for that cotton."

So I traded with her. Then I took the old mule up and tied it in the barn. It even made me happy to see how glad those poor, hardworking people were with that new mule, and what good care they'd take of her. She was a lucky mule. They'd treat her right.

Both of the parents got into the wagon, waving their hands at me. I didn't have any place to put this cotton, only outside the barn. Well, they hadn't been gone for more than an hour until I had more mule buyers than I'd ever seen anywhere else. And they all had a mule they wanted to trade, and they all wanted to trade a bale of cotton with it. I had twenty mules left. I didn't know what to do with the mules I took in trade. I didn't want to have them killed, but I didn't know what I could do with those old, worked-out animals. And I didn't know what to do with all those bales of cotton.

A sale was going on at the commission house; they held a sale every two weeks there. A commission man said to me, "We'll have a sale tomorrow. Why don't you put those mules up and sell them all?"

I put those mules up and sold every one of them for twenty to twenty-five dollars apiece. Then I thought, Well, I've got all that cotton up there and what in the devil have I done now? I don't know what cotton's worth or anything about cotton at all. And those mules I traded for the cotton cost a lot of money.

I was standing there looking at that mountain of cotton. Looked something like a snowfall all done up in big packages, and about as useful, I thought.

A fellow came up and said, "That your cotton?"

"Yes."

"You got a bill of sale there?"

"Yes, I do." I had made every one of those farmers give me a bill of sale. I didn't want to have my mules taken away from me.

"You want to sell that cotton?"

"I don't know what cotton's worth."

"I do. I'm a cotton buyer. I'll give you a dollar a pound for the whole lot." A bale of cotton weighs five hundred pounds, I knew that.

I told him, "You don't need to go any farther, you own the cotton." I slid out from under that snow mountain as quick as I could. I was figuring how much I got for all that cotton besides what I had already got for the mules. I had twenty bales of cotton piled up there. I didn't know anything about cotton, don't know yet, but that it's nice and white and has to be ginned and all.

It was something. I thought, Now I've found something. I've got the mule business. I'll go home and buy another load of mules, two loads of mules, and think about trading for cotton.

I went home, started buying mules and bought forty (two carloads), put them in the feed lot, and fed them just like I did cattle. I darkened the barn so flies wouldn't go in, got those mules all ready to sell. I loaded two cattle cars and sent them down to Atlanta. Got down there and I couldn't give them away. Never found a man who would give me a dime for the whole load. They just absolutely didn't want any mules. I turned around and sent those mules to Kansas City. Got down there and the mule market was not any good there. I couldn't sell those mules! Couldn't begin to get my money out of that investment.

There was a fellow from Houston, Texas, there and he says, "There's a good mule market down in my town. I'll get them sold for you." I was willing to try anything to get those mules off my hands. They were costing me more money every day. "If you think you can sell them and get anything out of them, I'll send them down," I told that Texan.

He said he could sell the lot, and I sent them down. He did sell them. I got $140 apiece down there, and the feed bills, the freight, and commission I had to pay, well, they came to just about $140 per mule. I lost all my time and trouble, without even a thank you. In the horse business, in the mule business, in any buying and selling business, you never know. You are a gambler, and the very nature of the business keeps you from ever forgetting that you gamble every day of your life. You can only smile on the lucky gambles. You can only make up your losses on the lucky deals. But that never stopped me, because I was out to take what I could find, wherever I found it, move it, and make something out of it.

I'll tell you about another adventure I had with mules. It was back when I was about nineteen or twenty years old. A man was buying a lot of horses, and I was selling to him. As I went through the country I'd buy horses, and I'd sell them whenever I could and wherever I could. This man bought a lot of horses from me. He had a contract to fill, maybe several. He had contracted with someone somewhere to supply so many of a certain kind of horse within a certain time. He knew he could get good horses from me; he trusted me, and I did right by him.

One day he said to me, "Lee, you're a good horse buyer, why don't you go down to Missouri and buy me a load of mules, colt mules."

I said, "I'd have to have an understanding about that. I'd have to get so much apiece when I get them up here. I'd have to get rid of them real quick once they're here."

Well, we came to an agreement, so now I was a mule buyer too. You buy a colt mule by the height. After those colts get away from their mother, they'll follow you right along. Why, I'd go out and a whole string of them would be following me. Looked like a game of follow the leader.

Another time I bought a bunch of mules from a man, and there was a big horse colt with them. I noticed she was following this one mule around all the time. I took them home, and even when they were loose the colt wouldn't eat, just stood there and worried all the time. Worry, worry, worry. I separated them for the night. Early next morning I heard this mule braying like she was fit to die. I went into the barn. Her udder was about to burst, swelled up until I guess she thought she'd like to have her friend back again. I milked her out and took her to get a drink of water. We went back into the barn and she laid her head down. I thought she was going to die. She was just homesick for that colt. It took some time, but she finally got over it. I took the colt up where she couldn't get out and get to the mule, and she grew up, after a while.

I had a similar experience with a hen that started mothering a bunch of kittens. The hen was setting in the barn, and the eggs got broken when some accident happened up in the loft. A cat had a litter of young kittens up there, and that hen chased the cat away and adopted the kittens. They knew their mother, of course, but the hen would call them and they'd come around like a bunch of chickens and she'd scratch—scratch and cluck—but she couldn't get those kittens to eat what she scratched up. Those kittens would crawl up the poles in the barn, and that hen would have a fit. It was something to watch. She'd call them and they'd come atearing and she'd start scratching for worms. Talk about a frustrated hen; she was as bad as some human ones. She was a good mother, though. She trained them till they got to be big kittens. People will be a lot wiser when they learn what goes on in the emotions of an animal. They'll know a lot more about people.

SIXTEEN

A Killer Depression
and Killer Horses

While Harry McNair and I were partners in the 1920s, we handled saddle horses, a few draft horses, and everything else. I'd have more horses when I'd go in on Monday than I had orders for, but I'd buy them and ship them on east to Chicago anyway. I'd sell until Monday night, then I'd start home, load more horses out, and send them on east and sell them. Then I'd go back home and ride all the rest of the week buying more horses for my weekend load. Saturday I had another load or two ready to go again. Hardly even had time to sleep in bed. Only bed I slept in was after I'd get home. Worked till way late every day. Snow, blizzard, rain, heat, and everything else, I never stopped.

I used to like to buy horses when it was real cold. Go out in my warm clothing with my sheepskin coat on. There was a trick to it. Most people, when weather is real cold, they rush out and do their chores, rush back, and sit beside the stove until chore time again. Being too warm only makes them feel the cold more. Well, if they had a horse to sell, I'd aim to get there before noon and if we were talking on the south side of the barn, I'd coax them around to the north side. I'd just stand there and talk to them until I'd freeze them out.

"Oh, my God, I'm just frozen," they'd say.

"Well, sell me the horse."

"All right, take the darned horse and go on with him."

I closed a good many deals that way, so in some ways, the colder the weather, the better I liked it.

My partnership with McNair went on for several years. It was hard to believe how much I got for some of those little horses. We really had a good thing those days—wars all ended, we thought, nothing to worry about but just getting along, getting some enjoyment out of life, seeing this great new world that everybody believed had arrived. We enjoyed life then.

Everyone knows what happened in 1929—the terrible Depression. All my hard work went for nothing. The banks all closed. I had a lot of money in those banks and never got a cent back. I lost all my farm except the eighty acres where I lived for so long. Everything went wrong.

I met one of my old friends on the road one day. He gave me some good advice: "Lee, the only way out of your trouble is not to lose courage." That wasn't easy to do. The next time I was blue I thought of what this friend had told me, but it was sure hard to go ahead. Still, he was right.

When everything was gone, my children went to work. They were pretty big by then. It wasn't much hay, but it helped. I gathered up some old machinery and I had an old saddle horse. My mother gave me a little money to get another horse. I found a good old horse and I plowed sixty acres for corn. I walked every foot of the way behind that plow, just like they did in the days before they had any machinery to do the hard work.

Then I started to trade horses again. I sold my saddle horse for fifty dollars and bought a two-year-old colt. I sold the old mare for a hundred dollars. I knew where there was a real good colt, two years old, so that gave me a good, young team. I traded the sorrel colt for a roan mare that a man couldn't work. That gave me a good team of roan horses. My brother Art had a roan horse that was a perfect match for the horse I had, so we made a trade. I'd planted and cultivated the corn, and my wife and I picked it by hand, but corn was so cheap that a load of corn wouldn't buy a ton of coal. So we burned the corn to keep warm that winter.

One day, after I had finished harvesting the corn, I was standing in the barn door just as blue as anyone ever could be. No idea what to do next, which way to turn. Three men drove into the yard and wanted me to buy old horses for the Clapper Brothers of Rockford, Illinois, a killing plant. I told them I didn't think I could buy that kind of horse, as I always bought the best. They said if I would go with them, they knew I could make plenty of profit. We started out, and before dark we had twenty horses (a carload), and my pay would be one hundred dollars. Believe me, that was the best money I ever made. I took a contract to buy five hundred head. Only thing was, where would I get the money to start with?

Mina and I sat there in our house and talked about that. Pretty soon she got up out of her chair and went into Kenneth's room. I heard some jingling as she walked into the girls' room. She came out after a couple of minutes with her hand full of small change. I looked at her, and I thought what a really wonderful wife she was to me. She had taken all the money out of the kids' banks. No matter that they were grown, each had kept a small amount of change in their old banks on their dresser tops. Mina looked at me and smiled. I stared at her a minute.

"You said you could start on ten dollars, didn't you?" I still couldn't believe what I thought she meant. "Well, I think if you'll count this, you'll find just about ten dollars here, maybe a little over."

Next day I started out with that ten dollars, and that was all the cash I could put together. I made up my mind I could buy and trade those old horses, but still it seemed kind of silly after buying so many great and wonderful horses the way I had.

The first place I stopped was north of Adair. I asked the man if he had a horse to sell.

He said, "I have, but I don't think you would buy her, as she is a kicker."

I said, "That won't make any difference." I gave him ten dollars for that mare, as I was sure I could trade her for three or four old horses.

I tied her on the car and drove slowly about three miles, then I stopped to let her rest. Three old gray horses came trotting up to the fence. Horses are as curious as people, they always have to find out what's going on. Pretty soon two men came out. They were bachelor brothers, I had seen them before.

"What are you going to do with that mare?" they asked.

"I'm just leading her along."

"Would you sell her?"

"I want a hundred twenty-five dollars and those three old horses there."

"We might trade them for that mare."

"I'll trade with you, but I'll have to have some boot. I would rather buy your horses, as I don't think you can work this mare. She is a kicker, and I got her off your neighbor. I don't want to misrepresent anything. She's worth a hundred and a quarter to me. To take home and break, she's worth a hundred fifty." Well, you've got to plan all these things if you're a horsetrader.

"That don't make any difference, we can work her. We know all about her, we've been trying to buy her." They told me they would give me a hundred twenty-five for that mare. If I would give them fifteen dollars for these old grays, I could have them. That left me a hundred ten dollars clear on the deal. So now I had that money and these three old horses, three to lead behind my car. By the time I got to Exira I had bought two loads of horses and had plenty of cash to start buying next day. I just kept a-trading, and some of those horses, when all the chips were in, didn't cost me anything, some cost a dollar, some five dollars. That was my limit for an old horse.

I filled my contract in a short time. I took another contract for a thousand head of old horses, and I filled that in a little while. I shipped those out, and I banked most of my money, but I kept out three hundred dollars. That was for three loads, three boxcars full of horses, sixty poor old horses who couldn't work anymore. The company was giving me ten dollars a head, and I was sure of making a hundred dollars a load. I took another contract and bought, oh, twenty or thirty loads of those old horses in Exira, trading every day. I'd buy a horse that looked pretty good and I'd trade him for two or three other old ones. I could fill a contract in a few days. I'd go out to the horse auction whenever I was near a town. The traders there would buy all kinds of horses for me. I was trading every day, filled one contract after another, sometimes for a thousand, usually for five hundred of those old fellows.

Killer horses are not horses that kill people or anything else. They are old or disabled horses purchased for the sole purpose of being killed for human consumption or as food for some other animal—dogs, cats, furbearing animals grown for commercial purposes, that sort of thing. After World War I the United States sent many shiploads of horses for human consumption to Europe. I filled several orders myself from England, France, Germany, and Belgium for horses for human consumption. Some Europeans and some from other continents seem to eat horsemeat all the time, and I see no reason why not, if they want to. Must be as good as beef, and less fat. It's all in the way you're taught to think about it.

The kind of old horses I was buying were usually killed to provide food for household pets which might have been out catching their own—cats, dogs, and so on. A horse seems an awful noble animal to be chopped up and fed to those smaller animals who can't (or don't) do any work to earn their keep at all. What do most dogs do? Sit around and lap their tongues at some person who feeds them. Cats? Aside from crossing the highway at night and getting hit, they seem to catch mice or other rodents, but for every one that's worth anything, there may be a dozen or a hundred who just lie around the house sleeping. So we kill those beautiful horses, who don't harm anyone and only ask the bare necessities of life. We kill them to feed these lazy critters who, if they were any good, would find their own food and live a better life for it. That's the way we do it, and we make out like we're doing the horse a favor because men used to turn the horse out to forage for himself when he was too old to work anymore. Why, I think that's downright ungrateful. And killing them off for money allowed the men to say they'd done the poor old faithful, overworked horse a favor. I never could quite justify horse killing in my own mind, but I bought and sent many horses to their death just the same.

After the animal is butchered and all parts possible used for animal feed, the remainder of the horse carcass is used for the manufacture of other products which can be made from horse tailings. By that I don't mean the tail of the horse, but bits and pieces of him left over when they've taken out all the dog and cat food they can get.

More and more in the early 1930s, I knew that Henry Ford had been right. The horse had really had his day. He was being finished off, at least for common working purposes. There wasn't the money in horsetrading that there used to be. It didn't pay what I needed now to buy good horses and sell them to work.

Some people used to worry about the horses who had worked hard for many years and still lived but couldn't work anymore. Some just sold them to be used by whoever bought them. They might lie about the horse's age. You know what they say about looking a gift horse in the mouth? That had to do with his age, because if you can see how much his teeth are worn down, you can see how old he is. Many old horses were overworked, left outside all winter, not fed, left to forage for themselves. They lived a horrible life, especially in winter. Lots of people had no appreciation for a horse, even after it had worked for them all its life.

Then somebody got the idea of butchering horses for dog food. I think it happened after we shipped so many boatloads of horses to Europe to be butchered for human consumption. Anyway, it became a big thing after World War I and a great big thing after the Great Depression. One thing led to another, and it was nip and tuck, I guess, whether any old horse would make human food or dog food. Even the cats put in their meow. That's how I came to start buying horses to ship for killing. Killer horses, old pitiful nags put out of their misery and sent to do good wherever they were needed, recycled after a long life of nothing but hard work.

I took care of my animals. I put half a ton of hay in each freightcar, and water enough so they wouldn't run out of it. When they got to the market they were killed immediately. They walked from the cars right to the slaughterhouse. They were put out of their misery in as humane a way as possible and made to serve a good purpose at the same time. At least, that's the way we looked at it in those days when man was supposed to know everything and be able to decide everything about all those helpless other animals he came in contact with. We didn't question our right to make such decisions any more than people today question their right to do some of the things my generation would never have considered.

People were beginning to think themselves fancy if they had a high-bred dog. Those fancy dogs were too good to eat food off the family table like any ordinary worthwhile dog would, like dogs had been doing all the thousands of years since they decided to latch onto human beings for protection and care. For mark what I say: dogs receive more protection than they ever give, unless they are working dogs, like those I had on my farm. And they demand a great deal of care and petting of we humans. I've seen people neglect their own children to take care of the darn dog. No trick at all to pay more to feed the dog these days than you spend to feed the family, especially if the dog's as big as an elephant. These dogs had to have something special, and it was horse-meat. I hate to think how many good old horses went to feed some silly-looking (and often silly-acting) dog who didn't know his . . . but it was a business that paid, and I had a family.

I want to tell you a story so you'll understand how some people felt about those old killer horses. The Adams ranch in northern Iowa was one of the biggest ranches in the state. They raised and worked hundreds and hundreds of mules and horses. I was buying in Omaha one day, and the commission man was sick or something. He asked me if I wouldn't buy a load of mules for Adams. He had a lot of mules at the yard, and he didn't want to be overstocked. It was a good buy, so I took a carload of mules and shipped them to Adams. At the ranch they were so impressed by the stock I sent in that load that I bought for the Adams ranch from that day on. I could buy there and get what my contractor wanted.

I had never been to the Adams ranch when I got into the killer-horse business. Then I had a contract for the government and I had to make a trip that way. The road, it turned out, went crosswise through the center of the ranch. I met the foreman, and he ordered me off the property.

I said, "I don't want to turn around and go back. It is a longer way than is necessary, and I'm pushed for time. This is a public road, isn't it?"

"Oh, it's public for most people but *you're* not allowed on this ranch."

"Well, maybe I'm not going through." As I went on I came to the ranch house. Mr. Adams and his wife were sitting out on the lawn. He appeared to be about seventy to seventy-five years old. They looked pleasant, and happy about what life had done for them. The house was sitting close to the road, so I stopped. In a strange country in those days it was good business for a horsetrader to stop at every place he came to. If you missed one house, it might be the best in the whole state for your business. You never knew what you might find.

Northern Iowa in those days was settled mostly by second- and third-generation Americans. In between you might find a little group of three or four families of Swedes or Germans, maybe Poles or Finns. There might even be a couple of Italian families huddled together here or there, and often some Irish. A horsetrader had his own feelings about "foreigners." He never for a moment thought of himself as one, or as only slightly removed from being one with these foreigners. He figured foreigners were not to be trusted. Guess he must have got wise watching the Indians, seeing what happened to them.

Mr. Adams wanted to know what I was doing, and I told him. He wanted to know how the killer-horse business was handled and all about it. I told him most of the details.

When I finished talking he said, "Daniels? Daniels? Where have I heard that name before? When did I know a man by that name? How did I ever come in contact with a man by the name of Daniels?"

I told him, "Well, Mr. Adams, I've never seen you before but I don't know how many carloads of mules I have bought for you at the Omaha market."

"Oh, yes, of course, I know who you are. You come right on in." I got out of the car and sat down in a chair. We didn't talk any business, we just talked about crops and how he handled this, that, and the other. He told me about his life experience. When he was a boy he was bailed out—kind of apprenticed, you might say—to a man about twenty-five miles south of where he then lived, in a little town. He was an immigrant boy. This man sent young Adams to the mill at Odebolt with a load of wheat. Adams couldn't make the trip in one day, so he camped for the night. The boy lay on the ground looking about him in a sort of daydreaming style and thought, Someday I'm going to own this land, I'm going to have a ranch here. He worked for that old man until he got enough money saved to make a small payment on a piece of land, and he had his start. He told me, "That's the way I got started.

Whenever I got money, I bought." His story was quite interesting. He wasn't the first or the last foreign boy to get his start that way.

Mr. Adams wanted to know a great deal about my business, where I found the old horses and how they were treated. I don't know when I enjoyed visiting with anyone as much as I did visiting with Mr. Adams.

But I was working for Lee Daniels, I wasn't working for anybody else. I was going to try to buy some horses I had seen as I came along. I had told him all about the use of these old outcasts, and he knew it was true. Come stormy days and the young working horses would all be in the barn while those old ones who had worked so many years stood out by the straw pile in the storm and weather. Oh, I made quite a story of it. The story was for my own benefit, because I figured the old man was going to try to sell me those old mules of his along with the horses. I told him how I took care of the animals, that they had hay and water all the way to Rockford and were immediately killed when they arrived, that they walked right from the freight cars to the slaughterhouse and they were put out of their misery in a humane way.

I stayed there a long time. Every time I'd get up and get ready to go, Mr. Adams would say, "Oh, don't go yet." Finally he said, "Say, I've got a lot of old cheapskates back there in the pasture. Why don't you come back again? Are you buying mules?"

"No, if I ship mules back there, they won't kill them. They don't have the equipment to kill a mule. I know where I could sell some mules, but I wouldn't care about buying any." He didn't say anymore about it then, but next day I was close to the ranch and here came the overseer who had ordered me off the road.

He said, "Mr. Adams wants you to come out to see him."

I went out and he said, "Well, I've been thinking about that horse-butchering plan. You know, that is a humane way of getting rid of those old horses. They stay out there in all kinds of weather, their teeth wear off, break off, and they can hardly hear. Nobody takes care of them. Often they starve to death or are eaten by wolves or wolverines."

It was true, as I had said the day before. These old animals were all put out of their misery in a humane way, and the meat was needed at that time in different parts of the world. Of course, I didn't remember ever hearing of anybody eating mule meat, but when I thought of it, I reckoned an old mule in a storm standing by a stack of straw, with worn-off teeth, might suffer as much as an old horse in the same fix. Yes, I was sure of it.

"Mr. Daniels, if I sell you those horses, will you let my foreman go with them?"

"Yes, I will. Now, Mr. Adams, about those mules, do you want to sell them?"

"Yes, I do. Will you let my foreman go with them if I sell them to you?"

"Yes, I'll get a railroad pass for him. If there are enough mules to make a load, all right, but I can't send them to Rockford. They'll have to go to Kansas City." There wasn't any place in Rockford that would butcher a mule. They weren't equipped for the job.

He said, "I'd like to send my foreman and have him tell me if you're telling me the truth or not."

"All right. His pass will take him there and back."

Well, I got the old horses loaded and I said, "Now, I owe you for these horses," and I pulled out my wallet to pay him.

Mr. Adams said, "Oh, no, you don't. I wouldn't sell an old friend. Every one of those old horses and mules is a friend of mine. They helped me to get where I am now. I wouldn't sell them. But I'm not telling you that I'm giving them to you. I'm putting the old fellows to sleep, where they belong. I wouldn't take a dime for them."

The foreman went up to Rockford with those poor old horses, and everything was just as I had said. And, you know, I made a friend out of that foreman. He was the key man of all that whole country around there.

That foreman said, "I used to let the neighboring farmers take those old horses out and use them, but you know, they abused those old fellows. They expected to do a normal day's work with them, and the horses weren't able to do it. Why, I couldn't sleep last night just thinking what a nice way that was to dispose of those horses in such a useful way, where they would not be abused but still didn't have to drag out their last long years foraging for themselves."

Before long I had a lot of men working for me in that part of the state. We got a lot of horses out of there.

SEVENTEEN

Sale Barn Days

By the 1930s the big companies were beginning to haul by truck and were getting rid of their horses. Some of these horses were too good to be killers, so I rented a pasture near Council Bluffs to keep them in until I could sell them for other uses. I knew there were a lot of old horses around Council Bluffs. Roads were good there, and snow was getting deep near home, so I rented my pasture where I could do the most business.

The first deal I made, I went to a place where they delivered ice and coal. They had changed their wagons for trucks to make their deliveries. I made a deal with the owner, gave him seven dollars a head for all the horses he had. Some of those horses I took right over to Omaha and sold at the auction. That's the way I worked there all winter. Finally I wound up with a sale barn of my own, and oh what a business I had there. I'd go over to the auction and buy those old killer horses, bring them over, and put them in the barn. I rented the barn behind the Neumier Hotel, and I lived at the hotel that winter. Business got too big for me, and I had to hire a man. I hired a young gypsy named Johnnie Wyatt. Johnnie and I ran the sale barn all winter, had a sale every Saturday. The Depression wasn't over, not by far, but I had whipped my share of it, and I wouldn't ever stand in the barn door and wonder what in the world to do, not again. Killer horses were my answer, and I guess I did them as much of a favor as I did myself. Starving and freezing cannot be desirable to any animal, and death we all get anyway.

I had some interesting experiences there at that sale barn. I decided I'd put some men on the road to buy for me, and I began to hire gypsies. They were all good traders, one fellow in particular, that little fellow, the first one I hired, Johnnie Wyatt. Johnnie had a cleft palate and could hardly speak. He talked through his nose, but he was one of the shrewdest horsetraders I ever ran across. He and I hooked up together as partners. He did the trading. Whenever anyone came in to trade, I'd send old Johnnie out to work on him. Johnnie'd trade them out of everything they had for an old plug of a horse.

A millionaire boy owned the property I rented, and he bought a burro and gave him to me. I didn't want that darn squalling, honking animal. I said, "Johnnie, take that burro and trade him for anything you can get. I don't want him around the barn."

Along about noon, here came Johnnie. He had a couple of dozen hens, a Victrola, a rocking chair, and an old trap of a wagon, all for this little dollar burro. Johnnie couldn't drive a car, so in the spring I started him out on horseback and gave him money to buy a load of horses. He went up toward Missouri Valley.

I ended up with forty-four men buying horses for me. I'm telling you, we bought a lot of horses. It wasn't any time at all until I had bought a lot of range horses and brought them in there, a lot of them broken, ready to work. Oh, we just had a business! You know, it was immense.

After I got on my feet I went to buying a better class of horse, trading and selling. I held an auction every Monday. I'd trade those old horses, a pair here, another pair there. Why, I'd go along the road leading a bunch of those old horses behind a car, and I might have eight or ten of them, some tied onto the bumper of the car, the rest tied onto each other's tails.

One time I stopped at a place near Soldier where a man was plowing corn. He had a pair of mules, an awful nice pair of big mules. He drove up, and there was a hedge fence between him and the road. Well, his mules saw those horses of mine. They got scared, and away they went. They threw the fellow off his plow and ran up through the cornfields.

I made my horses fast and went and helped him catch his mules, and we brought them back. They had stove the plow all up.

He says, "What've you got to trade me for those mules?"

Well, I had bought a pair of old gray mares that morning. They were fat, just as gentle as they could be, but they were old. I said, "I'll tell you what I'll do. You go over there and pick any two horses you want, and I'll trade you even for those mules."

He jumped over the fence and picked out those two old gray mares. Why, I'd only given ten dollars apiece for them.

He unharnessed the mules, put the harness on the mares, and said, "I want to try them out."

"All right. Just try them on your cultivator."

I tied the mules up to the fence and we hooked the mares to the cultivator. He drove that cultivator across the field a couple of times and drove back to where I stood. He said, "That's just what I want. Now I can cultivate my corn. I couldn't do anything with those mules."

Well, I led the mules along behind the car with the horses. When I got up to Soldier those mules went into pasture. Later I sent them down to Omaha and got $450 for them.

I had another pair of mules that I traded a fellow. One of them would crowd you in the stall, and the other was a little handy with his hind feet. I didn't sell them in Council Bluffs because I couldn't get in my stall. Monday morning, here came Mr. Hare from Fontanelle. He had a bay mare that I'd seen running in his pasture. He wanted to trade her off. I knew something was wrong with her, but I didn't know what. She turned out to be a balker. He wanted to trade for these mules.

I said, "All right, I'll trade with you." Now, that gave me the upper hand, because I'd price the mules high enough so the mare wouldn't cost me anything. I priced these mules at $350.

Hare said, "Well, if you'll give me a hundred dollars for this mare, I'll trade with you." I traded with him. He took the mules home, and they just never caused him a bit of trouble. He put them right to work, and they never crowded him in the stall or threatened him. He kept them as long as he had a farm.

That darn balky mare, she didn't cost me anything. I took her down to Des Moines. We had to hook up all the horses in the mornings to wind them before the sale. Came to her and I thought, Oh-oh, here's one that isn't going to work. I put her on a big wagon, her and another horse, and I never saw a horse dig in and pull like she did—stout, big mare, just took that big wagon. I put her with one that looked a good deal like her; they made a good-looking team. After we had winded them, we set the brakes on that wagon and tried to see whether they'd work or not. Why, they just lay into that harness and pulled with everything that was in them.

An old farmer bought that team. He took that mare off my hands. I saw him afterward and I said, "How did you like your bay mare?"

He said, "That's the nicest team I ever owned."

She wouldn't pull her tugs tight for Hare, but apparently she liked her new owner and liked the horse we had put her with, and now she didn't mind working. She never balked. We both made money, all the men were happy, and so were the horses. I believe an unhappy horse will not work, at least not as well as a happy one. I also believe there are more balky drivers than there are balky horses. If a horse doesn't like his driver, he can very well sit down in the traces.

Here's a story about the time when I was in Soldier—and broke. I had my men all at work up there, forty-four of them, and every Monday morning I had to have money to send them out to work. They would bring their horses in, and I would give them money to live on and to buy horses for another week. I hadn't seen my wife and baby for a long time, so Mina and the baby took the Chicago and North Western to Soldier.

Usually my company would wire money ahead to me, but this time they made a goof and didn't get the money up there. I took my baby and my wife to the hotel. Generally, if you have a suitcase, they don't expect you to pay every day. You pay when you check out. My money didn't come and it didn't come. I had a meal ticket, so we could buy our meals, but finally I was down to the last meal on the ticket. I just didn't know what to do. My money was gone. I wired my company again.

"Yes, yes, we've sent the money. It's been lying there in Soldier since the middle of the week."

But it wasn't there! I borrowed money from the hotelkeeper to telephone to the company at Council Bluffs. The boss sent money up by a messenger, who arrived at twelve o'clock midnight. Well, that cleared everything up, but I was one embarrassed horsetrader, staying there in a hotel in Soldier with a family to feed and not a red copper in my pocket. No meal ticket, hadn't paid my bill, I just didn't know what to do. No money for my men when they were ready to go out to work. That was one time a horsetrader didn't have the last word. I used to joke with my wife about that, because it was the first time in my life I had had to pawn my wife and baby to live a week in a hotel.

About this time I bought a few horses to ship to Chicago. One day I bought a pair of big farm horses. I gave a big price for them, and I asked the man, "Have you worked these horses?"

"Oh, yes, they are perfectly gentle."

He didn't say he had taken a razor or something and patched them up. In the winter a horse will wear all the hair off wherever the harness touches, and the skin becomes sore. These horses had had their sore patches covered up by the owner, a clever job of repairing their sore spots. I didn't suspect that these gentle, nice horses had anything wrong with them.

I sent this team to Chicago, and they were the first I sold out of my shipment. I sold them in the auction and got a good price. I had a man harness them, and I thought they seemed a little edgy about the harness. I was sitting along the top of a box stall nearby, so I could see pretty well what they were doing. When they went out of the barn I noticed one of them shake his head. He shook the bridle off and away they went, wagon and all. Two men were sitting high up on the seat of that big wagon. One horse without a bridle, why, two men couldn't control such a team.

They took off up Oxford Street, clear up to Center Street, and I hurried along after them. When I caught up with them I thought, Oh, my heavens, they're gonna go right through Sears and Roebuck's store, big plate-glass windows and all. But my driver got them turned, and they came back. Oh, they were running. They were running as fast as an automobile. They came in front of the yard office, and somebody had left a big Cadillac there. That street was reserved for livestock, wagons, and such. There weren't supposed to be any automobiles parked there by the stockyards. These horses took off right down the street. Well you know the tongue of a wagon sticks out in front of the wagon seven or eight feet, maybe more, and when those big horses hit that car the impact ran that tongue right through that car and everything inside it. The horses ran the car up to the mule pens, which were all solid cement or rock, and they just set that car on end. They broke the tongue out of the wagon, and the horses both fell down. We got them straightened up and got them out of there.

Oh, that man who owned that new Cadillac, he was just going to take everything I had. He was going to get the sheriff. He got the sheriff. He also got this fellow and that fellow and the other. Boy, I had worked hard for a year just to get ahead a little, and that one accident seemed about to wipe out everything I had. He was going to take me to court!

I said, "Well, all right. You go ahead, get a judgment against me. But I don't think you can. I don't know the law here, but I think you're breaking the law when you leave that car on this street. When you talk about damage, I think I'm the one gets the damage."

He cooled down a little bit and said, "How could that be?"

I said, "There's the wagon all broke up, my driver is hurt, and I don't know how badly those horses are hurt."

Well, that kind of cooled him off. I went downtown and got a lawyer. He said no, the man had no right to have a car on that street at all. That car owner never did sue me; he was just trying to bluff me. If it had been on one of the other streets, then I'd have been in for trouble, and bad. I'd have had that car to pay for, and a lot more.

Anyway, the man who had bought the horses ran after them, and somebody else helped him. They brought them up to the barn again.

I said, "I don't suppose you want them now."

He smiled as he patted the nearest one, "Oh, yes, I wouldn't turn them down for a thing like that. They weren't to blame. When I put a bridle on those horses they won't shake it off."

Imagine those horses running with that man way up there on that big wagon seat—way up high, you know, ten, eleven feet off the ground. I just looked for him to get killed. When he made them turn, that was a relief, but when they hit that car, boy, my heart did stop for a couple of beats. I just nearly fainted. The auction stopped and everybody ran out to see what was causing all the excitement.

After a few trips to Chicago I got along back to my Council Bluffs yard. About the first thing that happened was that I went over to the horse auction in Omaha one day and bought quite a few old horses, and I had to get them over the bridge across the river to my sale barn at Council Bluffs. I tied them head to tail, and the Humane Society happened to find that out. I'd done it before, and so had other people, but this day just happened to be their day to find out some things they couldn't understand. They notified the police.

Next day I took another band of horses over the bridge tied head to tail, and the police stopped me. They said it would cost me fifty dollars a head if I did that again. I tried to explain that I had to take my horses over to Council Bluffs to ship them on the Rock Island Railroad, as I had a special rate on that road. I said I also had a shipment coming in from Geneseo, Illinois, next day, and I would have to drive that band over to Council Bluffs. The policeman wanted to know how many there were. I said 180.

"Well, if you won't tie any more head to tail, we'll police a street for you."

The horses came in and we drove them through Omaha, and everything went well until we got to the toll bridge. I was ahead to pay the toll, and the bridge operator wouldn't take my word for how many horses I had. I said he'd get in trouble if they tried to count them as they were wild horses and would stampede, and that was just what happened. I got out of the way; I knew these wild horses would run over me if I didn't.

After they crossed the bridge, those horses turned south into the brush. We sure had a time getting them into the pasture. Everyone helped me or we never would have got them. I'll bet there never was anyone ever required to turn their horses loose on that bridge again. And I sure wouldn't like to try it again.

I had bought a lot of horses in Mullen, Nebraska, and I would have to drive them forty miles to a railroad or make some kind of a deal with the Chicago and North Western Railroad. I sent to their board to see if I could make special arrangements. The horses I had bought would lose me money if I shipped at their regular rate. The man in the office said he couldn't do that but that the railroad officials were having a meeting in Omaha and he would write a letter. I could take the letter to them and tell them my story.

I was busy that day, and the yards were slushy. I wasn't very presentable. The girl at the outer office didn't want me to go in to the meeting. She took the letter to the head man, who was meeting with the board. They wanted me to come in and talk it over. I went in there, and they were all dressed up. If there had been a hole in the floor, I would have jumped in, but as long as I was there, I told them in a few words what I wanted. They asked me to sit down and tell them all about the deal I had made and what I did with so many horses. The first thing I knew I was telling some of the funny things that happened in this deal with people and animals and things, and I forgot all about my muddy clothes. Still, I didn't get any satisfaction from them, though they laughed heartily about my stories. Came time for lunch, and they said for me to go with them to the dining room. They took me to the best hotel in Omaha. I couldn't get out of it. After lunch they still wouldn't let me go. I guess they wanted to be entertained. At last I told them I had to go, as my wife expected me at home.

"Well, we have had a good time at your expense, so you go home, and we will talk it over and write you a letter in the morning." Which they did, allowing me everything I had asked for.

I pretty near killed a man up at Manilla, and it happened to be little Johnnie Wyatt. I hadn't been home for a long time, but it got to where I had to go, so I gathered up the twenty-five horses my men had bought and put them in a pasture on a woman's farm about ten miles south of Manilla. Since I could trust Johnnie, I put him in charge and said I'd be back as soon as I could.

He had always been my best man, and he stayed with me most of the time.

In about a week I went back, and there was Johnnie and a couple other men in the yard of the woman's place. Johnnie was drunk as could be. I got him in my car and went to load the horses, but I couldn't find but five head. The others, it turned out, were clear gone. I asked Johnnie what he had done with my twenty horses.

"That's none of your business," Johnnie shouted.

I scolded him about letting my horses go. I told him in a few words what he would have to do. Johnnie made for me with his knife, caught me right in the shoulder, just ripped my leather jacket right down and went into my hide. I've got a scar there now that was about eighteen inches long but didn't go in very deep. Well, I hit Johnnie so hard that I just paralyzed him. I hit him as hard as I could, and for a bit I thought I had broken his neck. I beat the living daylights out of him, and when I finally looked I thought I had killed him.

One of the fellows who was with Johnnie took a hand in the fight, so I picked up a two-by-four and gave him a blow on the head. The other man ran. Now there were two men lying there on the ground.

The woman came running to the front door and said, "What're you doing out there? I don't allow that. Now, all of you get out of here."

I said, "Now, wait a minute. He jumped onto me and I had to protect myself. I want you to help me. I believe I've killed a man down here." Poor old Johnnie Wyatt. I couldn't see him breathe or anything. I said, "We'll pick him up and put him in the car, and I'll take him to a doctor."

I took Johnnie to a room in Manilla and called a doctor. We worked with him all night before he came to. Oh, he was the worst-looking sight I ever saw. I don't know how I ever hit anybody that hard. That man's face was just as black as coal, all of it. Eyes all swelled shut. He had killed a man some time before, and the other men were all afraid of him, all but me. I guess he had got to bullying the other men who worked for me, but he didn't know I wasn't afraid.

When Johnnie came to, he looked at me and said, "I don't suppose you want me anymore."

"Yes, I do, Johnnie. I'm sorry I hit you that hard. But Johnnie, never draw a knife on me—on anybody—again."

I got my shoulder patched up and took him along with me. I asked him where the rest of the horses were, and he told me he had traded them off while he was drunk. I asked him, "How does it come you got drunk, Johnnie? I told you when I hired you that the horse business and liquor wouldn't work together. I said I'd give you a job but that you had to keep clean." Johnnie, like most drunks, didn't have much to say for himself.

"Well, Johnnie," I said, "I can't get the horses back. No telling where they are by now, so if you'll tell me who sold you the whiskey, I'll try to make him pay for the horses."

I remembered well the Johnnie who had come to me for a job. He had been down to nothing, just begging for enough to eat, when I took him on. I had fed him up, got him in shape, and I paid him good wages.

I said, "Johnnie, I don't want you to quit. I'm not gonna let you quit. But never do that again." Maybe I really didn't have to say that.

Johnnie told me where he got that liquor. Since this was during Prohibition, I knew if I could find out where they got the liquor, I could make that fellow pay for the horses somebody had got away from Johnnie. I knew that liquor had come from Manilla. I walked along the streets of Manilla and happened to run across a fellow who was a good friend of mine. I knew I could trust him. After we talked a bit I said, "I'd like to have you go with me for a while."

He said, "What's up?" I told him, and he said, "Sure, I'll help out."

I told him my plan, then I said, "You know this man who's running the blind pig. We'll go in there, and you introduce him to me so I can buy a pint of whiskey."

When we got there my friend did as I asked. The bootlegger said, "Oh, yeah, sure, I'll let you have a pint of whiskey." So he got a bottle.

I handed the bottle to my friend and said, "Now open it up and test it out. Tell me what it is."

My friend did. "That's whiskey," he said thoughtfully as he tasted it. "Corn whiskey."

That was all I wanted to know. I went over to the bootlegger, placed my gun on the counter, and said, "Now, you sold one of my men whiskey, and while he was drunk someone got away with twenty of my horses. What do you want to do, pay for the horses or be turned in? You know what you'll get if I turn you in." Don't forget, this was Prohibition times.

He acted like he was trying to reach for his gun, but the man who was with me told him he had better not try that. "Just pay for the horses," he said, "and let's have no more trouble." The bootlegger decided to pay for the horses.

Of course, my other men heard about that. The news just went like wildfire. The boss had whipped that little gypsy and about killed him. Boy, they all were thinking about that. Whatever I said after that, nobody ever talked back to me. Old Johnnie never bulldozed the rest of my men again, either.

EIGHTEEN

The Wild Horse

There was a man in Wyoming who had a band of wild horses. He was an old horseman and rancher. I read an article in a magazine about him and his herd. He told a lot about the hardships of the wild horse, how he lives. I'm not so sure they had that much of a bad time. As I look at it, I don't doubt there were times when they were hungry, but that was freedom. Some of those stallions are very intelligent, and sly as they can be. How else could they exist with all the responsibility they have, guarding their family of mares and baby colts, fighting other stallions, foraging for food and shelter. I have often wondered how they managed to exist.

The horse has disappeared almost as needlessly as the buffalo did, at the whim of men who did not and could not care about anything but themselves. Wild horses have died off from old age, but much more from the smoking guns of the butcher, the assassin. Many of them were killed and left to rot, even as the buffalo. But thousands more were herded to be butchered for cat, dog, and human consumption and for the manufacture of goods for people, goods that could have been made from other materials. We had no thought but to destroy those beautiful bands of fine, intelligent creatures. I always loved a good horse. I've had lots of them. There is one thing about a horse, no matter how tame he becomes, if he ever gets the drop on you, he'll kill you.

A few years ago I'd hardly have known where to go to find a wild horse, but I might find one now, one or two. Idaho, Montana, Nevada, eastern Washington and Oregon, that's where I'd look today. Several years ago, too, I was down near the Mexican border, and I saw a band of about twenty-five wild horses. I was talking about that over at the sale barn one day. A man I saw at the sale hunts horses down near Mexico. He said there are quite a few left down there. He corrals them, captures them for training and, later, sale. He is a government horse wrangler. The wild stallions down there are considered a nuisance by the farmers and stockmen. Those stallions steal the work fillies and saddle horses from the farms and ranches. They're all Appaloosas there around the border, spotted, with a shave tail.

One stallion was known to be twenty years old at least. He had been a bad nuisance all those years. Well, I think if my wife was put into slavery, and my kids, I'd do what I could to get them out, wouldn't you? That's all that horse was doing when you look right at the problem. But man doesn't give other animals credit for having that kind of feeling. Man thinks he is the only one with feelings, but I wonder just whether he has any feeling, from all the things I see him do.

This wrangler was offered a hundred dollars to go down there and capture that stallion. He owned two beautiful Appaloosa mares. The wrangler rode one mare and led the other down, tied them out. He hid, with a roping horse tied nearby. By and by along comes mister stallion, up to his old mare-stealing tricks. The wrangler managed to get a rope on him, captured him, then began to wonder how he could kill such a magnificent animal. He tried to tame him, but the stallion was too old to change his ways. The wrangler had to slit his throat. He took the head off and sent it to a taxidermist. That was the longest horse head he had ever seen. Weighed way over twenty pounds. Shame to kill such a horse. The next spring one of those mares had a colt, the most beautiful thing you ever laid eyes on, looked just like that stallion.

When a band of horses is attacked directly by a hungry preying animal, say a mountain lion, they run as much as the colts can stand. But if they can't get away from the danger and the colts are wearied, then they circle the colts. Those old mares turn their tails to the center of the circle and their heads out. They protect the colts while leaving themselves free to paw or bite. But the stallion is entirely free to give battle. If this situation develops, the smart lion just leaves. On the run. The stallion may chase him off. He'll have to find a jackrabbit or starve.

Contrary to what some believe, a horse can think for himself, and he'll preserve himself and his family with much intelligence if you give him a chance. He provides what shelter he can, food, care for the young, training, education. A horse is nobody's fool. When they learned a man would be good to them, treat them with kindness, they seemed to appreciate it. I found, in my experiences with them, that they held fear. If they had to fight for their lives, they were mean in self-defense. They don't fight to hurt anything, just to protect themselves. When a horse learns to trust you, he is your horse as long as he lives, does anything you tell him to do. I guess you might say they are really conquered only on their own consent. They would be foolish to throw away all the comfort of barns and plenty of food for the privilege of remaining out in all kinds of weather trying to find food all year round, fighting wolves, dogs, man, when they did have a choice.

Today few people have any use for horses unless they've got a pedigree three miles long. Horses were pushed off the range for cattle and sheep, because men had tractors and trucks and they could sell beef and mutton. Horses are hunted with guns and dogs, jeeps and helicopters which send absolute terror through their beings. Man uses any way he can to get rid of the horse, one of the best friends he ever had.

I have captured wild horses and I've been in roundups where there were hundreds of horses. They were gathered in and shipped out to all parts of the globe, slaves of men. They remained slaves for the rest of their lives, and died slaves. I've seen them where they have been abused, and are scared, and scarred, shot down for no fault of their own through malicious reasons or misguided ones. Finally, like everything else in our time, they have become worthless as they can be. Or so man says.

We went through a machine age when there was no longer any use for the horse, but maybe Henry Ford wasn't so wise after all. Maybe there were some bugs in his combustion engine. Maybe the horse will come back a part of the way and become a bigger part of human life than he is today.

The greatest horse I ever knew—
ah, there's a story I'll have to tell you. I once caught a wild white stallion

singlehanded. The story could be pretty near a book by itself if I could remember it all. But it is one experience I could have done without.

Once in a while there's a stallion you never catch. Cowboys, ranchers, wild-horse hunters have all tried to catch this particular horse, but he's smarter than all of them. It takes a wise man to handle a wise horse, and those wild horses always were wise, especially the stallions. When they stop being wise, that will be their end. This white stallion was one of these, and he was one of the most gorgeous horses I've ever seen—pure white, great big eyes and a fine Arabian head, nice slim neck. He looked like a purebred Arabian horse, not an American horse. He had something about him. He was a beauty. I'm sure he wasn't wild, really. He might have been wild to start with, but he had been captured and I think he had been abused, maybe sadly abused, and had got away from his owner.

He ran like the wind. No one could ever get close enough to throw a rope on that horse. He was a kind of boss of the whole range. He'd go up on a mountain and he'd watch. If you ever saw him around, you'd have a hard time getting any of the other horses, because they all depended on him.

It is quite a science to catch wild horses. You've got to stalk them. You've got to take a field glass and go way up on a high place and locate your band. Also, you've got to have a gelding, and to be of any use to you in catching wild horses, the gelding has to have been fed at the place you want to use as your starting place for this maneuver. He will run back to where he gets his feed. Such a horse cannot have been wild, ever, to start with. He has to have always been tame. And get the fastest one you can find. Then hide your regular saddle horse until you spot a bunch of horses with your field glass. Then put your saddle on this gelding and hope he feels like running.

Every stallion has several mares, and he does not allow another stallion or a gelding to go near them. If one comes too close to suit him, he takes out after him to flip him out of his realm. Well, the gelding is scared, and he'll start to run for the corral, or wherever he has been fed. The wild stallion will take after the gelding and, of course, the mares will follow the stallion.

Now the rider, on his fast horse, should get behind, and he must be fast enough to cut the mares in on both sides so they can't, any of them, get away from him. But the rider can get in trouble in this situation. If there's an old white mare in the bunch, you want to have your eye on her all the time, because she's the leader if the stallion gets killed or has to go away for a time. She just might take off across the prairies as fast as she can go, and you've got to have a horse fast enough to head her. If you don't, your horses are gone, because all the other mares and the colts will follow her as hard as they can run. Get your horses into the place you have made ready for them and lock them in.

Another way to catch wild horses is to have a big drive like the one I was in in Wyoming. The ranchers got together and made a general roundup of the township. We had all the wild horses in a box canyon, got them in there in the evening. The year I was in the roundup there was a mound, about an acre of ground, right in the center of the en-closed area. A lot of stallions will get up there, and you'd think they were going to fight, but they don't. They just whinny and scream. I'm sure they are communicating. They seem to come to an understanding. Then they go down into the main herd and each one sorts out his own mares and takes them off into his own family area. He herds them all the time they're in there.

The year I was in the roundup they built a pole fence where they had to, to keep these wild horses in their pen. We had a pretty good catch of horses in that pen, but the white stallion was not among them. He just hung around outside the pen and wouldn't let himself be caught. And he wouldn't go away. He would come up at night and try to tear the fence down. He bothered us so much we had to do some-thing. We had to put a guard out to keep him away. The men took turns standing guard, one each night.

I had a turn standing guard one night. I sat my horse in the dark of the canyon. It was quiet and still. You could hear the soft breeze whis-per past. Everything else was quiet. I was just about asleep after a couple of hours sitting there when I first heard the stallion, but he didn't stay. I listened for a long time, but I didn't hear him anymore. Time wore on pretty well toward morning and I was about half asleep again, sitting there on that horse. There was a beer barrel sitting on top of some blocks. I heard a commotion near those blocks and looked down, and it was him.

I am not a good roper and I never was, but that morning in the dark, I was lucky. I threw the rope and caught the white stallion.

Talk about a wild animal! He beat everything! With that rope around his neck he just jerked my horse right off his feet. He would jerk my horse until the rope came tight around his own neck, then he would come right toward us. I was afraid if I got off my horse to run for better cover he might kill me. My horse was afraid of him too, but we couldn't get out of there because the lariat was tied to the saddle horn. Another man had used my horse the day before. He had tied the lariat onto the horn of the saddle. I didn't know that, hadn't noticed it, never used it that way. Now I couldn't get it loose. We went round and round and finally we choked him down some. We got close enough to a tree and I got my rope around it and fastened to it. I snubbed him down with a half hitch. Oh, I was just delighted. I thought, If I can just get this white stallion home, he'll be worth more than all the horses they could give me.

I tried to gentle him. I know every trick in the horsetrading business, and in the horsebreaking business too. I know how to train a horse or conquer him. But that was a horse I never could conquer. Tried to feed him, but he wouldn't eat, and he wouldn't drink any water. And for days I couldn't get close enough to him to get that rope off. I could have cut the rope and let him go, but he wouldn't allow me near enough to do that. If I let it drag and let him go, he might have gotten hung up somewhere and starved to death, or choked, or even hanged himself accidentally.

He was such a wonderful animal, a one-in-a-million kind of animal, that if there had been one chance in a billion that I could have tamed him, I would have tried. But I didn't think there was even that much chance. He didn't hate me, he hated all men. To his dying day that horse would look at me with all the hate that was ever in any animal's eyes. If he could have killed me, he would have died a happy horse.

Ah, he was a horse. *He was a horse.* A thousand men would have tried to get him. Maybe a hundred had tried. But I did. I got him. I lassoed him and he was mine. For one short instant he was mine. But he never was really mine, not really.

That horse starved to death. He died for lack of food and water, and he wouldn't touch a bit of either, though I brought them within his reach daily or oftener. Or did he die of captivity, and a broken heart? With a sigh, a tremendous sigh, he laid his head down upon the ground and he died a prisoner, my prisoner, and a part of me died with that wonderful horse. I have known that every time I have thought of him during these entire ninety years.

NINETEEN

Trick Horses and Trick Mules

Trick horses? They are a law all to themselves. The horse has to be smart, and he has to be able to laugh to himself, and at himself, and at people. Yes, even if most people think a horse doesn't laugh, when you work with a trick horse you find out he has a sense of humor and he knows who the joke is on. After that, he has to be trained.

Yes, the horse has to be smart, but you know, even before that, the man must know more than the horse does, though maybe not more than the horse can figure out. You may never know about that part of the game.

To train a horse, you've got to use a lot of different methods. Some horses you can train one way, and some you train another way. Some you train with a whip, some with kindness. A few you have to train by force. I always found horses to respond to kindness and gentle treatment better than to anything else.

I once trained a little outlaw pony, a half-blooded Shetland. I got him from one of my neighbors. You couldn't ride him, couldn't do anything with him. He was just naturally mean, but he was smart too, you could tell. He just wasn't going to be handled, he wasn't going to be driven around carrying a man on his back. He wasn't going to be driven. They couldn't do anything with him. I saw this pony one day when I was going along the road, and I asked the owner what he'd take for him.

"Well, if it was anybody but you I'd price him, but I have those little kids up at the house, and they'll get hurt with him, fooling around in the barn sometime."

"What's wrong with him?"

"Well, nobody can ride him. He'll buck and kick and bite and do anything that's mean."

. I said, "That don't bother me. I can gentle that horse, I know I can." So he sold the horse to me.

I went down to get the horse. I had to rope him to catch him, and I choked him down and put a halter on him. I thought he'd just as well learn what a bridle is, and I had a bridle in the car. I got it on him and tied the reins around his neck so he couldn't drag them. Then I tied him on behind the car.

My second daughter, Opal, was with me, and she was, as I already said, quite a horsewoman. From the time she was five years old there wasn't often a horse she couldn't ride. After we had made that pony run two or three miles, Opal wanted to ride him. She thought she'd like to get on him. So I stopped the car and she got into the saddle. I left the horse tied to the car and we went home that way. No trouble.

I started training that pony the next day. I soon learned that he was fond of tricks. To teach them one trick, you show them how it is done about three times and they'll do the trick for you if you know how to handle your horse. There are several ways of doing it. You can use a whip with a tack on the end of the lash. You can use a bribe—sugar or apple. But sugar is as bad for a horse as it is for a human, so I didn't try that.

There are different things you might teach them. You might make them waltz or make them stand on their hind legs. If you want them to stand up, you tap them on the belly with that whip and tell them to rear, and they'll come up. If you tap them on the legs, they'll raise a foot up, and that's the way you start training them. Before long that old pony would do everything but read numbers. I taught him to waltz, to rear up on his hind legs, to go down on his knees and pray, and to get down on one knee to let Opal get into the saddle. He learned fast.

A man came in one day, and he wanted a pair of big gray horses I had, and I sold them to him. He saw this pony in the barn and said, "Will you sell that pony?"

I said, "No, I wouldn't sell it. It belongs to my little girl."

"I'd like to have him. Have you taught him any tricks?"

"Yes, he can do anything."

"I'd like to see him perform. Would you mind taking him out?"

I took the pony out and put him through his tricks.

The man said, "Do you suppose your little girl would sell him?"

I said, "I don't think so, but she's in the house. If you want to talk to her, go ahead."

He went up to the house and asked her, "Would you sell that pony?"

"Oh, if I'd got enough hole in my head."

"How much?"

"How much would you give?"

"Two hundred dollars."

"Oh, I wouldn't sell his tail for that. What're you talking about, anyway?"

She got him up to five hundred dollars, and I said, "Well, just sell him, Opal." He took that pony and sold him to a circus in New York City.

Two years later I was in Omaha one day, and the circus was there. I thought I recognized that pony on the billboards outside. I went to the show and, sure enough, it was. I went in back after the act to make sure. Sometimes, you know, a horse remembers a person. But though I was sure it was the same pony, he didn't recognize me. He had been around too many people. He had forgotten me.

Another time I had a spotted mule and I trained him. That was a queer deal. He was an odd-colored spotted mule. I had to take him in order to get some horses that I wanted. The man wouldn't sell me the horses unless I'd take that mule too, so I bought him and brought him home. He was a regular clown. He would do tricks without any training. He knew tricks of his own. I'd put a pillow in my overalls and he'd kick me in the seat of my pants, you know, and run between my legs (he wasn't very big). He was the cutest thing you've ever seen, and I used to spend just hour after hour with that doggone thing, just playing. I think someone had trained him, but it was also natural for him—he was a born clown, he just loved it. You'd get on him and ride him, and he'd go tearing around, and first thing you know, off you went. He'd stop dead still and kick up his heels to be sure to get you off. Then he'd prance around and prance around. You'd go to get up and he'd kick you in the seat and you'd fall over. He almost seemed to laugh.

Well, I took him to Chicago. I had him out in the street playing with him, showing him off, and I suppose there were a thousand people around there watching him.

A fellow came up and said, "What will you take for him?"

I said, "Now, I'll tell you, he ain't worth fifteen cents as far as value is concerned, but it takes fifteen hundred dollars to buy him."

He said, "Oh, you wouldn't ask that much. Why, I'll give you a thousand for him."

"I won't take a thousand. I want fifteen hundred. I just brought him up to show what he'll do, let people see what a personality a little mule can develop. I just had some room in my car with the regular shipment, so I brought him along."

"I won't argue with that, but I'll give you eleven hundred dollars for him."

"All right, I'll take it."

Well, they showed that little fellow all over the world. For years I saw him in rodeos, saw pictures of him in different kinds of shows and circuses dozens of times.

I had another trick mule at the same time. They were in no way related at all, but they looked alike, people said. I was over to another town in Iowa and saw a nice pair of sorrel horses, and I wanted them awful bad. I had a hard time buying them, too. I also noticed this little spotted mule around there. Seemed like he was a little precocious. He was loose in the barn, the door was shut, and when they opened the barn door and let the stock outside, I watched. That mule just couldn't behave himself. He went over to the watering trough and was pestering the horses.

The man said, "You'll have to take that mule along with you if you buy the sorrel horses. He's just always some kind of a pest here." So I took him home.

He only stood about thirty-six inches high. He was out of a little

Shetland pony, spotted as a leopard. The other trick mule and he were the only spotted mules I ever heard of. I trimmed him all up so he'd look good among the mules, roached his mane and tail. He thought he was a dandy when I finished him.

One day after he'd been around for a week or ten days I thought, Maybe I can make a trick mule out of him. I didn't have much time to fool with him, only Sundays. Some time later I shipped some big horses to Chicago, and he made such a fuss I let him go along. I sold him on a trick deal. I don't remember now whether I got anything out of him or not. My kids had a lot of fun with him while he was on the farm. They weren't so happy when I took him away.

Most animals learn to be cautious about electric fences pretty quickly—overcautious, you might say. When I raised hogs we used electric fences to keep them in, but we had some trouble. The hogs kept getting out all the time. I had an ear of green corn on a wire. I knew one old sow would come up and try to get out. She came up, all right, and saw the corn. She took a bite of it and, boy, she went back, right into the middle of the yard. That hog was afraid to move. You couldn't drive her over a little piece of wire an inch long after that. You couldn't get her near a wire. I don't know why that fellow Pavlov had so much trouble teaching his dogs. My old sow learned in just one lesson.

Same way with cattle. Put an electric wire up and have it up there all summer, and you'll have an awful time getting those cows out of the pasture, just an awful time. I worked for a whole day just to get them to go out of the gate, because the electric wire had been up there to keep them in, and they couldn't understand that I had taken it away.

But it doesn't always work out that way. Once I bought a good pair of Percheron mares. They were beautiful. I was still at the sale when a man and his boy came in with a whole truckload of little mules. This was after the mule business was played out, and they put these up for sale and couldn't get their bid for them. The old man who owned them came to me and wanted to know if I would buy that load of mules. I didn't have any use for mules, but I could see the man's position.

I said, "No, but I have a large pasture and I could put them in there. Maybe I could handle them if you could sell them cheap enough."

He didn't seem very happy, but he asked, "How cheap would that be?"

"Twenty-five dollars a head."

"All right. I've had them to two or three sales and couldn't get rid of them."

Well, I didn't want them. After a while I was wondering if I could haze the old man a little and maybe pick some fault with his mules and make him take them back. I got another man who was a little feisty, a mule master. I said, "Come on, I want you to see these mules."

We had put them in a pen in the barn and had them just crowded in there as thick as fleas and not much bigger. I took a rope and pulled one up to the fence and I looked in his mouth. The first one I looked at had a parrot mouth, the lower jaw was pointed one way and the upper jaw pointed across it like an *x*. A parrot-jawed mule has trouble eating, chewing his food. I called the old man over, with his boy.

I said, "How many of *these* you got there? I've just looked at one, and if I had known it was parrot-jawed, I wouldn't have wanted these mules. Parrot-jawed animals are not worth a nickel. That's the reason you couldn't sell them. Just take this mule out and put him in a pen."

He took that one out of the bunch he had sold me. The next mule was overshot just a little, but not enough to hurt him. His upper jaw stuck out beyond his lower jaw a little, that's all. "Take him out," I said.

Finally, of the nine head, he took out five. I made the old man and the boy look at them and admit that they were overshot. Four of the mules were all right.

He said, "Well, what'll you give for the four?"

"I'll give you twenty-five dollars a head, and you just throw in the five others."

Just a little grudgingly he said, "All right."

When I got home I put those mules in the pasture with the big mares. Of course, the mules took right after those horses, and there was one mare there, she had more sense than a lot of people. If you'd ever show her anything once, she'd never forget.

A neighbor from about three miles away called one night about nine o'clock and said, "Hey, Lee, your mules are all over here to my place. I know they're yours 'cause I don't have any more mules in my pen."

I got in the car and went over, herded the mules home, and put them back in the pasture. I checked all around the fence, but I couldn't see where they'd got out. I had put them inside the electric fence to be sure they wouldn't get out. I checked the wires clear around the whole fence. Not a chance for mules to get out, not anywhere.

Two or three days later they got out again! This time they went about nine miles before somebody noticed them and called me. Well, I got them back, but I figured there was something wrong someplace, that somebody'd been letting those mules out. So I just got in my car along about sundown and I drove off to one side to watch.

By and by this mare, she went up to the fence. The mules and other mares followed like they had it all made up, and I don't doubt they did. At least, they knew what they were doing, and they did it after dark so they couldn't be seen. That mare just quietly put her foot on that electric wire and pushed it right down with her hoof. She had no shoes, so she didn't get shocked. Over they all went. Then she took her hind foot, put it on that wire, and she stepped right over herself. That electric wire never touched her.

Quite an electrician, I thought. Here that big mare had done that three times now, had let those mules and mares out of the fence I had built to keep them in. And how did she ever know how to handle a live wire? Even Ben Franklin spent more time figuring it out.

Well, I gave her a good shock. I fixed it so when she went to put her foot on that wire she got a shock right on the end of her nose. I may have frustrated genius at work, but I broke that old mare of letting those other animals out.

Later two men came along, one was an old mule buyer, and they wanted to buy those mules. I priced them, the men liked the price, and they took all the mules. Then they wanted to buy those old mares. I priced them, and they bought them too. Earlier I had given my grandson a pony, a colt, and the colt outgrew the boy. She grew too big, and I told them I'd send a man over there to buy her, because the family had no other use for her. That's the kind they ship down south, small-like mares. These buyers went over and looked at this mare and bought her, then they started home with all their new stock.

They had driven about three or four miles when a car ran into them, killed one of the buyers and put the other one in the hospital for three or four months. All the animals came back to me to care for. Well, I had several chances to sell the horses and the mules, though I didn't like to do it. But it was a lot of work and a nuisance and an expense to feed all those animals, which didn't even belong to me anymore. After a few weeks I called the wife of the hospitalized man and asked her what she wanted to do with all those animals. I said I'd had them for a long time, but I didn't mind keeping them, pasturing them if she wanted me to.

She said, "My husband's still in the hospital, and he was talking about this the last time I was down there. He wants to call you as soon as he gets out of the hospital, but I don't know what he wants to do."

This situation went on clear from October to Christmas. He kept calling every little bit, wanted to know if I was tired of keeping his mules. Of course I was. I had a lot of cattle and mules and other animals of my own to take care of. It was just a plain nuisance. I wanted to get rid of these extras that didn't belong to me anymore. Finally they sent a truck for them. I put the old mares in the truck first, thought the mules would follow. Get mules in that truck? We just had the awfulest time getting those mules into that truck! Then when they did get in and we shot the gate down, they tried to crawl over the top. Some of them tried to get their feet clear up on the top rung of the truck bed.

I said, "If you ever get those mules to Kansas City, you'll be a wonder." But that driver got them down there. They put those mules in a barn, and they'd never been in a barn in their lives. It was funny, too, but I was glad it wasn't my barn. Those darn mules kicked the whole side out of that barn.

TWENTY

Trick People

Just like other animals, people have their own tricks they like to play. Some of them are kind of funny, like grownup versions of the pranks I told you about that we played on people when we were kids, or like Buffalo Bill and the bird shot. Others aren't so funny, and some of this kind of trick are what we call crimes. I guess I've run into my share of all three kinds.

Take the time I was in South Dakota on a buying trip, and a man rushed right up to me and said, "You a cattle buyer?"

"Yes, I'll buy cattle."

"I've got some."

"Yes? Where are they?"

"Right down here."

"Those along the road?"

"Yeah." They'd had a fire and there wasn't a spear of grass you could see anywhere.

I said, "Those cattle are in good shape. You must have some feed back in the hills."

"No, we haven't. I drive them up as far as I can, up there on the hills. I wait until they get good and thirsty, then I start them back. The grasshoppers are pretty thick here this year, and the cattle are so hot and they get so dry they get to running with their mouths open, and they swallow those grasshoppers. That's the reason they're so fat. You know, there's a lot of protein in grasshoppers."

I said, "Yes, that's what they tell me, there's a lot of protein." I never cracked a smile.

Pretty soon I heard an old man laughing in the back room. "Hee hee hee, haw haw haw. Mister, I'll bet that man you're trying to fool has owned more cattle than you ever saw." Half an hour later they were still razzing him about trying to make me believe his cattle were eating grasshoppers. I still laugh when I think of that story.

                         Once I rode in a rodeo. There was one at a town near Adair called Wiota. I took the kids over, and oh, there was a great big old western fellow, he was dressed up like Buffalo Bill. He made an announcement that he had a horse nearly twenty years old that had never been ridden by any man. They couldn't stay on him ten seconds. A lot of my neighbors were there, and one man said to me, "Lee, why don't you go over and take that fellow on?"

Several others said, "Yeah, Lee, give it a try."

I said, "All right."

We went over and I said to the owner, "Did you say you have a horse that has never been ridden?"

"Yes, and there isn't a man living that can ride that horse."

"Where is he?"

"He's right over there."

"Would you bet a little money that a man couldn't ride that horse?"

"I would, indeed I would. I have a standing offer of fifty dollars for anyone who can ride him." I thought he looked a bit sorry when he said that, but he sounded brave.

"Get your fifty dollars in sight, because I'm going to ride him. But I'll say this much, I'm going to ride him my way. I'm no cowboy, but I'm going to ride your horse."

"Well, you can't ride him, and you can do anything you want with him just so you don't take his front feet off."

"I'll let him have all his feet, but I want to ride him my way."

They put him in the chute and I got set in the saddle, got a good hold on those reins. When he went out there I just brought his head right up to his breast. He made about two little crow hops and that was it. I loosened up the reins and trotted all around the crowd and brought him back and got my fifty dollars.

The owner said, "Oh, I wouldn't have had that happen for anything in the world. That horse was my bread and butter."

I said, "Why, any kid can ride that horse. He's no bucking horse. If you want to see a bucking horse, come over. I've got one that really can buck."

"I'll be right over," he said, but he never showed up. He moved on to the next town to see how many other suckers he could fool, I guess.

I had a horse I don't believe anybody could ride, but that little old pony of his was so darn old he couldn't hurt you if he did buck. He was just a drawing card, bread and butter for a slicker too lazy to work.

Sometimes I guess I was on the wrong end of a joke to see the humor in it, if it had any humor in it. Once I was traveling through northern Iowa and bought a big bunch of horses. A man came out and said, "I got a horse I want to sell."

A woman and some girls came out and crowded and fussed around. They hated to see their old mare go, an old pet.

The man said, "Yes, she is an old pet. She never harmed anyone anywhere."

I had fixed nosebags to feed my horses, and I went to tie one on this horse. That old devil kicked me on the knee. Oh, it hurt me. I yelled with pain, "You damned old bitch!" I took my cane and just laid it right to her.

That man and these women just went into convulsions. They laughed like they were having fits.

"That's a hell of a pet you've got there," I told them, and I just whopped that horse a few more licks. You bet. I laid the cane on their dear old pet right in front of the whole family. Then I began to think they'd be worried they'd sold her to me, but I didn't care, they could take her back. Only they never said a word. I guess someone thought that was the way to play a joke on a horsetrader. I didn't agree.

Some tricks get played just because nobody's paying attention. Once I had a contract for a thousand horses and I had to have room, so I rented from the son of a millionaire. His father had died, and he had about twenty-five acres of the best alfalfa you've ever seen and a hay barn with I don't know how many tons of hay in it, baled alfalfa hay, and it was filled clear to the top. Well, that was just what I wanted. I'd go over there and buy a carload of old horses and turn them in there. That was my trading place.

Every Monday morning I'd sell from ten to twenty-five outfits to the Red Cross and other organizations there, for the poor people. They'd come and buy a single horse and wagon with harness. About the middle of the week here would be the welfare recipients all coming back, and I'd buy back all the horses, wagons, and harness and sell them again the next week. These organizations would give the poor these horses and wagons to make a living with and oh, those snakes up there, they'd do anything. Just as soon as they'd got possession of the equipment and got a few dollars ahead hauling wood or garden goods or some such thing, they'd bring the horses and wagons in and sell them back to me. I wouldn't give them much of anything, a ten-dollar bill lots of times, though I was getting twenty-five dollars for these outfits. An old horse, an old wagon, and an old set of harness cost me four or five dollars, ten at the most. I never could figure welfare out.

In an auction, you don't know who the animals belong to. It doesn't matter; they go to the highest bidder. Knowing this, I've played tricks on sheepmen a good many times. For instance, when I was working for Iowa Pack, sometimes I'd go to a sale and some smart aleck, he'd jump in and outbid me for some sheep. I'd just let him have them. But I'd bid them right up. Oh, he'd think, if he's bidding them that high, they're worth ten cents a pound more to me. A lot of times it's been my own stock, and I've bid a dollar or two dollars a hundred more than I could expect to get for them, just to catch a smart aleck. Oh, I'd bid on the other fellow's stock, too, a dollar or two a hundred more than he could expect to get for them. Those fellows were so sure they knew all about the market, thinking that if those animals were worth a dime more to me, they were also worth a dime more to them.

One time they had a big sheep sale at Anita. I sat there and bid on every sheep that came in. And all the sheep that came in, the other bidder got them.

The auctioneer, Speck, said, "Well, what's the matter with you anyway?"

I'd known Speck since he was a little boy and had hung around the barns wishing he could be an auctioneer. Now he was one, and you'd look far to find a better one.

I said, "Why, Speck, you know me well enough to know that I was stopping that fellow. He'll never be back here."

After the auction this dude just came in there a-bristling. He knew more about sheep than anybody else. He got back in the yard among the fellows, and they all knew me. Oh, he was telling about the wool on the sheep and all he knew. Told how he put it over on me. One man told him that I bid a dollar or two over the market price to let him know he didn't know the market, wondering would he change his mind. My friend told this smart buyer that before he sold those sheep he could lose five hundred dollars or more. That stopped him, I guess. He never came back.

Another time when I was on a buying trip something happened to me at Roswell, New Mexico. Everybody knows that after the Mexican people eat their noonday meal everybody then has a siesta. They sleep for an hour or so and then get back to work, whatever they were doing—a very healthy thing to do. Well, this was a sale barn. Down there they sold sheep in the morning and cattle in the afternoon. I was at the sale, interested in sheep. Came noon and everything stopped. I was walking down through the stockyards, and I saw a two-year-old bull in a pen. He seemed pretty ferocious. I wondered what made him like that. He was behind strong steel gates and there was a husky latch holding them shut. That bull was just raving mad. Everybody who'd come along there, he'd just jump at the gate. Then I saw what it was all about. Every time any man would walk that way he'd tease that bull, throw something into his pen, poke him with a stick, pester him. Oh, he didn't like that. He'd tear them apart if he got a chance. But he was in there nice and safe, and nobody thought he'd get a chance at them. Well, everybody that came along his way, that bull would just jump at the gate. Oh, he was mad.

Over alongside the barn was a bench about shoulder high to me. After they ate, those Mexicans would line up on that bench, stretch out, and take a nap, a siesta. Every man in the place seemed to be up there sleeping, I thought. That bench was as full as they could lay.

Either somebody let that bull loose or he got out himself. He started at one end of that bench. It was just the right height for him. He could just take his horn along there. He'd prick each man as he moved down the bench. They'd get down off the bench before they were really awake and then all they could do was run. You never saw such a scramble. He had them up telephone poles, atop the fence, everywhere they could get to. That bull was clearing everything in those yards in less time than I can tell it. I was in a good, safe place. I was right behind a big gate where I could see the whole performance. Now, I wonder who turned that bull out. I know I didn't.

I bought five hundred yearling ewes down there, the very best sheep I ever owned. They were just like that many peas. I shipped them home, and everybody liked them too well. I wanted to keep them myself, so I priced them high. I didn't think anyone would buy them. I didn't have them three days until every one was gone. That was a short story.

I have to tell you this story about an experience I had at Ida Grove. I had been home for a week or ten days from my Council Bluffs sale barn, getting some home business taken care of, and I had to get back to the sale barn. I had bought a Chevrolet car, and of course we had to try that out, so Mina and I decided she and baby June would go with me for a few days. June was still too little to be in school, and our other children could stay with a woman we hired.

We drove out to Ida Grove and got there about three o'clock on a Sunday afternoon. When I drove up to the sale barn a man was waiting for me. He had a horse he wanted to sell, so we got into the car and drove six or seven miles out to where the horse was pastured. A wild bronco! That's what he had. A wild bronco he had tried to gentle and couldn't. But I bought her, and we put a halter on her and I tied the halter rope to the back of this new Chevrolet. We went along slow enough for the horse and got back into Ida Grove after dark.

Anybody who buys and sells like I did has to carry a lot of money with them. Several times I had just escaped being robbed. I had a lot of men working for me, and I had to furnish the money for them to buy and sell, too. When I left home that day I had money enough with me to stake all my men to keep them at work.

By the time I drove up to the front of the stockyard with my wife and baby June, it was real dark. There was an office next to the stock pens where stockmen weighed their animals when they brought them in. Every stockyard had such an office, and it was always unlocked and open to anyone who needed to use the scales. I drove through the front gate of the stockyard and up near this office. Mina turned on the car lights so I could see to put this wild horse in the corral. Just as I came even with the office, leading the horse, four men stepped out of the darkness.

One of them said, "There he is, we've got him now."

I didn't know what to do. I couldn't even run, knew I couldn't get away from them. I looked around and thought perhaps I could make it to the car. I had a gun in the car.

My wife had presence of mind enough. She picked up the new crank that we used to start that car (this was before they put self-starters on cars), and she pointed that crank out at those men. As those men came toward me and into the lights shining from the car, that crank looked just like a gun.

Mina yelled, "Run, you devils, or I'll shoot you all to death!"

I'll tell you, I never saw anybody run as fast as those four did in all my life. From the crank of the car! I don't know what would've happened if Mina hadn't done that. They thought I had driven there alone, and usually I did. I suppose they had already checked and knew nobody else was around. They were waiting not just for me but for the first trader who came in there, and they intended to rob whoever came and make a getaway before some other trader showed up.

Later Mina said when she picked up the crank it just seemed to be the only thing she could lay her hands on, and she thought of hitting them over the head, which, of course, she couldn't have done. Then when she got the feel of the weight and size of that crank, it made her realize what was the best way to use it. As soon as they saw it those men started begging, "Don't shoot! Don't shoot!" It was a different matter when they were in danger.

I had another odd experience while I had the sale barn in Council Bluffs. (Wasn't so odd, really. I ought to have had better sense.) A man came to the sale barn one morning with a nice team of black horses, practically a new set of harness, and a new wagon. He drove up just as I was opening the doors of my office and said, "Heard you was buying some horses and wagons."

"Yes, I'll buy anything you bring in here if I can buy at my price."

"I want two hundred dollars for this whole outfit."

I looked at them and thought if he'd asked any less than that, I'd be suspicious. But it was a fair price for them, so I bought them off him for two hundred. I took them and unharnessed them and ran the wagon in the shed. I had another black team there, and one of them was quite a bit bigger than the other one. Well, the same was true of the new team, so I just split them up. I put the little horses together, took the big horses and put them together in stalls at the other end of the barn, and now I had two matched teams. I hung the harness up behind the little team—not for any particular reason, I just happened to do it that way.

Johnnie Wyatt came in about that time and said, "Say, where'd you get the big black horses? You sure done a good job matching them up."

I said, "Yes, I just bought them this morning."

"What'd you give for them?"

"I gave two hundred for the horses, wagon, harness, and all." We were just standing there looking at the four horses when another fellow drove up.

He didn't bother to get off his horse, he just said, "Did you see a man with a new wagon, bright new set of harness, and a team of black horses?"

"Yes, I did," I told him.

"Well, he stole those horses. I'll have to take 'em back."

I said, "I don't just know about that. You'll have to identify your horses before I'll let them go." I was thinking fast now. I said, "The first thing to do, I've got the horses and I bought the wagon, according to your description, but I don't think the man has had time to get away. He said his wife was sick and he had to catch the train. He went out of here on the run. It isn't very far to the depot, and we better get down there."

We went, and he was busy buying his ticket, so we nailed him. He had the money with him, and I took it away from him.

We went back up to the barn and I said to the real owner, "Now, go in and pick out your horses and harness. Be sure you get the right ones." I wasn't just exactly satisfied with the way he acted. He went into the barn and looked first at the bigger pair of black horses. No, they were too big, that wasn't them. He went on back to the other two. They were two or three stalls down. He thought these were the ones, he said.

I said, "Are you sure?"

He scratched his head. "That's their harness there, that's it." So he took the little horses and left me the big team. I didn't tell him the difference. No, I didn't tell him anything. Let him be his own judge. If he beats himself, that's all right. I never tried to mislead him, never lied about it. I told him to identify his horses. I'd bought them in good faith, not knowing they had been stolen. I got my money back. The only difference was, I got a two-hundred-dollar horse for a hundred-fifty-dollar horse. I had a matched team, but then so did he.

Some of the tricks I ran into while I was running the sale barn weren't funny at all. They were just outright crimes. One time I was interested in buying some horses from the Indians over at Walthill, Nebraska. There's a reservation up there, near the Missouri River. I hired a man to buy horses from the Indian agent on that reservation. Some of them were too good for killers, so I took them out and put them in my pasture. I didn't look at them very close, but I got thinking one day, Well, if those are government horses, they ought to have a brand on them someplace. I caught one of the saddle horses and looked under his mane. There was an "O" brand right under the mane. One of my buyers was there. I said, "Now, did you buy those horses or did you steal them?"

"I bought them from the agent."

"You got a bill of sale on them?"

"Yes, here it is."

I sent him back up there. I told him, "It's quite a way over there, and you've got to find out where they got these horses. If I'm not mistaken, there's something wanting in this deal. There's a ferry across the Missouri River near where you bought these horses, and that's the only place for miles and miles that a person could cross that river. You might just as well bring me two loads in a couple of weeks, because I'm pretty well loaded up here at the yard right now. I'll get my men started out and sell off what I've already got. You buy two loads of horses while I sell what's already here." That'd give me forty head when I'd about sold out my present stock. My man went right up there.

I was pretty busy for about two weeks, but I kept thinking of that man, though I didn't hear from him, not a word. Three weeks and I didn't hear anything from him. I began to wonder, Where's my money gone? I got in my car and went over to Whiting to find out about that man, any trace of him, if I could. He might be over there drunk. Buyers could do that sometimes, many would. I had to be on the lookout all the time, you know. They'd get drunk and be in jail, and I'd have to get them out, which I did a good many times. My crew of forty-four men, all gypsies, wanderers, well, they were not an easy lot to handle. I was about to start out looking when this one phoned me. "I've got a bunch of horses over here for you," he told me. He'd had quite a time getting them across on the ferry. They were a wild-acting bunch. When I got out there he had them on the Iowa side of the river, a hundred head of them. I took one look at them and I knew that fellow had stolen those horses. There were horses in that herd worth a hundred fifty to two hundred dollars. He says, "I wish you'd pay me now so's I can let my men go back across on the ferry tonight."

I said, "I haven't got much cash with me. I left everything up at the hotel, and I can't see these horses anyway tonight. I'd like to see them first thing in the morning."

"All right."

These men built themselves a campfire and herded those horses along the river bottom. I went back to the hotel. Hadn't more than set my foot inside that hotel than the sheriff walked in. "Did you see any Indian horses?" he asked me.

"Yes, I did."

"Did you buy any? Did you buy a bunch of horses that went across the ferry today?"

"No, I didn't. I agreed to look at them in the morning, but I didn't buy them. It was dark and I couldn't get a good look at them. They didn't look like killer horses to me anyway. I'd have to see them by daylight."

The sheriff said, "That fellow stole those horses from the Indians up at Walthill. We know he's got them and we're gonna catch him. I'm gonna deputize you and you're gonna go out there with me."

"Oh, no, you're not gonna deputize me. I'm not going out there, I'm not ready to die yet. There's five, six, maybe seven pretty hard-looking customers out there. If they stole those horses, somebody's gonna get hurt."

"I'll deputize whoever I need," he said.

He deputized fifteen or twenty men, and we went out there about twelve o'clock midnight. There they were, all around the campfire. The men who were deputized had every kind of gun you could think of. We surrounded that camp, walked right in on those horse thieves, never had a bit of trouble capturing them. There were seven of them. We took them in, put them in jail. They had a trial and got five years in the pen for horse stealing. The authorities took the horses and gave them back to the Indians. If I had bought those horses I'd have been out whatever money I paid for them. It sort of makes you think. Of course, I was out what I'd given my man to start with three weeks before anyway.

I also had quite an experience down at Redfield in 1934. I went there with a man to look at some horses he had, and as I parked my car and walked through this gate some men stopped me, then let my friend and me pass. I thought they looked kind of like pictures I'd seen.

I said to my friend, "I wonder if that's the Dillinger gang."

He said, "I don't know. They act kinda funny, don't they?"

I didn't waste any time. I started walking pretty fast, but carefully, not to give alarm. I said, "I believe we'd better get out of here. We don't want to get mixed up with them."

We got in the car and drove off. They didn't bother us. We went down to Dexter to have a late dinner or an early supper. The United States marshal was down there. He had his deputies and asked if I'd seen anything of those men in my travels.

"Why, yes, there are some people down at Dexfield Park."

"What do they look like?"

I described them as best I could, the ones I'd seen. There was quite a gang of them, about ten, I think. One was a woman. That marshal gathered up a posse and went out there and shot it out with them. The outlaws saw them coming and opened fire. I didn't go out, didn't want to get mixed up in the trouble and was lucky enough not to be deputized.

I guess the bullets were flying pretty rapid for a while around there. The gang leader was killed, the whole gang except the woman. She was shot twice in the arm. She had a machine gun. She was down behind the dam alongside a little lake. She got to mowing the grass and everything else around there. Luckily, not one of the posse got hit. They took this woman in, gave her medical treatment, and took her to Des Moines. She got life imprisonment. All the men were killed. Nine of the ten were shot to death there that night. It was Bonnie and Clyde's gang. The leader was a robber and murderer, didn't show any mercy, shot to kill. But one of those deputies was a dead shot. When anyone stuck his head up he got a bullet right between the eyes. Why, they fought for two to three hours that night. I saw them when I came in from another job. I went on about my business, and when I came back to stay at the hotel at Dexter that night, that town was just rocking with the news.

There's one story I hesitate to tell, because it involves some high-ups that I had a lot of confidence in, and I didn't think they'd stoop to such things. But I'll tell you the story

anyway. They're all dead now. Maybe some other people have had similar experiences.

I was in Des Moines, and I was selling quite a number of mules at
the time. A man came and sat down beside me as I talked to another
horse buyer. This third man was an elected representative from a
nearby county, he was sent to take part in state government. Now, I
won't tell you even what county this man was from. A promise is a
promise, and I said I wouldn't tell, but a lot of time has passed, and if
I keep out the names of the people and the county, it shouldn't matter
to anyone now. So I'll tell it now to show what people will do for a few
measly dollars.

This man came in and sat down beside me, a representative from
one of the counties in Iowa. He said, "We're gonna sell the mules off
our prison farm. Now, if you want to buy them, I can work it so's you
can get a bargain."

I said, "I'd like to buy those mules." I knew they had rented the
prison farm out and they were going to sell these mules to somebody—
anybody.

He said, "I know you're in the mule business. We'd like to have you
come and make a bid on these mules."

We talked a while, and I said, "How much commission do you want
out of them?"

"Anything within reason."

"How many mules are there?"

"We got forty head of them."

"So you want to sell 'em all?"

"Well, I'll tell you, I think you ought to give me two dollars and a
half a head."

"That's fine. I can do that."

"But, ya know, I gotta see the governor about this."

Next Saturday I saw him. There came the governor. They sat down
on the seat next to me. The governor said, "You the man that was gonna
look at the mules?"

"Yeah."

"You can make good money on those mules."

"Sure I will, or I won't buy them, I'll tell you that, mister."

He looked at the toe of his shoe a moment and said, "I can fix it so you can buy 'em. It's up to me." He kind of hemmed and hawed around a little, and then he said, "How much commission would I get?"

I didn't let on. I answered him, "I told your representative here two and a half a head. Now if you want two and a half a head too, that'll be all right with me."

He nodded his head and said, "That's fine with me."

"All right, I'll go down and buy your mules tonight." It was Saturday night, and I added, "I'll bring my trucks along. There's one way you can do this and you won't get into any trouble. You price those mules to me at a hundred forty dollars apiece, and I'll take the mules and give you two and a half and the other fellow the same. We'll make it a hundred forty-five per mule to me."

He said, "All right, I'll do it."

I didn't look at him too close. "Now, I want a bill of sale for those mules. You have a bill of sale down there at the farm."

A job hauler who often worked for me had a semi truck that could haul the mules. There were other mules in there too, so I just took him and hustled down there, got my forty mules, and hauled them away. When I saw those mules I just couldn't wait till I got them into that truck and started down the road. It was a pretty good buy.

As we passed the governor I yelled, "See you at the bank in Des Moines Monday morning!"

He yelled back, "We don't want any check, but we'll see you there first thing Monday!"

I had a little account in Des Moines, money I thought I didn't need but that might come in handy someday. I drew this money out of the bank and paid for those mules. I paid that deal off in cash, took those mules to market, and netted a hundred dollars apiece profit, and nobody would ever know if I didn't tell it now.

How many such deals do you suppose there are, using up the tax money we all pay into our local, state, and federal governments? This governor was a man trusted by enough voters to land him in the highest office in the state. That was the way he treated the taxpayers who voted him into a good job, to look after their interests. He was willing to take two and a half dollars per mule, a total of one hundred dollars, instead of putting that money back into the public treasury. A pitiful amount for the chance he took of being found out. And he shielded his buddy for the same amount. You can't tell what people will do for a measly hundred dollars. If they had asked me two hundred dollars apiece for the county's mules, it would have been honest. All the other horse buyers had been trying to get those mules, but they just never pulled the right kind of string.

TWENTY-ONE

Sheepdogs and Sheepherders

People who have not worked on farms or with cattle or sheep don't realize how much the stock grower depends on his dog. A sheepdog is a really wonderful little animal. Now I think of it, not many of them are really big dogs. I've had some wonderful dogs. One was called Ted. He was one dog I could send from town to home with a bunch of sheep and not go with him—four miles. I was lambing ewes—I had three hundred ewes and lambs—and I had shut the ewes and lambs in the barn at night so they'd be warm. With all that body heat, the barn was as warm at night as it would be during the day. Then, too, some heat from the sun stayed in the barn after sunset. This kept me from losing some of the lambs. I had made the barn all tight, covered the cracks, and it was a good place for little young lambs.

When about two-thirds of these ewes had dropped their lambs the weather got rainy. I was sick. I'd been sick for some time, and one night I didn't shut the lambs up. The next morning I was just about tuckered out, had been up every night for a couple of weeks lambing ewes, so I didn't stay in the barn long, just went into the house and lay down. It started to rain some more. I'd been asleep probably about an hour or so, and the dog came to the door and let out a yip. He jumped right against the door, too. Mina went to the door, and old Ted went across the yard as hard as he could run, out toward the lambing barn. Mina said, "Lee, there's something wrong with the sheep. You'd better go out."

I went out there, and a ewe had had twin lambs, right out in the rain. Ted had got one of them and taken it into the barn, but with the

189

other the ewe was fighting him, and he couldn't get hold of it. When I got there I kept the ewe away and the dog picked the little lamb up and took it into the barn. Of course, I let the ewe follow them in. Now, just think of it! A dog had sense enough to take those two little lambs and put them in the barn out of the rain. It doesn't seem possible. The human animal doesn't always appreciate the canine animal.

Well, Ted guarded those sheep every night they were in the yard. There was a hole in the high board fence, not a big hole, and I didn't suppose any dog would ever try to go through there. And, carelessness on my part, I thought the little lambs wouldn't go out. But they did go out, one of them did, and three killer dogs came down there.

You know, if a dog once finds out he can kill a sheep, he's no good anymore. If you're smart, and it's your dog, you shoot him and save yourself and the neighbors trouble, and money, and sheep's lives. You'll never break that dog from chasing sheep.

Well, these three dogs came down there at night and tried to get through that hole in my fence. Ted went over the fence to fight them all at the same time. They tore him all to pieces. Oh, he was the worst-looking sight I'll ever see. The next morning when I went out there he was lying on the ground. They even tore his chest up, the guts were falling out of him, but he was still alive. I tried to sew him up, but I couldn't. He died about noon. I'd had trouble with dogs before, and I knew these were the same dogs. I trailed them right up to their owner's place, and I took my gun along with me.

I said, "Now, here's a shotgun. Those dogs of yours killed that good collie of mine, and I wouldn't have taken a thousand dollars for him. I want you to kill those dogs, or I'm going to kill them."

"Would it be all right if I killed the two older ones and kept the pup?"

"That'll be all right. I don't believe the pup would do a thing alone, but I want those two others." He took the gun and killed the other two.

That darn pup. Mina and I and the kids went to town one afternoon, and when we came home that pup was down there chasing the sheep in that little pasture. I grabbed the shotgun. I didn't want to kill the dog; I thought I'd just scare him. But I was a little too close to him. Boy, I shot him so full of lead! He went home.

His owner came right down. He says, "Did you shoot that dog?"

"Yes, I shot him. He was down there chasing my lambs, and I told you I was going to kill every dog that came onto my place. From now on no dog better come here, 'cause they ain't here for any good. As far as that dog's concerned, he'll get all right. I just peppered his face with fine bird shot."

Well, the pup stayed home after that. But I still marvel at old Ted, fighting until he lost his life there in the middle of the night, protecting those sheep, keeping those dogs from going through that hole, and no help coming until it was too late. He just laid down his life for his duty. What more noble animal could man hope for as a friend?

I needed a dog after Ted was gone. I got one from my grandsons. They had a collie, and she was an extra good dog. She had nine pups, and there was one pup in the litter that was the boss of them all. That's the one the boys wanted to keep. After Ted was killed I went over there. I had to have a dog right away. I asked my grandsons if they'd sell that dog.

No, they didn't want to sell it.

I said, "Sell it. You'd get money enough for it."

Yeah, they believed they would. They started thinking what they could do with the money. I gave them five dollars for this pup, but I had to promise they could come play with it whenever they wanted.

I took him home, and he didn't know anything. He was just a little bully. He'd bossed all the other pups, that's the reason I wanted him. But I had to take some sheep about three miles, so I made the pup go along. That poor pup. He'd get so tired he'd cry. He wanted me to pick him up and carry him like the boys used to do when he played with them, but I wouldn't do it. I just said, "Well, now, you come along. Come on."

I'd go ahead, and pretty soon he'd come toddling up. We got the sheep out along the road and, oh, I thought he'd give clear out. We drove the sheep all up to the gate, ready to put them in the pasture, and a cat jumped out of the grass! Away went the dog. Away went the sheep. Well, I got him, and I gave him a good tanning for that, which is something I'd never done before with my dogs. But I felt it best to train him right then and there that he must never chase anything while he was working sheep. Oh, he cried and he blubbered. I made him come and make up with me after I'd given him his tanning, then I put him in the car and took him home. From that day on he was a sheep dog. He'd guard them at night as well as in the daytime. He got big. That dog would weigh 140 to 150 pounds. He was stout. The kids would come over there, my grandsons, the boys I had bought him from. I told them they could come over and play with him. Well, they were over to my place about two-thirds of the time for a while. This pup was more fun for them than all the others. I fixed them a wagon, fixed them a sled, made a harness. They'd come over there to my place and pull the darndest loads with that dog, everything they could think of. That was just what he needed, because he developed his muscles, you know. Not only that, the kids always felt bad because they didn't have their dog. This way they felt they had him, and he had work to do. He was a dog who needed to work. Finally I began to call him Toughie. He was tough, and he didn't let anybody forget it, but in a nice way. He was with me all his life, a great dog, a noble dog.

When Toughie was grown but still young, I saw three dogs jump into the sheep pasture, and they were chasing the buck sheep. Toughie was at the house on the porch and he saw them. Away he went, way up the road to that pasture, running hard and me after him with a shotgun in my hand. He went over the fence in a great leap and threw one of those dogs clear across the fence, almost in one motion. Then he made for another dog, and while he was busy with that one the third dog got away. Toughie caught the one and got him inside the corner of the fence and darn near killed that dog. When he let loose, the dog left and none of them ever came back. Neither did the dog that was thrown over the fence.

Another night we heard a commotion out in the pasture. It was hot and I was tired. Sheep had been lying up around the trees and in the barn all day long. I thought I'd leave them out that night, let them cool off. Sheep will graze at night when it's cool and the days are hot. I heard a commotion out there and saw Toughie. There were three other dogs, and they all jumped onto him. They were after the sheep, and he was protecting them. Those three dogs were all fighting him, had him down. Oh, they were just chewing him up. I went out there and took the shotgun with me. Soon as I got one of them away from my dog, I let him have it. I killed him. Then I got another, but the third got away. Old Toughie was pretty sore for a few days. There wasn't any one dog he couldn't handle, but three dogs at a time was pretty hard. They tore him up pretty bad, but they didn't stop him. I thought of that little baby dog crying to get me to pick him up instead of him herding sheep. Old Toughie had come a long way. From then on, every night when the sheep went out he went with them.

Eventually Toughie got so old he couldn't get around very well. He'd try, but he got all stiffened up with arthritis. I had to get a new dog, and I hunted everyplace and I couldn't find one that would suit me. After Ted and Toughie and the others I'd had, I guess I was dog spoiled. Maybe I was dog-eared. I wanted a dog I could depend on, and I wouldn't settle for less.

One night a man was buying hogs in Adair. He phoned me and said, "There's a white dog here and he just wants to work. I believe he'd be a good dog for you."

I said, "Put a rope around his neck and I'll send my boy right up after him." So Ken went after this big white dog.

Well, that big old collie Toughie, he'd sit in the middle of the yard when I was handling sheep and he'd boss that new dog. He'd make a little bark, or get up and start someplace, and that dog would watch him all the time. Old Toughie made a first-class sheepdog out of that pup. I never trained him, never. He trained himself, with old Toughie looking right down his shirt collar. If that pup didn't do what Toughie wanted him to do, he got thrashed right then and there. And Old Toughie limped along, taking it easier and easier. One day he got hit by a truck and died a few hours later.

A man couldn't raise sheep without good sheepdogs. A good sheepdog's worth more to you than any horse that ever lived, if you're raising sheep. Herders usually take a bunch of dogs with them. They always take a female and let it have puppies. She trains the puppies herself. You never pick up one of those puppies. If you see one of them played out, never pick him up, or he'll not be any good as a sheepdog. I don't know what happens to them, but if he's beat out, worked out, tired, and you don't pick him up, he just shifts for himself. I've seen those pups come in so bone tired they could hardly wiggle. But that old dog would just thrash the dickens out of them if they didn't do just what she told them.

It is wonderful, you know, how the female trains them. Six or eight or ten puppies, she'd take them all out. She'd start taking about two of them. Eventually she'd have them all out there working sheep. They'd just walk around the sheep where they were grazing and they'd spread out over the pasture. Those dogs fan out to cover the entire herd while the grazing sheep seem not even to know what's happening or how they are being herded. At night you don't need a fence, the dogs are still out there.

One time, years ago, my brother Gene and I came to know there was a little dog living in a clump of trees in my pasture, a little wild dog. While I was working in the fields she'd come up within, oh, ten rods or so. Like that white stallion, she was afraid of people, but she was also attracted to them, or maybe she was curious to see what I was doing. Maybe she wanted to be there if I dug out some small animal she could use for food. She wanted to be close or she wouldn't have come close. She could have stayed hidden.

I knew that some way, sometime, she had taken a liking to me, but I never tried to get close to her. I imagine someone had abused her when she was a pup. She took that fear and turned it into hate for any man. If a stranger came near her, her hair would bristle up. Why she was there I never knew, just a wandering dog who kept out of sight better than most, I guess. But she came of her own accord and left the same way, when she was ready. We had known about her, my brother and I, for two or three years. In a way we tried to tame her, gentle her. Gene even tried to pet her once, but she didn't allow anyone that close, badly as she needed people.

Well, she came to the house one night and oh, it was storming. The wind was howling, the snow blowing. I heard her whining on the porch. I got up from my chair and opened the door. She popped right into the house. She was covered with ice and snow. I fixed a blanket for her and put her behind the stove. She just acted like she was wild, afraid of anybody and anything. Seemed she had never been near a house in her life, but she had sense enough to know what to do when trouble came. She was just heavy with pups, and the need to protect those pups was what made her come in.

After a while she got all warmed up and went to sleep. We all went to bed. The kids were making plans about whose dog she would be when she became gentled. Along toward morning I heard a little racket in the room. I got up to see what was going on, and here she was on the sofa—and she had three pups. I got her out of there and fixed her a box. She got in it and soon she had more pups. When I got up next morning she had five babies. I went out to do my chores and she up and followed me out, left her pups and went out there in the cold and mud. I was feeding a lot of sheep at that time, and some of them broke out of the pen and ran off. I was trying to cut them back. I cut back what I could of them, got them in the corner of the fence to let the other sheep through. You know, that little dog, she was guarding those sheep when I got back out there. She held them in the corner till I got back out.

After that she worked all the time. She'd leave her pups no matter what time of day I went out. If I was out there working, she'd leave her pups and she'd come out there to help me. The pups grew up, good pups. She taught them how to handle sheep. I sold four of them. Everybody who got one was happy to have it.

Well, that old dog, she stayed around till—oh, I was shipping sheep out so it must've been November or December. Helped me all the time, even after four of her five babies were gone. I never named her. I'd just whistle for her and she'd come. One day I was moving out a lot of sheep in some trucks and she wanted to go along, but I wouldn't let her. She'd been with me almost a year and I thought she ought to know she had a home. By the time the last truck left there wasn't a sheep on the place. I suppose she got lonesome, or thought her job was done. One day I missed her. She had gone away, and I never saw her again. Just because I took her in when she was in trouble, seemed like she wanted to pay back. She knew I needed her, but she needed me, too.

That was home to her for a while; maybe the only home she ever knew. They say home is where you can go when nobody else'll have you. Seems like that's how it was with that little dog. During all those months I never took a step but she'd be right there. This little dog and I had done each other a favor.

Basques are the most wonderful sheepherders in the world. None better than them. They come from a small region along the border between France and Spain, high up in the Pyrenees, but the men I knew were from the Spanish plains, where they had herded sheep since they were big enough to walk, I guess. They certainly knew all about it, must have been at it that long. You'll find them out on the West Coast, but not very far inland. Occasionally they'll come as far as Wyoming, but they're mostly in California and Washington. When I was working sheep I'd see a lot of them, and some came from southern Spain. That's sheep country, and they don't know anything but sheep. One man will take a bunch of sheep out, and they know their business, they take care of their animals. They come up into the mountains and go to work for a rancher and they save their money. They're a very thrifty kind of people and save what they can from a small wage until they have a herd of their own. They do their own shearing. If you hire a sheepherder, send him out with a thousand ewes, and the lambs will drop, and they'll all be taken care of. Come fall and they come in off the range, the sheep are all sheared and the lambs all tended to. Oh, they're great herders, experts.

Being out there alone with nothing but a bunch of sheep for all those months can sometimes get to a person, and there's always a lot of joking about the sheepherder. I'd like to tell you about a sheepman who came into Omaha from Casper, Wyoming. He drove his sheep into the market, and after selling them he was looking around for some stock to buy. I guess he went out with another shipment of feeder lambs, but he was in town two or three days that time. This man, kind of a recluse, was standing there like he was lost, and I guess when you've lived months on end with nothing but the bleating of a herd of sheep you can feel lost when you find you're all alone with humans and no bleating sheep.

Once he was just standing there by the fence with his sheep, and I walked up and said, "Are these your sheep?"

"No-o-o-o-o." Just like a sheep.

"Well, where do you come from?"

He said something, but I wasn't sure I knew just what.

"Are you a sheepherder?"

"Yes-s-s, I'm a she-e-e-pher-r-r-der."

I looked the sheep over, and I saw that one of them had a red ribbon around its neck. I said, "How did you come to put that red ribbon on that one?"

"Wel-l-l-l-l, she was-s-s sick with a cold when the she-e-e-pherder brought her-r-r in. If she could just have co-oo-oked . . ."

Sheepherders led a boring life in the old days. They often lived alone for months with nothing but that continual baaing. I've known herders to do some unusual things, such as darn socks. One I knew used to crochet. Made all kinds of lace, even window curtains for his wife. She was real proud of those. He'd walk along behind those sheep from sunup to sundown with nothing to do, so he'd crochet and crochet like mad, walk along, step by step. Pretty dirty lace by the time he'd finished, but his wife washed it up, and it came out as nice as what you see at the county fair.

A sheepherder is supposed to take a thousand ewes and a thousand lambs. That's one man's job, to take care of them—two thousand sheep, and every one's got two thousand bleats in him. I've heard about some herders going stark raving absolutely mad from the terrible boredom of all those months of baaing and no one to talk with. No man can stand more than whatever his own limit is.

They drive their sheep from place to place, you know, to feed and water them. If there's another herder, they're not going to argue, but they think it's wonderful if they can bring in a few more sheep than they went out with, and they steal each other's sheep. Then, after so many years of that they take to thinking everything's sheep. That herder just thinks like a sheep, talks like a sheep, sleeps like a sheep, and I guess he even eats sheep, especially when the wind blows. Eventually they've become more sheep than man, I guess. Seems that way when you try to talk to one of them.

After all that time with a herd of sheep, a man came back to his own kind unable to communicate with them sensibly. Lonesome? Why, sheepherders didn't get to see a man more than once a month. They couldn't read because of the nature of their work. Had to watch those dumb animals all the time, see they didn't stray. There's just that monotony and lonesomeness and so many sheep around them, and at night, you know, the herder's got to be right close with the wagon in case of wolves or some other danger to the sheep. They baa and they baa and lay themselves down all around the wagon. The sheepherder is king of his community, but he doesn't hear anything enlightening. A man gets so every word he says sounds just like those sheep.

Now the law has stopped all that. They won't let one man go out alone anymore, and they have radio and TV, so they don't lose track of who they are. It was an inhuman practice, it really was, all that time alone with a herd of sheep.

TWENTY-TWO

Slaughtering

You want to know about cattle? I
can tell you what happens every step of the way from the pasture to
the can, from the time they get off the train until they are ready for
people to eat. Now, with cattle, each one of those pens at the stockyard
is under a different commission man. The stock raiser can assign his
cattle to a commission man, who goes ahead and sells them to the
highest bidder. The packing houses have their buyers who ride among
the pens. When they see something they like, they put a bid on it.
When four or five bids have been made, the commission man sells the
lot. He usually sells to the highest bidder but sometimes to some other
bidder if the bids are satisfactory. If not, he can turn them all down.
After they are sold, the cattle go to the slaughterhouse.

Many of them don't go thinking, Man willed it, so we must go. When
they realize what this place is, they try to escape, but man already
knows this. He has built the fences too high. There is no hope for a
cow once in the train, no hope, yet they will fight for life, what little
they can, you might say, with the deck stacked against them.

Killing a cow is a nice clean operation. They run the cattle up into a
chute and take a small sledgehammer, a nice round ball peen hammer,
and hit the cattle in the curl, right on their forehead. That knocks them
unconscious, and they drop down into the skinning floor. They don't
cut the throat. A man stands there and stabs them through the breast,
chips the artery there next to the heart. They bleed the animal and
make blood meal out of the blood, for fertilizer. Then the carcasses are
cut in half, right down the spine, then into quarters, and then sold to
retail men. The quarters are cut in different ways to make different food

products. The hide goes to the tanners, the horns and hooves to the glue factory. The offal goes for tankage. They use everything but the bawl, and I think they use that nowadays. It must be what they make rock-and-roll music out of.

With those old canner cows, workers take their flesh off, peel it off in big chunks. The packers can that meat. All the fat has to come off; the lean is all that may be canned. Then they send the bones to the bonemeal factory, horns and hooves for glue and so on. There is some use for every part of the carcass.

A boner cow is just one grade better than a canner. Today a boner cow brings more money per pound than the fat cattle. A fat cow has too much waste on her. That tallow is worth only eight or ten cents a pound. Some of those boners are sold as high as twenty-three or twenty-four cents a pound. They bring more than a fat cow. If we have a meat shortage, as sometimes happens, prices run much higher.

Of course, those big, fat animals, the corn-fed ones, they go to the high-priced hotels and restaurants and all the other fancy places. That meat can sell for around five dollars a pound, before inflation, maybe more. You go into a restaurant and you pay all the way from ten to fifty dollars a plate for that meat. It can be eaten with a fork, it is such fine meat, like you might eat a piece of pumpkin pie. It has that corn flavor.

The old bulls make lots of foods; you'd be surprised. They buy those old bulls because they're muscular. Hardly any waste to an old bull at all. They have big muscles, the bigger they are the better the canners and processors like them. They butcher those bulls, then take the carcasses and put them into a vat of water and leave them there for twenty-four hours. The fibers of the meat take on a lot of weight that way. The stripped carcass, when it comes out of the vat, will weigh just about the same as the live animal did before all the insides and hide were taken away. That's the reason why they pay such a high price for these animals. There's no waste to a big bull, no waste at all.

The Chicago stockyards, like many another business, attracted great numbers of men specializing in certain activities. Many were champions in their own field, and one of these fields was beef dressing. I remember, from way back, Mike P. Mullins, the Champion Beef Dresser of the World. He had bills printed up that said

CHALLENGE: I, the undersigned, challenge any man to a beef dressing contest for a stake of $5,000.00, the contest to be governed by the American rules governing beef dressing contests. Signed: Mike P. Mullins

Now, to me a beef-dressing contest is much more interesting than a prizefight. The rules are stricter than those of any prizefight. First, there must be three judges, and they have to be thoroughly familiar with the rules and the butcher business, and be strictly honest. Second, cattle must weigh at least 1,400 pounds. Third, a man is allowed twenty-five minutes to dress a steer, and the judges call time when the front feet are off and the right hind leg is broken. The dresser calls time when he is finished. After he calls time he must stay a certain distance from the hide and the carcass until the judges have made their inspection. Mullins held this championship for maybe as long as twenty years.

Hogs are butchered in much the same way as cattle. The difference in butchering hogs is that they are hung up alive, by the hind legs, on an automatic carrier, a belt. Hogs go along this belt, and at every station there is a different process. They squeal when they are raised up. A man stands there with a long knife and sticks that blade in near the heart, like with the cattle, and they bleed. By the time pigs are bled out, they're ready for the tank of scalding water.

After the hog is scalded, they have scrapers that scrape all the bristles off. A hog is just covered with stiff hair, you know. That's all the covering they have. It's thin, too, compared to the coverings of other animals. After scraping, hogs look like they'd been to the barber for a shave. Then they go into the washing room, where they are sprayed with cold water. They are then slit down the underside, the insides are taken out of them and they just keep moving along the overhead belt they've been hanging from.

That conveyor belt never stops. Each man, at his own station, has a quick job to perform on every one of the hundreds and thousands of hogs that pass him daily, weekly, monthly, yearly. Everything is automatic. It is like one big machine, every part of which has to work, and lots of times one man could not do the work of some other man. But I have never seen a man miss a trick. They get every one of those hogs as he passes, but I don't know how they can do it. They stand there, every one of them, and do that same old thing over a thousand times, a thousand thousand times, as if they were not even human beings anymore. Sometimes I wonder if these men don't go berserk and murder their whole families at night, like they murder helpless animals all day. I wonder if they ever do that.

The old male of the hog species can also be used for food. You might think their flesh is too strong, but there are ways. Perhaps I ought not to tell this, it might hurt the packers. But it hadn't ought to. I'll tell it anyway.

Now you have a pretty good idea how your meat gets to your table. What I have just told you is a part of the canning and curing process for every piece of meat on the market today. This is the meat you buy to serve at your own table, to your own family.

When I was working for a packing company we had a goat, an old Judas goat. I saw those old Judas goats in many places where sheep were handled. He would lead the sheep up the ramp to the slaughter. It was quite a steep approach, a wide board with cleats nailed on so the sheep's feet wouldn't slip and make them fall off. We'd count those sheep off and Judas would take them, all crowded in the alley, must have been four or five hundred at a time. This old goat would open the gate, start up ahead, just a-bouncing along, and away would go the sheep, bouncing along like they were going to a picnic. Judas would wait until they all got in the slaughter pen, then he'd hike into his own pen until they were all in Hades, or wherever it is stupid little white sheep go when they die. Then back he'd come as hard as he could run for another bunch of sheep. I never had a man that ever got sheep into slaughter pens that easy. They wouldn't respond to a man like that.

You use practically the same methods for buying and selling one animal as you use for another. Almost the only difference is that there is a great deal of romance attached to horses that you don't find with other animals. Cattle, sheep, hogs, mules, all are strictly for making money, for feeding the human race. They are a liability until they pay their debt to their owner with their lives—with the exception, of course, of the milk cow. She usually pays with her life when she stops giving milk, or when her owner, as sometimes happens, doesn't need her milk any longer because he is not in the dairy business and has too many milk cows for the use of his family.

Killing is bad, always bad, but when you live with it as much as stockmen do, or as slaughterhouse workers do, and your money that you live on comes from the killing of animals, you get so you don't even think about it. It is like a logger who can cut down the most beautiful, the most aged, redwood tree and cuss it if he gets smacked by a limb as the tree falls. It is like the farmer who goes out and mows down fields of hay. He is killing that grass, those plants, for his own good, and so it is with the cattle, sheep, and other animals. Man kills them for his own gain, and if he thought of it that way he couldn't do it. But he has chosen this way to earn his livelihood, and he becomes immune to feeling about it, and after a while he is unconscious of it in a way. That's the way life is. In a war, soldiers don't feel guilty about killing other soldiers, the enemy, or about burning homes and making people live like they have to in a war. That is a way of life. The soldier is trained to kill and kill again.

The stockman believes he has a right to do as he pleases with the lives of these animals. Men used to feel that way about their wives and children. I don't know how it all happens, but I felt that way about the animals I handled. I guess slaveowners in the Old South felt that way about the people they considered to be their property. I've never heard anybody explain that. I was just one of those who lived with it.

The horse, however, is a romantic figure, always has been, and I believe as long as there are horses, they will seem romantic to the human beings who come in contact with them. In the first place, horses are superbly beautiful. They have spirit and intelligence, which holds the human being in awe. They are loyal to a point surpassed only by the dog. Then, too, they are pure pleasure. Did you ever hear of anyone having fun with a cow? Or a sheep? Oh, yes, there are bullfights, but they seem cruel to me. Oh, I saw one or two, but they didn't impress me. But how many pleasant hours can a person spend riding a horse? And they are intelligent. They can learn things other animals seem not to care about, and all these traits make them very good companions for man.

TWENTY-THREE

Changes

The Council Bluffs sale barn got to be a big operation, I was a whole lot busier. This was hard work, and there was never much time for a rest. I bought fifteen thousand horses in three years, and at the end of that time I had forty thousand dollars clear.

Running that sale barn took me all over the country. Sometimes I had to leave within a few hours and didn't know when I'd get back. After so many years of long hours seven days a week, nights too, it can get to you. Anybody can kill themselves with work, but when you've overdone, the smart thing to do is stop and get yourself back on your feet. I decided that time had come for me when the doctor got hold of me. He said, how could I live like that and expect to stay well?

He was right. I sold the sale barn.

I went out of the horse business at Council Bluffs. I sold all my horses. We used all tractors and heavy machinery on the farms by then. Horses were no longer any use. About all the old killer horses had been bought up, there weren't many of them anymore. I even sold my saddle horses. But a love of horses never left me. If I see a good horse even today, I want to go up and touch him, look him over.

Closing the barn was something I looked forward to. I had been tied to it too long to suit my taste. I called my men all in and had a picnic for them, a big feed. It turned out to be quite a sad affair. Some cried when I said farewell, wanted me to take another contract. But I was tired and had worked so hard I just had to quit. I had to be with my family.

I came home and rented some more land and started farming again, but really, I needed a rest. After one year of farming I decided to take an extended vacation. I had enough money for a while with my forty thousand dollars, and believe me, that would buy a lot more then than it will now. I always had Kenneth as a partner at home, and we raised good crops, fed lots of cattle and hogs. When I decided I had another idea, Ken always took over. He did it again when I needed a rest.

I turned the farming all over to Kenneth and started again to buy horses for the Chicago market. Harry McNair was still there, and we got along like we always did, just fine. Adair had a name for raising the best horses in Iowa, and the best buyers from the East always came to me before they looked anyplace else. I sold most of my horses before the autumn, and that gave me the advantage over other buyers. Well, I still hadn't regained my health, was still just dragging around so tired I could hardly keep going. At last I knew I just had to take that extended vacation. I had overworked myself to where a lot of people begin to be old. Not me. Only hard, killing work had finally caught up with me. I couldn't work at all, just had to lay around for a while.

My doctor said he thought if I'd go down into the hills of Arkansas, where people weren't so tense, perhaps that might help me. Anyway, that's the way I found the people of Arkansas. They just lived from day to day back in those hills, never in any hurry, and I guess that's the way a person ought to live, away from this rat race we have here in the Middle West, everybody on the go day and night. I found it really a relief to be there where people didn't worry their heads off, work their lives away.

I had quite an amusing experience in Arkansas. I stayed with a family who had nine boys and one girl and the old gentleman and his wife. There were so many of us that we kind of used up his pork supply, so the old man said we better butcher. I looked around, but I didn't see any hogs to butcher.

He said, "I'll get one. We'll go out and get one. Don't worry about that."

I had noticed—couldn't help but notice—and often wondered why they had so many dogs around. Thought maybe they just happened to. Anyway, the boys called the dogs.

The old man looked among that horde of dogs and said, "Where's

Old Bull?" His old bulldog was scarred from head to tail where he had fought those wild hogs. He would catch a hog and lie down, and no matter what they'd do to him, bat him or anything, they couldn't make him let loose. He'd hold that hog until the other dogs drove the other hogs away.

On top of this mountain the grass grows tall, something like the grass that grew here in Iowa when this was all prairie. The dogs didn't any more than hit that grass before it looked to me like the whole thing exploded. Razorback hogs were coming from every quarter of the globe. They were sure in there, squealing and grunting, and the dogs barking. You could see the dogs' tails waving above that long grass everywhere you'd look.

Then the dogs made for us, guess they were outnumbered. We made for the trees. As fast as it could happen I went up a tree. I climbed as far as I dared, but the darn tree started to bend. It bent pretty low, and I thought sure I was going to get dumped right into that squealing and snorting bunch of hogs. Well, I managed to keep out of reach, and the old bulldog, he went in and grabbed the hog they told him to get and laid down. Then the battle began between the dogs and the wild hogs. Soon you could see the dogs were too much; they chased the hogs away. I had a front-row seat, except I missed a few plays when I had to renew my grip on that sapling or climb back up when it bent low. Then the dust kind of died away, and we got down out of the trees and put a rope around the captured boar.

We drove that hog about five miles through the timber to the old man's place. We put him in a log pen that was a good eight feet high and about eight feet square, kept him there for a couple of weeks, feeding him corn. He wasn't in too bad a shape, but the old man thought he better be fed a while. Then we butchered him, and that was about as good meat as I ever ate. These pigs live on acorns and roots and other natural things, and they taste altogether different from those we raise in the Corn Belt.

That was enough hog hunting for me, even if the meat did taste so good. After a few weeks I got to feeling myself again and went home and got into the stock business again. Kenneth had filled in for me while I was away from home, like he always did.

All my life I listened while people talked about growing old. I know this is a thing people fear, but I still don't know what it is. I felt the same at eighty, ninety, a hundred, as I did when I was twenty, only I have a lot of experience behind me now to help me make better decisions, and because of my experience I understand better what to expect of the other fellow. I understand the markets better, I know what my animals will do and how much I must do for them if I want to make a profit. Only thing is, my darned legs don't do what I want them to, and my eyes don't see as well. But for that and a few little things, I'd be a much better man today than I ever was in my earlier times. So if your body holds up, it seems to me you've got it made. Of course, some people's minds don't hold up, but I haven't had that problem. Nothing wrong with my mind today, only I don't have enough to do to keep it busy.

As far as I can tell, the reasons for my long life are that I lived clean. I always aimed to make a fair deal because I wanted the other fellow to come to me again and again, to know I always made a fair deal. It does you no good to beat the other fellow, because if he doesn't come back, it'll count up on you, and in the end your business will fall off and you won't make it. When you hurt the other fellow, you hurt yourself more.

And take care of your own body. Some people can stand a lot more than others, but a body used to its full capacity is healthier than one that doesn't do much. And natural use is better than exercise, getting out and doing artificial things such as running too many miles and all that. Physical use is what flesh and bone bodies are made for. Now, I learned to chew tobacco before I was old enough to know it wasn't good for me, and I kept it up through my whole life. But I've never drunk much, except for a few times when I was busting from a kid to a man. I found it was a serious punishment for my body, and I didn't think that would pay off. When your body gives out, you're gone, or as good as gone. Maybe worse than gone if you're laid up for five or ten years. Better treat it right while it still is right if you want it to last. Man was not meant to be fragile, to last only sixty or seventy years. I still didn't feel like an old man when I was ninety-five, but my physical body held out quite a while after that, doing many things I'd always done, feeding sheep, calves, hogs, what-have-you with the best of them, and maybe trading a few horses, too. To say nothing of nursing three wives (but not simultaneously) through their last days and right into death itself.

My father died in 1933. At eighty-eight he had been sick or disabled for several years, a great care to my mother, and Amy was there too. My mother got to looking pretty worn and old herself during those years. My brother Gene had taken charge of the old home place several years before Dad died. Dad had bought a house in Adair for himself and Mother and Amy, and it was best for them, it made housework easier for my mother and a good home for them.

We all worried about Amy all the time. She was always on our minds, always there. You couldn't forget how much she needed help and what a problem she could be if something went wrong. What would happen to her when the folks were gone? Like so many brain-damaged persons, Amy didn't die young, she suffered on, suffered because she knew she couldn't do the things other people did because she was different. She had no choice. She suffered every moment of her life because of that, but we couldn't help her, we didn't know anything to do for her. Mother and Father worried about her all the time. So did all of us, her brothers and sisters, and even the grandchildren and her nieces and nephews. We all worried about her, but didn't any of our worrying do Amy any good, didn't change her life. Only Amy didn't worry. She couldn't know what a big problem she had, so, because she didn't know, it was a bigger problem for all of us.

Dad made his will long before he died. I wasn't too pleased with a great many of his ideas about what was fair, but I did like what he did for Amy. He left her 160 acres of land and eleven thousand dollars in cash for her keep. She was also to have the rent for her land. It was all to be a trust fund. He had it figured out so the interest from that money and the rent from the land would care for her as long as she lived. He also said the house in Adair should be Amy's home as long as she wanted to stay in it, even if we had to keep someone there to take care of her. But Amy still had our mother, Josephine, and except for a housekeeper, they didn't need any help.

My mother, Josephine Paine Daniels, died in April 1944 and we buried her there in Eureka Cemetery at Adair. She was eighty-eight years old. Of course, we all missed her very much, but now we, her children, had to solve Amy's problems as well as our own. Amy couldn't live there in the house Dad had left her, all alone. We looked around and hired a woman to stay with Amy. It seemed a pretty good arrangement. Amy never said much when mother was alive, and she didn't say much now.

Many times I've thought that Amy didn't worry, but who knows? Why else was she so determined that no strange person come near Mother? Why else would she throw things and hit Mother and Father? Why else would she glower all the time and so seldom smile? When I think back on it, I think Amy worried nearly all the time and never knew why she worried. Maybe worry is part of the terrible problem Amy had to live her long life with. Things just were never right with her. Who can say? She couldn't know what a big problem she was to us or to herself. Her whole world was a very sour, a very threatened world, an insecure place where anything could happen to her, for hadn't she fallen down that long staircase in her infancy, and hadn't everything been wrong for her ever since? And had life ever been a happy circumstance, ever, since that fall? And hadn't others been in better situations than she? There was nothing in Amy's life to make the living worth the trouble. Or did she, in a different way than we understood, find her small world a comfort in some way different than we could understand? Anyway, because we felt she didn't know, she was a problem to all of us now, more than ever before.

Amy was in good shape financially. Dad had done all he possibly could do for her in his will. Now, with both Dad and Mother gone, Amy's brothers—Gene, Arthur, and me—and her only living sister, Mattie, were left to care for her. It was all up to us, though we all had our own families. As long as Mother was there, it wasn't too much of a problem. Being older too, Amy was a bit more placid than she used to be. Now we brothers and sisters had to do all the planning for Amy, and we had a difference of opinion. It was a big problem finding someone to stay and keep house for Amy, but we finally did, and after we got the woman everything seemed to go along smooth for a while.

Then one day I was in town and someone came up to me and said,

"Lee, you don't know it, but that woman is abusing Amy." Well, if anything would make me mad, it was anyone picking on Amy, because she was helpless to take care of herself. She hadn't even known to tell any of us. I went down to the house and I just took that woman bodily and I threw her out of the house. When I found out what she'd done—well, it wasn't for any human being to do. She was less than a dog to me, and I couldn't tolerate having her around Amy another instant. If she had any brains at all, she'd not even think of doing such a thing. I just kicked her, furniture, clothes and all, out of Amy's house. I told her what I'd do to her if she ever stuck her head back in the door, too.

Again, there was Amy, alone. I knew of a lady who lived in the town who thought quite a lot of Amy, and I got her to go stay a few days until we could find a place for my sister. We finally found a place with a family living in Anita. They were awful good to her. She stayed there and lived with them all the rest of her life, and she lived to be eighty-four years old. The last years of her life she got to talking so I could understand her. The people she lived with had a daughter with a similar problem, and maybe that was companionship for the two afflicted women.

About this time Kenneth was in World War II. Esther had married Clifford Williams in August 1936. Opal had married Keith McDowall in November 1936. June married Ambrose Fagan but not until June 1946, so she still was home with Mina and me, which was a big help, because Mina didn't get around as well as she used to, and I had to run the farm. But June was working too, part of the time, after she finished high school.

Kenneth was away for four years. He went to Europe with the Ninth Armored Division, and he was all through those war-torn countries. Then the war ended and Mina and I couldn't wait for our only son to come home. I decided I'd retire when Ken got home, turn over the whole farm to him, and Mina and I would grow old together. He would be getting married soon anyway, we thought, and it would give him a chance to get a good start before he found a girl. He could raise his family right there on that farm, which had been so full of sandburs when I first bought it, but which had done so much for all of us.

Family life kept me close to home in the early 1950s. Mina wasn't well, and more and more had to be taken care of. Kenneth and I were farming pretty heavily at that time, so we had lots of outside work, but we had to keep up the housework, too. The girls helped as much as they could.

Kenneth and I were buying all the animals we could feed on the grain and hay we had raised, which was quite a lot of feed. My son was with me most of the time and we were busy keeping our feedlots full. Our capacity at home was three hundred cattle, four thousand lambs, and eight hundred hogs at the peak of our farm operations. We made a lot of money in this operation. Then bad luck struck as Mina's illness cost so much in emotions, cash, and time.

I had been married to Mina fifty years and three months when she died on September 19, 1956. We had raised a wonderful son and three fine daughters. The girls were all married to fine men and living near us. Mina and I were not happy to see Kenneth still a bachelor, but it looked like that was the way it was going to be. Of course, he would always have a home with us, and I supposed the farm would be his someday. We all expected that to happen.

Mina and I were married a long time. When our fiftieth anniversary arrived we had a big celebration, a golden wedding anniversary. My daughters got up a big party for us. I've never seen such a crowd in any place in Iowa as there was there at our place that day. People came from all over, hundreds of them. I had been in business so long, all over, everywhere, and they came from miles and miles around. At one time during our anniversary celebration eighty-five cars were parked in the south pasture outside our yard, and they kept coming and going all day. My grandsons did the parking, and they had cars parked clear down pretty near to June's place, half a mile away. It was a grand day for Mina and for me.

Mina's Aunt Prue and our friend Mrs. Clide Smith received the guests as they came into our house. The guests passed on through to Mina and me. Then they had cake and ice cream and other good things and visited and then went their way. Everybody had a gay time that day, and it was a real accomplishment to have a golden wedding anniversary. It was the greatest.

I have often felt glad this happened the way it did. Less than a month after our anniversary Aunt Prue died. Two months after the anniversary Mrs. Smith died. Mina died three months after the big day. You know, it was a lot better that way than if they had all been gone before it happened, and a few weeks more or less could have done that to us.

When Mina was gone I was pretty much alone. Kenneth was with me, and we tried being bachelors together. The girls, all with their own families, helped us all they could. Traveling around as I had, I figured I'd lived half of my life as a bachelor, more than half my life. But it was different from what I had now. I felt like the world had dropped out from under my feet. Time, they say, is a miracle healer. Nature has a way of softening the blows it deals as time passes. That is life. I had quit the horse business because Mina had been sickly for so long. I had to be home to take care of her, and Kenneth and I had a pretty big job with the farm and taking care of Mina too, but now we both would have been willing to do it all over again if it could have brought her back. During the past few years my brother Lewis had died of tuberculosis and my sister Abbie of strokes. In twelve years we had lost them, my mother, and now Mina. Our family, as families do, had gotten smaller on the older side and larger on the younger side. We boys all had families, some of us had grandchildren, but none of my sisters ever had any children.

Now to pick up the pieces and make a life after my wife had died.

Time is really a miracle healer, but waiting for time to heal is another matter. For a while it seems nothing in this world can help you and there's nothing you can do but mourn. That fifty years had been a long time, but Kenneth and I had our animals to take care of, so we were busy, and that helped the time to pass. After a while I got to keeping company with a woman I met, and then another one. Seemed if I couldn't get Mina back, maybe I could find someone to kind of take her place. There must be other good women in the world, I thought, and it just didn't work out for Ken and me to go it alone.

Right after Mina's death there had been a letter from someone I hadn't thought of in years. At the time I didn't think much about it, had other things on my mind. It was from little Lena Bennett, who had married Frank Patrick because her father thought I was too tough to court his little girl. Lena was out in Washington State. Frank was dead, their only son had died as a young man, and Lena and her daughter were both nurses. Well, I answered the letter just like I would anybody's letter. Nice of her to write, nice to hear from her, but I didn't think any more about it. We kept writing for quite a while. I had plenty of lady friends after a while, and it was just fun to hear from Lena now and then.

I got engaged to one woman who had a son, and Kenneth didn't like that at all. He didn't like that son, said if I married that woman he'd leave for good. I got to thinking about it, and that wasn't just the right thing to do, it seemed. Kenneth had to have a home. He shouldn't be out in the world all alone with no home of his own. Besides, I didn't think I could stand living with that other son myself. Then I kept getting more and more letters from Lena Bennett, and pretty soon I decided I wasn't so sure I wanted to be engaged to that other woman. I decided I'd be as cross and tough with that overgrown baby of hers as I knew how to be. I insisted on having my way about everything, and finally we had our last differences. I took them home from a trip we had made to Colorado, and she broke it off. I felt like jumping in the air and throwing my hat up, but I managed not to until I got out of their sight. I was afraid she'd try to sue me for breach of promise if I broke it off. She might've, too. I knew that I had something else to do with the rest of my life, and I thought I knew what it was, but I couldn't say so for a while yet.

TWENTY-FOUR

Little Lena Bennett

The last few letters I'd had from Lena, she had said she was having some kind of trouble, and the doctor had set her up to go to the hospital for a little surgery. Well, it was supposed to be just a small thing, but you never know when you go into a hospital. All kinds of things can happen that you don't expect. I decided I'd go out to Washington State to see Lena, and before long she was opening her front door and there I was in my Sunday best, hat in hand. She sure looked good. We had real fun getting acquainted all over again after more than fifty years. Lena was always the cutest little thing I ever saw, and she hadn't changed—any more than I had. We still looked good to each other, we sure did. There wasn't any end to the visiting, and later the things we had to say to each other, experiences shared long after the happening and new experiences shared together. We knew we wouldn't ever have time to get finished with all the things in life that we needed to share. There wasn't anything left to do but get married, and we did that on the second day of February 1958 at San Gabriel, California. Lena's sister Belva and her husband stood up with us.

Well, life was sure rosy after Lena and I got married. My only worry was how Lena and Kenneth would get along. If Kenneth had a family and moved off alone, that wouldn't be so bad, but if he was alone and felt like he didn't belong, or wasn't wanted, then I'd feel real bad about that. I thought about this a lot. Maybe, I thought, I shouldn't have been in such a hurry to marry Lena. Maybe she and Kenneth should have met first and we should have taken more time, but I knew I'd have married Lena in the end, no matter what. Only thing bad about that was now it seemed I should have gone after her back when we were kids, no matter what her daddy said.

Lena had one daughter, who was married and running a rest home with her husband. She also had a sort of foster daughter, Daisy Melick. Lena had nursed Daisy's mother in her last illness, and Mrs. Melick had been worried about Daisy after she found out she wasn't going to get well. She and Lena had made an arrangement that Lena would act as Daisy's mother, or foster mother. They got along fine, and Daisy and I got along fine.

Well, those first months Lena and I traveled, and we lived in her house in Riverside, California. Didn't make any difference where we were; the world was a more perfect place than it had ever been before for both of us, and we had a ball wherever we were. Finally I decided to go back to my farm for the summer.

Lena really seemed to look forward to returning to Adair. She hadn't been there since she was a young bride and had left with Frank Patrick. We drove back about mid-April, saw the sights along the way, and all the time I kept thinking how to handle this problem of Lena and Kenneth. Well, I didn't need to have worried. They just took one look at each other and fell into each other's arms. He always called her Mom, and she always called him Son. Seemed he kind of took the place of that son she had lost, and he felt about her that she kind of filled the empty place that had been there since Mina went away. He maybe had missed Mina more than he realized, though we both missed her a lot, that I know. I felt a lot better, didn't have to worry about Lena and Ken anymore. That was sure good to see.

Still Kenneth felt left out, too. He wished he could find a wife but never seemed to meet the right girl. It just didn't work out for him. He said he felt like a fifth wheel.

Lena and I decided to stay in Iowa that winter. She was having a great time meeting all the people she had known so long ago and visiting with them, getting our house straightened out after two old bachelors had spent so much time there alone. Believe me, she brightened things up there pretty fast. Kenneth and I got our feed in and bought up our feeders for the year, and then one day we went to the airport to meet Lena's friend and foster daughter, Daisy Melick. We made quite a foursome. Wasn't long till we could see Kenneth and Daisy just seemed to have been made for each other. They were married on September 7, 1959.

They didn't even need to buy a home for themselves, because now I knew Ken would stay right there on the farm and benefit from all the hard work we had both put into it, especially my getting rid of those blasted sandburs. Besides, now Lena and I were free to come and go as we liked between my farm in Iowa and her home in California. We both liked to go places and do things. I'd retire and just be at the farm during the busy season when Kenneth needed me, and he'd be free to do as he pleased with the farm. We all thought how this was about the best arrangement we could have hoped for. The only thing wrong with Ken and Daisy's marriage was, they were so late in finding each other they couldn't have any children. They both wished they had even just one or two children, and I wished they did too. Somehow, Ken having always been such a fine son, I thought it wasn't quite right for him not to have a complete family.

A nephew of mine came up to my place one morning and said, "We're going to sell Amy's farm."

I said, "Oh, no, you're not. You're not going to sell Amy's farm. That never can be sold so long as Amy lives. You better look at your granddad's will. That farm can't be sold while Amy is alive."

My youngest brother and I, we always saw things the same, and we stuck together. I went to see him and we went to Greenfield and hired a lawyer and brought this thing to trial. We found they had overdrawn Amy's bank account. The banker got kind of leery about it and asked me what had happened. He wanted to know where the money would come from to pay that overdraft. He had told them they'd have to sell Amy's land to make up that deficit, to pay off the bank. As it came out, they either had to pay back all the money which had disappeared or go to prison. This included one of my sisters, one of my brothers, the auditor of the estate, and the judge who had allowed the sale, because they had spent that money. My younger brother and I talked it over, and he didn't want to go ahead with it, but I didn't care. If I hadn't just happened to find out about that, Amy's property would have all been gone. I thought they needed punishment. I thought it over for a few days. My other brother was sickly. He had been kicked in the leg by a steer and was just in bad shape, with a nasty sore there. We finally got it settled without anybody going to prison.

Amy lived through it all not knowing that her support was threatened by the very ones she trusted most. She wouldn't know what you were talking about if you tried to tell her. I couldn't say she was happy. Amy never seemed happy, but she was unaware of anything unusual. It was my own need to see that she was the same that caused me to go see her several times during all this fracas over her money and her property. I visited her a bit more than usual.

One thing I must tell you about Amy. After Lena and I were married, we went to see Amy. I knew she had not seen Lena since we were all kids around age twenty.

I asked Amy, "Do you know this girl?"

Amy nodded her head and said, "Yes."

I waited a minute and then asked, "Who is she?"

Amy answered softly, with a smile, "Lee's girl."

After I married Lena we lived in California quite a lot. The farm got to be too much for Kenneth to do all the work, so we dissolved our partnership, and Ken and Daisy bought a big farm out west of Atlantic. They had adopted two beautiful little kids, Cecelia and Paul, and by now the kids had got pretty big. Ken milked fifteen or twenty dairy cows and raised corn. Cecilia was a great tractor operator; she could drive one as well as most men—a cultivator too, and other big farm machinery. They were great kids, those two.

Later on, Daisy began to feel sick, and she never seemed to get better. Ken and the kids had to do most of the housework and wait on Daisy. Her heart got worse and worse, and the farm and the kids and all were too much for Ken. Finally the kids left home, and Ken sold the farm and moved to Atlantic. Daisy was in the hospital while he was moving. She got home to see her new house, and in a day or two she was back in the hospital, where she died on March 3, 1971. All this was pretty rough on Kenneth, and he made up his mind he'd had enough of farming on his own. He took a job and was very happy with his new arrangement for several years. Later he retired, and he still lives in his home in Atlantic.

By this time all my family had died, brothers all gone, only Mattie and me left. Her husband, Fletcher Hunt, was dead, and they had never had any children. Lena was sick about half the time and recuperating the other half. We still spent most of our winters in California in her house and most of our summers in Iowa, and I raised a garden in both places. I fed stock in Iowa—usually sheep, but pigs too—and raised calves and sheep in California. We were as happy as two birds in a tree.

Lena and I were living all alone on my farm. I was feeding pigs and a few lambs. A lamb will never hurt you, no way he can but to butt you, and it wouldn't hurt if he did. They're not vicious, not dangerous. But a hog can kill a man, and will. I never had much trouble with hogs, at least until one day when I went out to the pen to find out why a pig was squealing so much. Boy, he was setting it up. He had got out of the pen, couldn't find his way back to his pals. I caught him, and fool that I was, I opened the gate and took him back into the pen. I could as well have hoisted him over the fence, but didn't think. I should've known better. The gate opened into the pen and I never thought, just let it swing shut.

Those old sows charged me and, trying to move fast enough to get away from them, my foot slipped. Down I went in that slimy mud, and one old sow took after me. I couldn't quite make it to the fence, didn't dare run or they'd all be after me. I grabbed a piece of board lying there on the ground and swung it, backed against the fence. I knew I was no match for them. You might think a sow is fat and slow. Well, you just wait until she's mad. Then she can be quicker than any other animal I ever had to calculate. I didn't know, maybe they thought I had hurt that pig.

Anyway, I couldn't get up on the fence, couldn't get out of their way. I kept my back against it though, so they couldn't get behind me. I swung that broken board at them with both hands, hard as I could. I aimed to kill. Every time I hit a hog, that board splintered. My weapon wasn't going to last very long. Must have been fifteen, twenty hogs ganged up, pushing me against that fence, grunting, squealing, rooting their old flat noses at me, with the slime dripping off their nostrils. I thought I was gone. I thought I'd sooner or later beat my club to pieces or fall in that slick mud and I wouldn't be able to make my getaway. All I could do was keep hitting as long as my old board would last. Those old sows were at bay in their half circle, just out of reach on both sides of me as far as the fence would allow, and they really set up a row. I thought, Lee, for all the dangerous animals you've handled all these years, looks like you're gonna be done in by a bunch of old sows. I could see my family picking up my bare bones, but I kept on fighting.

Suddenly about half of those hogs took off toward the gate. I thought maybe they'd knocked the fence down over there. I didn't dare take my eyes from that vicious mob, but in the corner of my eye I could tell somebody was there, doing something. I kept on fighting—had to, or I'd have been dead in a second. Then I knew it was Keith. He had a board bigger than mine and he was beating away at those crazed hogs. There was Opal beside him and she was beating hogs too. We all beat pigs, beat pigs to keep them from getting us. Beat for our lives. We were all fighting pigs, whaling them alongside the head, hitting them across the nose. You know, that hurts a pig worse than anything else. If you're ever attacked by a pig, or want to get him where he belongs when he's in your garden, just whack him across the snout. It sends him squealing, and he won't be back for a while. But they're stubborn, and they thought they had us. We beat them back. We kept edging toward the gate. Opal and Keith covered me while I got out, then they slid out too, beating all the way. Nothing like getting away from those hogs.

Well, that sure put an end to my feeding hogs, and I'll tell you one thing, it didn't take me long to send them to slaughter. One bit of advice I'll never forget: never go into a pigpen when there's nobody else around.

Lena was feeling pretty good in 1967, and we went back to the old farm in April and stayed until

November. I raised several crops that year. I had soybeans, oats, rye, corn, alfalfa, calves, beef, goats, everything you could think of, and a nice garden right near the kitchen door, which furnished a lot of our food that summer. The girls brought over jars of food they had canned, and we always had a stock of food in the cyclone cellar right outside the kitchen door.

That was the summer Helen Herrick and her son came to visit us, and when I got started telling tales just for fun she said I ought to write a book. Well, I had thought about writing a book, and it would be fun, but I knew I'd never do it. But she kept after me, and she kept turning on that tape recorder every time I'd tell a story. She said she'd help me write it, and in the end, here it is. Took a lot longer to do it than I thought. Whether I was in Iowa or California, seemed like whenever she could Helen would find me and we'd work on this book again.

California is a place I don't like at all, never liked it from the beginning, but I lived there a lot of the time because Lena was sick so much, and it seemed best for her. I'll take Iowa every time. I used to be curious to know what California was like. Now that I have lived there many years, I know it is all artificial. Everything there is artificial. I love nature, I don't want anything artificial. You can make an artificial flower as pretty as any flower that ever grew, but it's not even a flower to me. Nowadays you see artificial flowers, trees, plants everywhere, perfect as the real thing, it seems like. Sometimes you even touch one to be sure, but still it is not a flower or a plant. I understand these plastic things are made in Japan, mostly, but it makes no difference where they are made. What's important is what they cheat us out of, and they cheat us out of reality.

I don't like artificial things, and I don't like California, because the whole thing seems artificial to me—*is* artificial. People often don't act like people but like something man was never meant to be. All I feel when I go to California is a strong urge, which I sometimes can hardly control, to get away from the place. If I could manage that way, I'd never go back to that state. But I know there must be other places as bad, or worse.

Lena was sick a lot during the 1960s, so we were back and forth, Iowa to California and back, Belva took care of her and I took care of her and my farm. Wasn't easy for any of us, but it had to be that way. I couldn't leave my wife, and I couldn't leave my farm unattended, though Ambrose and June lived nearby and kept an eye on it. So we got along as best we could; that's all a body can do sometimes. In 1967 we were in Iowa, but Lena wasn't well. Several times she got into long sick spells, and I thought I was going to lose my girl, but she liked the life we had and she'd come back again and again. We were almost the same sweethearts we might have been when we were kids, if her dad hadn't stopped everything. Sometimes Belva would come out to Iowa and stay for several months helping take care of Lena.

Once when we were living in River-side, California, where Lena and Belva both had homes, I went to trading with little calves. There were so many dairies there, I got the idea of buying the day-old calves and feeding them until they got to be stalker age, old enough to be out in the pasture on their own. I rented a big yard about a mile from Lena's house. I went to a dairy and contracted to take all the calves that man's cows produced when they were one day old. That way I got them cheaper than if I'd bought each one separately, and he didn't have the problem of trying to find a place for each calf. You know, the dairyman wants to get the calf away from the cow as soon as possible so all the milk will go to the market. If a cow dries up, stops giving milk, you cannot get her to give milk again until she has another calf. That's the only way to get more milk out of that cow.

Now, I supposed that those cows would string along, just a few producing calves at a time, and that's the way they did—for a while. Then they got to coming in so fast I couldn't take care of so many calves. I'd just have to load them up and take them to a sale, sell them for whatever I could get for them. Then they began to get sick. They were too young to be taken from their mothers; they could not be healthy if taken so soon. Also, it seems that the cows don't get enough exercise, so the calves don't have much vitality.

For a while I was getting along with them all right, then some disease got into them and I thought I was going to lose them all. I knew a pretty smart Mexican, knew that he knew a lot about cattle. I wanted to ask him what to do with my calves, but he couldn't talk to me and I couldn't talk to him, we didn't speak the same language. So I went to his boss and talked with him. The boss went out and asked that Spanish man what he does with his feeder calves. He had charge of all the calves and raised all the heifers. Of course, the little bulls were all sold off for veal. The Spanish man said, "Bottle, this way, this way, this way." I knew he meant that he was giving his calves Pepto Bismol. Well, I got them all straightened up.

Later I was over at the sale yards one day and was talking about the problem, and a man said to feed them goat's milk. Lena had to have goat's milk, so I was already milking one goat, but I brought home five more and fed their milk to the calves. Then I got to putting the calves to these goats and letting them do their own milking. Say, that was the best plan yet.

Many calf buyers wouldn't buy the big calves from the dairies because they were afraid the calf had been hurt during the birth process. This doesn't happen, but these calves don't look like they are worth anything because they're so wobbly. I thought, Well now, I'll just try them; I'll get some of those big calves and put them on a goat. I got two or three of those great big wobbly calves and put them on a couple of little nanny goats that wouldn't weigh over sixty or seventy pounds apiece. The calves sucked those goats for about six weeks, and you have never seen fatter, nicer calves in your life. That's all they had, goat's milk. It would seem funny, a great big calf sucking that little bit of a goat. Before long they were bigger than the goats.

The way to do this, if you wanted to go into the business, would be to fix a chute to put the goats up high enough off the ground, and then fix it so the calves couldn't butt them—you know, a calf thinks he hasn't eaten until he has butted the cow enough. Sometimes he could knock a man down. The goats are too small for this. Get your goats into the chute, then turn the calves in, and it wouldn't make any difference which goat they got onto. I never got around to that, I got sick of the calf deal. But that's the way to raise calves—put them on a goat. The milk is very rich and apparently it agrees with calves. They didn't like cow's milk after being on goat's milk.

I had a yard at Riverside, back of my house, and I also had a feed yard where I was feeding calves. That's where I met one dog I couldn't control, the only dog I ever met that I couldn't handle. A neighbor just across the alley had a big German shepherd, and that dog didn't have any brains at all. I went over to my feed yard to feed my calves, across the street on a couple of vacant lots. When I went to get into my car, this dog jumped over the fence and made for me, jumped right for my throat. I grabbed ahold of him and held him away. Then he bit me on the arm. I got loose from him, but I couldn't get into my car. He wouldn't let me into my own car. I just stood there and kicked at him and did everything I could to make him leave me alone. The more I fought, the worse he was. Finally the woman who owned him came to the door. She hollered at the dog, he turned his head, and I got into my car. You know, I was afraid to go back there. I wouldn't go near the place.

I said to the owner of the feed yard I was renting, "George, you either tell them to keep that dog locked up or I'm gonna turn this feedlot back to you. I won't come over here again. I don't want to get torn up. Look at these teeth marks on my arm where that dog bit me."

George went over and told the owner he'd kill that dog if he ever came over that fence again. Oh, yes, they'd keep the dog chained, they didn't want me to do anything about it. Wasn't more than a day or two until the dog attacked a man down the road, got him down and pretty near killed him. He didn't have any brains at all, he was crazy. The owners thought he had hydrophobia and all that, but he didn't; he was just one of those mean dogs with no brains, maybe not much training.

Aside from that one I can handle about any kind of dog. I still get tickled when I think about the experience I had with a dog up in Little Denmark. That's a place in northwest Iowa where a lot of Danish people settled a good many years back. A man had this dog chained to his doghouse, had a log chain on him. Boy, that was a big brute of a thing and oh, he was just a-jumping against that chain, and every time he'd jump, that doghouse would move.

I said to the Dane, "What in the world do you keep a dog like that for?"

"Oh, I turn him loose at night. By golly, nobody come around here at night, not anymore."

I said, "Oh, I don't think he's so bad. He just wants somebody to pay attention to him."

"Vell, I betcha ten dollars you can't go up dere."

"All right. I'll betcha ten dollars I *can* go up there, and I'll betcha that doggone dog won't bite me, either."

"By golly, I don't tink so."

We put up the money and I walked up to the dog. I didn't seem to pay any attention to the dog, and he just jumping against that chain and bow-wowing and bow-wowing. I just walked up and took him by the ear. I pulled his ear a little bit, and he sat down and licked my hand.

That Dane said, "Gott tam him, I'll kill him."

I got up to that dog about as easy as I ever did to any animal.

TWENTY-FIVE

Belva, and a Bit of Advice

There came a year when Lena didn't want to come back to Iowa for the summer and I just couldn't stand any more of California. Finally I got her to come back, and got a housekeeper to be with her days so I could farm. I took care of her nights and sometimes seemed like I'd be up half a dozen times. I could get pretty tired, too, some days, with all that responsibility. Then we stayed in Iowa all winter. We had bad storms, very bad. We were cooped up in our house with snowdrifts ten feet high, and our housekeeper couldn't get to our house for days and days. I thought it would be the end of Lena right there. But, you know, after about three weeks of that kind of weather Lena was better than she'd been in a long time. We'd just had to do for ourselves, and besides, I'd had to feed some of the stock Ambrose had there because he couldn't get to my barns from his farm half a mile away, a sure enough bad winter. Well, Lena got better, and when the storms let up and we got our roads shoveled out, she was in great shape. It was always good to see her come out of those sick spells.

We had stayed on the farm that summer, fall, and winter, and I had raised feeder lambs, but I didn't do much more except garden and take care of Lena. Winter came and we were alone again, but not snowed in. Christmas came and went, and we had the usual great time with family, gifts and all. It was a great season.

One day in January 1972 we decided to drive in to Adair for some little things. The weather was cold and the yard where I kept the car was muddy. The ground was thawed a little in midday by a tired-looking sun. I was helping Lena into the car and she slipped. I grabbed at her to keep her from falling. Suddenly I knew something was wrong, and later I found out that I had ruptured myself lifting her to get her safely into the car. Now, wasn't that a mess? I had to go to the hospital right away for surgery.

I got a woman to stay with Lena for a week or so, but the day after I left she had to be taken to the rest home. She wasn't well. Even Kenneth couldn't cheer her up. She wouldn't eat, even for Ken. I had my surgery, but Lena got worse. I had to check myself out of the hospital and go home to her, and the next day my little girl left me. She just couldn't stay any longer. She was eighty-six years old, and she died on January 17, 1972. We buried Lena in the little cemetery here in Adair beside Mina and not far from Hattie and all the rest of the family. Of course, Lena and Frank Patrick had plans that she would be buried beside him, but with me sick and the dead of winter and all that I couldn't see going clear out there to western Nebraska for her funeral, just couldn't do it. Besides, I couldn't take care of her grave if she was out there. None of our family's there anymore.

Those months after Lena's death were the most lonesome of my life. I didn't have anything left to live for, and now I realize that the depression from my surgery, not having proper care, and checking out of the hospital too early, all that didn't help at all. I was just no good to myself or to anybody else. I went and bought some sheep and spent the following summer feeding them. Guess that's all that held me together. Then I went back out to Riverside to my sister-in-law's home and spent the winter there. Got there in time for my ninetieth birthday. That was quite a day. I got letters of congratulation from a great number of friends, and among them were letters from the governors of Iowa and California, congratulating me on my reaching the age of ninety years. I had a great birthday party with lots of friends. Well, it was pretty nice to have reached the age of ninety years. I don't know why the Lord has been so good as to leave me and take so many younger people away from this life he gives us.

Lena's death left me more alone than I'd ever been in my life. I couldn't live in my little farmhouse; that was no good. I spent as much time as I could with Belva after she had strokes and couldn't care for herself, but she wouldn't marry me, and I'd get depressed and blue about that and go back home to Iowa and feed a few more sheep and grow another garden. Then my three girls and Kenneth thought I ought to get rid of my farm and go live with him, so I did that. Kenneth was real good to me. I couldn't ask for any better, but he had to work, and that left me home alone. I had some good neighbors, but it wasn't right to bother them too much. So here I sat with my dreams of the past, and I wondered why I hadn't made more of my chances when I had the opportunity. Oh, well, what is the use crying over spilt milk?

I spent a week with Opal and Keith on their farm, a great week. Maybe I was never meant to live in town; I regretted that I had sold my farm even though I wasn't able to do the work anymore. We went to a fancy horse show Saturday night and I really enjoyed it. Such beautiful horses. Made me think of the time when I had the same kind of animals long ago, so many years ago, like so many other things. I couldn't seem to get used to just living from day to day. I knew the only thing I was good for was to help someone that needs help.

After selling my home I just didn't feel worthwhile anymore. I thought if I ever got sick I'd have to go to some home, and you always read about fire in some of those homes and elderly people being burned to death. That wasn't for me. It wasn't for Belva, either. When I was at her house we often talked about that. We weren't either of us going to be put in a home. Then Belva's daughter and her husband thought Belva should live with them. I was in Atlantic, living with Ken, but if she wasn't going to marry me, it seemed she had better live with her family. That was all she could do unless she went to a home.

She went, and they were awful good to her, just took great care of her. But it turned out Belva didn't like being in somebody else's home any more than I did. After she'd been with her daughter for a while, she just got as lonesome and blue as I'd been. One day she phoned me, in about September 1975, and she was crying. Well, that was it. I hopped a plane and arrived in Riverside shortly after that phone call. I had to present my case all over again, and she accepted!

We were married on October 12, 1975, in the little house Bert Carrigan, Belva's first husband, and I had built for them years ago. I was married just sixteen days before my ninety-third birthday! Oh, I don't know what people thought of us. I never really cared; we did it anyway. Lots of Belva's grandchildren and great-grandchildren were present. We had the minister, we had flowers, a ring, a cake—a great big cake—we had everything, and now we could live there in that little house together and I could take care of her, and it was nobody's business! Nobody was going to snoop around and gossip, there was nothing they could talk about, and we were able to get along together.

Belva was a left-handed person all her life, but a stroke paralyzed her entire left side. She could only manage a few things with her right hand and foot. She could walk with a special cane-like walker. She mostly dressed herself and fed herself. She could get from her bed to the couch and the table without help, but she could never cook, wash dishes, and do all that for herself.

But I could. I'm the best housekeeper you ever saw. Why, after seventy or more years wrangling horses and men, think I can't cook as good a meal as anybody? And run the automatic washer, wash the dishes, clean the floor, make the beds? What else? Well, I grew a garden each year, sold off the extra produce, fed a few lambs each spring and any other time I wanted. I had them butchered and put up for our own use, and sometimes I sold one and had it butchered for the use of the buyers.

We rented Belva's little house next door to some very fine people who looked in on us every day or so, and we could call them anytime we needed help. We just had a great life, better than most folks have. We had plenty of money, plenty of food, and we kept busy and happy. I wish more people had it as good as we did. Our friends came often. We had a great thing going, and I guessed I could live another ten years, twenty, whatever the good Lord wants me to have, and be grateful for it all.

Yes, Belva and I did just fine after our marriage, and we calmed down a few people who were shocked at our marriage. I guess they just didn't understand how it is for two elderly people who are used to doing what people do—work, travel, and all that—and suddenly, it seems, finding themselves doing less and less, and then strokes or some other curse falls on them and they are left high and dry, like a seagull on a post, with none of the things they used to be involved with. But we made it.

We took care of ourselves with very little help, and nobody had to worry about us. The man next door had a stroke and a heart attack and died, so his wife had to move away—a young couple, too, in their fifties, but that's life, the way it sometimes happens. Then Ken used to come out from Atlantic. He would sometimes stay a week or two, or more. He'd see we got to be in good shape again. Sometimes Helen Herrick came with her son Tim, and they'd help us, and we'd have a ball, but they had their own lives to live. When they'd go we were sorry to see them leave, but that's life, too. My daughters stopped now and then when they could, and neighbors dropped in. But Belva kept getting worse, and sometimes she had to be in the hospital for a few days and then for a week or so. Sometimes it did her more harm than good, and I'd have to get her all straightened out again after she'd been there.

I was all alone when Belva got real bad, and it didn't seem anybody could help me except the neighbors, and they did what they could. By April 1979 I knew she wouldn't last very long. I brought her home to die, and I nursed her almost by myself those last few days. I couldn't get any help. I did all that could be done for her, and finally on April 22, 1979, she was gone. We buried her beside her first husband.

Kenneth said that if I wanted it, I had a home with him. That was sure good to hear, and at last I was ready to go be somebody else's problem, though Kenneth always said I was no problem to him. So that's where I've been all these years, shaky hands, failing eyesight and hearing, and all.

We celebrated my one-hundredth birthday in 1982. Hundreds of people—family, friends, even some I'd never heard of—came to wish me a happy birthday and to help eat all the cakes I had, and drink the punch. It was a great day, and when they were all gone, I was beat, and I think Kenneth was too. But he says he's not tired of his job looking after me, so here is where I'll be as long as I need bed and board on this earth, and nobody could give me better care than Kenneth does.

Times change, you know, and man changes a lot too, changes the way he does things. Every day he has an idea, and usually he puts it to work. Well, after he's done that for a few years, you look what he's done and it doesn't even seem like the same thing. Why, there I was, shipping cattle from Adair, Iowa, to the stockyards in Chicago, riding along on those trains night and day almost as if I was some old cow myself, living in that caboose, eating what I could get at a restaurant. I'd never have guessed what they're doing now, neither would you.

Why, I talked to a man the other day, and he said now they ship cattle by airplane. That was one up on me. I talked with him quite a while, and he said they have sections of aluminum fence that they just connect together to make a pen. Use a regular passenger plane, just take out the seats and put in those pens. Darndest thing I ever heard of. They ship cattle all over the world like that—other animals too, I guess. Seems like some of the foreign countries have decided to give each child a cup of milk a day, so they're buying up cows, mostly Holsteins, and milking them. Don't know why they don't use some of those Brahmas they have over there.

I asked him more about it, and he said cattle have to take more tests than humans do before they can go flying off somewhere else. Then they put five or six in the little pen, and the cows can walk around. They don't have to wedge them in like we used to do in the stock cars of the railroads (of course, a lot of stock is still shipped by rail and by truck). Cows feed and walk around very much like they'd do in their own pasture, but much more confined. Sometimes a cow even delivers a calf on the way to Japan or India.

They have to pack the plane pretty carefully to balance the weight and keep the tail from tipping backward. Takes about eighteen hours to most of the Asian countries, and they have attendants right there in the plane. They haul about ninety to the planeload. Those cattle just walk right up the gangplank onto the plane. The attendants herd them into the tail of the plane first, then pack the rest of the pens right up to the main door behind the pilot. It is about the most important part of the job, balancing the plane so the weight is evenly distributed, and those aluminum pens keep the animals from shifting their weight too much. Why, those cattle hardly lose any weight at all. They're calm, feeding like they're used to in their own pens. Well, there's always something new going on. Just makes it all the more interesting to live long enough to see what's going on around you.

I've been a horse dealer and a dealer in livestock all my life. I'm way over a hundred years, and I've lived a life of adventure, and there's a good many things a person will learn in that length of time. I've dealt with everybody and I've had some strange experiences, as you can see in the stories written here, and I want to give the young folks some advice.

When you're trading, it isn't just what things look like, but what your judgment tells you they are. Now, in trading horses you never want to trade if it's an even trade. If you think it's even, always ask boot. You'll nearly always get it. If you don't get it, don't trade! That way, if there's anything wrong with the horse you traded for, then you have something to fall back on and you don't lose money. But if you trade without trading for yourself, first thing you know you're leading a halter with nothing in it. Many and many a horsetrader has wound up that way. So when you trade, trade for yourself, not for the other fellow, and be careful. Judge what you're trading. There's nothing to it. There's a good living for anyone who is a good trader today.

I've always made money trading. I've raised my family, sent them to school and everything. Mostly it was done through trading and livestock, and I learned one thing: No matter how little you've got to pay for anything, if you keep going far enough and you've got the money in your pocket, you can buy what you want, because someone will sell. People are funny. They get excited when they go to trading. That's one thing you never want to do. Even if you know you've got the best end of a deal, never get excited about it. If you do, you're going to make a mistake. Remember, they have the property. If you go to a man's place, and you want to buy something, and he wants to sell, that is all it takes to make the selling scene. You have the money in your pocket and he has a horse, animal, automobile, whatever. He wants to sell, or he wouldn't offer his property for sale. You've got the money and you've got the advantage. Now, it doesn't hurt him if you walk out and leave him with his property, and eventually that man will see that maybe he has made a mistake in letting you get away. You want that property, but you've got the whip hand. You have the money and he's got the property that he wants to sell. That's something for everyone to remember.

If you start in the trading game, be careful. There are times when you'll have to take a loss. If things are too high and you can't afford them, never hold on. If you lose a few dollars on one deal, make it back on the next trade you can. Eventually you'll come out all right. Another thing, if you lost your pocketbook (as in that experience I had many years ago), where would you go to find it? You'd naturally go back to the place where you lost it. Same way in dealing. If you lose money on a deal, there's no use to cry about it. Keep your mouth shut and go right back and try it over again, and next time beware! That's my advice to anyone starting in the business of trading, buying, and selling.

This brings me to the end of the old oat burners. Whenever I came to the natural end of a deal, when something I had started ran to a finish, I always went back to the farm and bought more land or found some feed yards to rent and filled them with cattle, sheep, or hogs to feed all the grain and hay we raised—which was quite a lot of feed. My son was with me most of the time, and we were always busy keeping our feedlots full. But through the years Kenneth became used to my retiring. I did that oftener than any man ought to retire, and it got to be a joke, but he always took up the slack for me. When I'd get away from work or the farm, I just didn't feel right, and soon I'd get another idea that I knew would work, and as soon as we could clear off the stock on hand, we'd get into something else. I think Kenneth kind of liked it that way—at least, he never complained about it.

I hope the readers of this book will get a kick out of some of the stories I have told. My days are getting short, and I sit in an easy chair and think of the things both good and bad that have passed, and I wouldn't like to live over some of them. All my children have good homes, and the girls visit me often. My parents, brothers, sisters, wives, everybody is gone. Lots of luck to all who read my story, and a little advice to all the traders: don't come home leading an empty halter.

Afterword

I first met Lee Daniels and his family in 1926, when I was sixteen—I spent a September night at their home near Adair while I was enroute from northern California to southern Florida. I passed through Iowa again in July 1965, renewed my acquaintance with the Daniels family, and discovered what a wonderful storyteller Lee is. He has since become an important part of my life.

Lee's father, Lewis, was a half brother to my great-grandmother, Lucenia Ser-Vis Ish, who died in November 1919. Lucenia was the mother of my grandmother, Alice Ish Strawn. For all practical purposes, Lee might have been almost unknown to me but for the accident of my stopping there in 1965, at which time he started spinning those fascinating tales. I had never before heard such stories. Right there I was caught up in his stories, his life. In 1926 Lee also sat me down and asked questions about northern California. I hadn't realized I knew that much about my surroundings. I left the Daniels home next morning a wiser teenager.

Upon my return thirty-nine years later, Lee and I again hit it off. When I stopped at his farm four miles south of Adair, he immediately began relating the tales of his experiences, and one story led right into the next. He seemed to be a compulsive storyteller. His family ignored his stories completely—I could see they had heard all this a thousand times, knew it all by heart, and wouldn't care if he never told another tale. But I knew that they should be in a book so everyone could enjoy them. At first I thought, Oh, well, someone will write them up. No, I decided, I wanted to capture these stories myself. Although I had two other book projects researched and partially written, I could think only

234

of these stories, and well, perhaps I had been lured, like the fly into the spider's web. I couldn't get out. Lee couldn't stop telling stories, and I had to write them.

We recorded the first tapes in July 1967, and for the next several years this was a constant occupation, not only transcribing them but wishing I had more stories and planning how I could get them. I was living in Philadelphia, teaching kindergarten, and Lee lived half of each year at Adair and the other half in Riverside, California. I planned to spend some time during the summer of 1970 in Riverside, and my son and I bussed out. But Lena was in the hospital, and Lee was seriously occupied with caring for her. Luckily, Lena's sister, Belva Carrigan, offered to share her home with them. Each weekday I would visit them there for several hours, and many of the tapes were recorded as we sat in Belva's kitchen while she baked luscious pies and cooked wonderful meals. Luckily for me, she refused all assistance, and I taped as many stories as we could in a two-week period. These two collections are about all I have.

Transcribing Lee's stories from tape to paper was a huge problem to start with, and it didn't get any smaller. Slowly and painfully, however, tape by tape, the job crawled toward its end. Lee's voice is so low it did not always come across clearly. Sometimes certain sentences or phrases had to be played back repeatedly. On some occasions I couldn't understand them at all. I paid typists to work on the most difficult tapes, and even then we couldn't always learn what was said. Eventually all the tapes had been transcribed, with the exception of one that was lost by a typist, and I started editing. But after several publishers turned down the manuscript, I put it aside, realizing I was simply saturated with the book.

Lee's stories really do show what life is all about—I felt very certain about this idea. Starting in December of 1984, I edited the manuscript all over again, had my cousin Daisy Dean Gerig edit it also, typed it over, and sent it out.

Well, here we are, you, me, and the book. And best of all, Lee is still here to enjoy it, probably at least as much as anyone else.